WRONG MOVEMENTS
A Robert Wyatt History

Researched, compiled, edited and written
by
Michael King

Computer work and editorial assistance
by
Allen Huotari

First published in 1994 by SAF Publishing Ltd.
Reprinted 1996

SAF Publishing Ltd.
12 Conway Gardens,
Wembley, Middx.
HA9 8TR
ENGLAND
TEL/FAX: 0181 904 6263

ISBN 0 946719 10 1

Printed in England by Redwood Books, Trowbridge, Wiltshire.

ACKNOWLEDGEMENTS

Wrong Movements could never have been realised without assistance from any of the literally hundreds of kind souls who contributed uniquely to assemble the 'great puzzle'. From translators Ann and Herve to Bill and Hugh who opened their diaries, my heartfelt thanks to you all.

Alessandro Achilli, Daevid Allen, Kevin Ayers, Rob Ayling, Roy Babbington, Laurie Scott-Baker, Herve Bassett, Carla Bley, Ted Bing, Nick Bodnar, Joe Boyd, Mark Boyle, Mick Brannan, Manfred Bress, Pete Brown, Chris Burgess, Pascal Bussy, Diane Cleveland, Andy Childs, Al Clark, Larry Coryell, Richard Coughlan, Lol Coxhill, Ron De Bruyn, Elton Dean, Lyn Dobson, Nick Evans, Chris Everest, Steve Feigenbaum, Fred Frith, Bruce Gallanter, Ken Garner (author of *In Session Tonight - The Complete BBC Recordings*), Ernst Giesking, Paul Haines, Paul Hammond, Jimmy Hastings, David Heale, Brian Hopper, Hugh Hopper, Mike Horovitz, Phil Howitt, Ken Hyder, Lady June, Andrew King, Heather Kinnear, Nicolas Klotz, Pierre Lattes, James Levine, Harold Lüss, Bill MacCormick, Dave McCrae, Ian MacDonald, Danny Manners, Lawrence Marks, Peter Marter, Phil Miller, Donald Muir, Jim Mullen, George Neidorf, Evan Parker, Gord Phinn, John Platt, Chris Probert, Pam Pyle, Pip Pyle, Mike Ratledge, Noel Redding, Philippe Renaud, Victor Schonfield, Gilli Smyth, David Sinclair, Richard Sinclair, Veleroy (Rab) Spall, John Stevens, Dave Stewart, Chris Stone, Ann Strong, Andy Summers, Sean Murphy, Julie and Keith Tippett, Geoff Travis, Roger Turner, Terry Valderos, Charles Van Waalwijk, Erella Vent, Martin Wakeling, John Walters, Trevor Watts, Graham Weston, the late Gary Windo, Honor Wyatt.

Special thanks to the photographers who kindly offered their work; Alfreda Benge, Anton Corbijn, Mark Ellidge, Jak Kilby, Laurie Lewis.

Above and beyond gratitude goes to:
Chris Cutler, whose valued support was instrumental.
Barry H. King, newspaper and library researcher extraordinaire!
Elizabeth Khodabakhsh, the scanning whiz.
Allen Huotari for his unconditional commitment, his wisdom and friendship.
My family, Lori, Hailey and Ryan (and Allen's too!) for their sacrifices and support.

Robert and Alfie for saying Yes!

PHOTOGRAPHIC CREDITS

1945-64   All courtesy of Honor Wyatt collection, except page 2 Alfreda Benge; page 7 courtesy of Rob Ayling collection.

1965   Page 6 courtesy of Richard Coughlan collection.

1966   All Mark Ellidge, except page 1 courtesy of Richard Coughlan.

1967   All Mark Ellidge, except page 17 courtesy of Caesar Glebbeek/Univibes collection.

1968   Page 4 courtesy of Pam Pyle collection.

1969   Page 2 Mark Ellidge; page 5 Jean-Luc Ourlin; page 6 &7 courtesy of Hugh Hopper collection; page 9 Jean-Pierre Lebir.

1970   Page 1 Mark Ellidge; page 10 Barry Wentzell.

1971   Page 2 Barry Wentzell; page 4 courtesy of *Radio Times*.

1972   Page 5 Philippe Renaud; page 7 Chinese poster courtesy of Randy Johnston collection; page 10 Mark Ellidge .

1973   Page 4 by kind permission of Virgin records.

1974   Page 4 Jak Kilby, page5 & 6 courtesy of Robert Wyatt/Alfreda Benge collection.

1975   Page 2 Piero Togni first published in *Muzak* #4, Italy; Pg 3 Rita Knox courtesy of Cadillac records.

1976   Jak Kilby.

1980/81   Alfreda Benge.

1982/3   Anton Corbijn.

1986   Page 1 Alfreda Benge; page 2 Alessandro Achilli.

1991   Brian Conlon.

1992   Alfreda Benge (Louth), Simon Russell (NYC).

1993   Page 1 Phil Nicholls by permission of Blanco Y Negro records, page 2 Alfreda Benge.

Addenda   Courtesy of Robert Wyatt/Alfreda Benge collection. Steve Rapport courtesy of Rough Trade.

INTRODUCTION

Why Robert Wyatt? It's a question with many answers. In a sense this book began back in 1976 when an old friend confronted me pointedly, "How can you call yourself a fan of progressive music having not heard Soft Machine?", as he plonked *Volume Two* on his turntable. It was this singular listening experience that so profoundly unshackled the conventions I'd accepted as 'progressive' and thrust open the door of discovery for jazz, new musics, and all things Wyatt. Here I found a so-called rock musician who'd eschewed the traditional expressions of Blues and Classical idioms to create an original music overflowing with wit, whimsy and warmth from a wondrous voice. All this and more from a genuine artist (as opposed to a prefabricated star) with possibly his finest work yet to come!

Over the years, as bootlegged radio sessions, concert recordings, and various interview clippings were collected, a fascinatingly different perspective emerged of the artist and his body of work. As with many musicians who swim against the corporate mainstream Robert Wyatt has led a largely unknown career path parallel to the formal recordings that established his legacy.

What began then in the Spring of 1990 as a general career overview to earn a free subscription to the UK fanzine *Facelift* quickly escalated into an impetuous excavation for the contents of what you are now holding. Nowhere during the odyssey could I have predicted what I found, specifically the many strangers turned friends who provided the foundation of knowledge and material. Moreover, it was a joy to witness Robert's many friends recount their musical experiences with great affection and admiration.

But an endeavour such as this cannot be undertaken without various reservations, and the two worth mentioning here concern possible trappings suggested by the chosen format. *Wrong Movements* does not offer analysis or critical evaluation on my part of Robert Wyatt's music nor its socio-political context, however deserving. The who, when, where, what and why's within these pages constitute factual signposts, existing as indicators and identifiers throughout a thirty year travelogue. As such they are ripped out of life's myriad experiences; profound, common, and otherwise which have surrounded and informed the music in question. The intent has been to empirically document all known occasions when Robert has performed before a public and recorded in a studio. Entries are presented chronologically in context with reflections, current and archival, from Robert and his many associates. Sources range through all media, private interviews and correspondence.

The second reservation concerns the possibility of romanticizing the vacuum surrounding these musical events, as encouraged by the current nostalgia fixations of mass pop culture. Put simply, The Soft Machine was not a happy family. Personal, musical and managerial struggles were rife during the sixties and seventies, a period for which Robert holds little to no nostalgia. Where comfortable memories remain is with friendships enjoyed, which is a sentiment I often found in speaking with other musicians. Quite literally *Wrong Movements* chronicles two remarkable and remarkably different careers. Its a division laid between the folly of youth and the responsibility of maturity and delivered through a debilitating accident.

When I first spoke with Robert Wyatt to seek approval for a career biography, I remember closing our phone converstaion with something like, "Well, I only hope that I can in print do justice to what you've done in music", and without skipping a beat the laugh returned, "Well, I hope you can do better than that!". I hope you enjoy the attempt.

This book is dedicated to you who've been listening, and to the dogma that art and politics are simply not to be mixed.

Mike King.

"I remember somebody describing his voice saying it was the best non-voice in the business, which of course is a very good description of it. But it sort of gets you in the solar plexus his voice I think, I find that I must say." Honor Wyatt

Footnotes
1. All concert events and recording sessions took place in London, England unless identified otherwise.
2. Where session period remains unknown the record is entered by the release date.
3. Record Matrix number denotes initial British release, except exclusive foreign releases.
4. Preferred reference format is analogue vinyl.
5. Unless identified otherwise, all entries:
a) January 1965 to June 1966 are for Wilde Flowers
b) August 1966 to July 1971 are for Soft Machine
c) January 1972 to September 1972 are for Matching Mole
d) Post 1973 are for Robert Wyatt

History is nothing but a collection of fables and useless trifles, cluttered up with a mess of unnecessary figures and proper names.

Leo Tolstoy (1828-1910)

"Mostly, when I look back, I just shudder with shame at all the mistakes I made, compensated by the pleasure of discovery. I think it was Wim Wenders who made a film called Wrong Movements. Now there's a title!"

Robert Wyatt (1945-)

On January 28, 1945, the family of Honor Wyatt and George Ellidge is enriched with the arrival of their only child, Robert Wyatt Ellidge. Half siblings include brother Mark Ellidge, a photographer for London's Sunday Times and from Honor's previous marriage the celebrated actor Julian Glover and sister Prudence, a mother of five. Just after his first birthday, Robert's family move from Bristol, Somerset to West Dulwich, London where childhood unfolded.

While Honor experienced a long and rewarding career in broadcasting and teaching, George's profession as industrial psychologist is cut short by the onset of multiple sclerosis in 1955. This prompts another family move, this time to the town of Lydden, ten miles south of Canterbury, in the county of Kent. Together George and Honor write of their experiences with this debilitating condition in the book 'Why Pick On Us?' George's last years are lived out confined to a wheelchair; his final days spent in Italy with Honor in 1963.

George Ellidge and Honor Wyatt

"My parents were part of a little gang of intellectuals, I guess you could call them bohemians, who went to Majorca in the thirties. My father was a psychologist, my mother a journalist and dropout from a posh family. They were friends of Robert Graves, who was very important to me."

Honor Wyatt:

"My first husband and I lived in Majorca, back in 1933, 34, 35. We lived in the same village as Robert Graves and so we got to know him very well and we were life long friends. In due course Robert went out there too.

"Robert's father was a very likable man, very amusing, and was very popular with everybody. He loved music and taught Robert all about music. We used to take him to the opera when he was eight or nine. It's always saddened me that George didn't get to see Robert's career, I would have been very interested in what he would have thought."

Robert Wyatt Ellidge, May 1948, with Lindy Palmer

"A characteristic which I've inherited from my mother and father which is I suppose you have to sum up as iconoclasm. But if you have this consensus in your home that we are an iconoclastic home, how does a child react to that with their parents? For example, if my mother comes from a generation that rejected material wealth and so on, in favour of culture with a capital C. My iconoclasm seems to have manifested itself in even rejecting the aristocracy of high culture. What that means is that I don't believe in Beethoven, and this really shocks people, although it even shocks my mother, but nevertheless I've inherited the desire to be able to say that, I think probably from my mother. That's the irony."

Honor Wyatt:

"Looking back one should have seen the signs early on. When he was about fourteen there was a book in the house about the French poet Rimbaud and Robert was absolutely fascinated. Not by the poems I may say, but by the fact that Rimbaud simply rejected every social standard that existed. He threw it all aside and even went against poetry in the end and what did he do, gunrunning or something dreadful. One should have realized how his mind was working then cause he thought it was a wonderful story.

A weekend in Dieppe, France, 1955

Honor Wyatt:

"We realized that music really meant a great deal to him when he was about twelve and he started this skiffle group, you know skiffle groups were the thing of the time. We had a big cellar in the house we lived in near Dover and they went down there with, I cannot remember what incredible instruments they were, they were bits of wire tacked onto a board and saucepan lids and buckets and everything you could think of! We used to laugh at this and my husband used to say 'Well, it's quite an interesting noise.' But Robert became obsessed by it and there were boys from the village, then of course friends from school.

"We had first thought that he was going to be a painter because he was quite good at art but in fact I think his art was nothing special, he had a facility for drawing and painting but it didn't really develop into very much. From then on we realized it was going to be music."

"My father used to play Shostakovich, Hindemith, Bartok, and my mother played Monteverdi. I didn't hear much rock 'n' roll and I never liked it. My dad introduced me to jazz, I think he'd seen 'Stormy Weather' as a younger man. I thought it was so wonderful that it took over my ears completely. My dad got alarmed because I stopped playing the Bartok. That was it really, I was in love and I've remained so.

"My father at that time had done various things. He'd got a degree in law at Liverpool, and then he did modern languages at Oxford, and then he got on to do psychology at Cambridge. A very bright bloke. But he was also a pianist and that's definitely where I got my ideas from. The house was full of music."

Honor Wyatt:

"We had always played records to him, I mean there was always music in the house and some of it he liked very much. I remember he liked Virgil Thompson, we had gotten an American record from the American Embassy and so on. And of course we played the classics and pop music of the time so he was always surrounded by music."

"My brother played me Duke Ellington, bebop, Cecil Taylor, the first quartet of Don Ellis with Jaki Byard, Mingus Presents Mingus, so all this was mixed up and just exploded in my head. The late fifties was a wonderful period for jazz records coming out, which kept me interested in life.

"I'd go to a youth club, to the juke box, and think 'Oh, I know what would sound good to hear, I won't put on anything like Ornette but Dizzy Gillespie Big Band at Newport, that will really groove, simple really great stuff.' And you could put it on for two seconds and they'd go 'What's that rubbish!' and you would think 'I don't understand what's going on here.'"

Honor Wyatt:

"I remember when he did hear some music...Bird something....who was called Bird? Yes, Charlie Parker, playing some classic thing. I can't remember what it was, maybe the Michaelangelo Sonnets or something, I cannot remember, but it was a mixture of Charlie Parker and this classical thing and Robert said 'Ah, Charlie Parker playing, that's the thing that makes me happy' and he meant happy. So that was how it all started."

"Hugh and Brian Hopper, Mike Ratledge, Dave Sinclair and myself were going to the same school in Canterbury. But Hugh and myself were younger than Brian and Mike and Dave was younger still. I was seeing Mike and Brian perform at school, doing duos for piano and clarinet, Debussy and things like that, really good. The first time I saw Mike he was singing in the school choir at the Canterbury Cathedral. I had just started school."

Hugh Hopper:

"I first met Robert at Simon Langton in 1956, September, it would have been. He was one of the people I got on with, he was not necessarily my closest friend all the time, but, yeah, we were both interested in each other cause we were quite different and from quite different backgrounds. I just remember he had fairly long blonde hair, long for those days."

Ted Bing:

"We went to school together. Robert was probably a couple of years younger than me so we didn't have that much contact in the very early years. At school there were various extra-curricular activities and amongst other things there was a Jazz Club. So we more or less met at that point. we used to give little lectures during the lunch hour, that sort of thing. Illustrated lectures."

"I had done a series of jazz club talks, we had a jazz in the dinner hour of school where me and a couple of friends would play records and talk about them, instead of having lunch. We'd get a record player and put it in the science room, ten or fifteen of us, and they'd sit around, I'd sit around, and we'd say 'I'm going to play you some Art Blakey today, or Ornette Coleman, or Fats Waller.' But Mike didn't come to those cause we were younger; age apartheid in schools! He did come up to me once and said 'I hear you have some Cecil Taylor records, can I borrow one? I haven't heard him.' And I had Cecil Taylor at Newport with Steve Lacy, so I lent it to him. And I was very honoured, you know, Mike Ratledge senior prefect wants to borrow one of my records!"

Mike Ratledge:

"I just listened to classical music until I was seventeen (1960) because that's all there was in the house. I slowly developed an interest in music outside, music you weren't supposed to get into. My interest in jazz started rather late, it was actually backwards, I was just into the purist avant garde, anything avant garde. It was my main interest at the time, everyone at eighteen then was into that, Cage, Bertram, Haydn, Stockhausen, Berio, all of the American born...anything, as long as it was avant garde, I didn't have any stipulation at that time. So when I got into jazz it was the other way around. From Cecil Taylor I worked my way backwards and discovered I liked less obscure people like Mingus, Monk, Miles, Coltrane, and all the way back to Charlie Parker. About that time I started to play jazz and losing touch with the classical, all on the piano. I started playing group music, before that I had played chamber music with friends. I started playing with Robert, just drums, Hugh and Brian on sax and guitar. We were trying to play jazz since it was our main interest, it wasn't too good though."

Brian Hopper:

"Mike and I were contemporaries at school. We started off basically because we both had a classical music education, he on piano, myself on clarinet, and we used to get together. It was sort of Saturday morning sessions at Mike's house basically. We used to record and play completely free improvised things between us, based loosely on modern classical things but increasingly with jazz overtones. We were also into photography and other things as well. We were very interested in early multi-media type things at that stage. We did concept photographs and Mike was doing quite a bit of writing, poetry, and other things. We were all trying to find our own way."

"Me and my school friends would, I don't know how, but we'd save up money and we'd read somewhere, I don't know Melody Maker probably, that there would be a Duke Ellington concert in London. We'd go up and somebody would let us sleep on their floor. I've been listening to jazz since the age of eleven and the cultural references I got from my parents were all about things that you could only really get to in London. So it's not anything specific about us. Anybody in England, one of the things they do if they're interested in painting or music or anything else is to make trips to London."

On one such visit to London during the very early sixties, a group of friends make a couple of vocal recordings in a public pay recording booth. These booths would directly cut a low-fi acetate disc of two minute duration.

a) Hugh Hopper, Robert Ellidge sing 'Round About Midnight' (T.S. Monk)
b) Brian Hopper, Phil Catlin, Robert Ellidge sing 'Evidence' (T.S. Monk)

"Music was my way of escaping from school. I did have a romantic association with pop records of the time — Roy Orbison, Buddy Holly, Eddie Cochrane — but that had to do with where the girls were. Wheres jazz was my comfort when I was struggling with homework that I couldn't make head or tail of. Miles Davis' voice, getting lost inside a Mingus arrangement, being carried along by the band, chucked from one soloist to another — that saved my soul as a schoolboy."

Ted Bing, David Gray, Robert Ellidge at Ted's home, Herne bay

CONTRIBUTIONS

A WALK WITH ROGER

So we decided to go after all, though when Roger suggested a walk I didn't think much of it. It was a sweltering hot day; but my cup of tea still went cold, so I called Fido (which, strange to say, is the name of our dog) and hooked on his lead. It was hot, as I said before. The leaves crinkled up with it, and the old house looked damn silly sitting there in the sun, but Roger didn't seem to get what I meant. He wouldn't. We walked along the road, which hasn't got a pavement, even though it is a main road. (We live in the country). Fido tugged on the lead hard and panted and hung his tongue out of his mouth. Roger shouted to cars going by that they were road hogs. It wasn't true, but it was fun shouting.

The hills were green and tufted with sheep; the sun still beat like gold on our heads and our legs were sweating because of the walking; the trees pathetically wavered a bit, but the heat was too much for them so they rocked gently and shed green blotches all over the road and ourselves. The lane we were on twisted a lot; we never knew what rotten moss-covered tree or swinging-inn-signed pubs we would see next. We came to a muddy pond which was more like a puddle, but the villagers liked to call it a pond. Fido got loose and jumped like a hound that was fox-hunting into the deliciously cool looking-deep water. But it wasn't very deep, for Fido got his head a wallop on a rock a foot or so under water. Then the wretched dog came out bedragglesome and all affectionate; which was annoying because he was soaking wet and splattered with water-weed. An old lady hobbled up, grumbled at us, and went away, tapping her stick on the ground. When she'd gone we giggled and called her a (blank).

There were trees all over the place, all different and blotted—this was a dank village—so after eating an unwelcome cheese sandwich (giving the cheese to Fido; I don't *like* cheese) we got going. There were so many leaves about you would have thought it was Autumn. Going through the tree-zone we went bang into a chunk of sunlight, where it smelt of earth, dead flies and the stinking water drying hard (it was so thick with squirms) on Fido's back and ears. The weeds had already peeled off in cakes. I told him not to stink; he can't have heard me because he stank to high Heaven. Roger told me it wasn't all that bad. Perhaps he was right. We then turned back, and decided to get lost, which we couldn't argue about; we were completely lost already. Just by following the road and searching a bit, we at last found the right way and saw the familiar trees and barns. Dusk came and a slight breeze was up. We came over the curve of the hill, and the house was still there.

R. W. ELLIDGE (IIu)

WHAT WOULDN'T?

There won't be so much as there would have been,
If there wasn't so much as there is:
But he hadn't as much as should have been had,
As there would be too much if there was.

He had much more than he should have been had,
As there will be too much (as there was);
But it wasn't as much as he shouldn't have been
When there won't be so much as there is.

Where there wouldn't as much as there shall have had
He shouldn't have been where he is;
But there won't be as much as there wouldn't have been —
If he won't be as much as there was.

R. W. ELLIDGE (IIu)

Above and left, a poem and short story published in the summer 1958 edition of The Langtonian, a booklet of school events.

Below, excerpts from a 105 centimetre wide photo scroll from Simon Langton Grammar School for Boys, July 1961.

Ted Bing
row 3, right

Hugh Hopper
row 5, center

Mike Ratledge, row 3, left
Brian Hopper, row 3, right

Dave Sinclair, row 1, left
Robert Ellidge, row 4, 2nd from right

Robert and Wellington House, 1957

Throughout the late fifties and early sixties, a fourteen room Georgian home named Wellington House provides a social milieu for informal inquiry, experimentation, and absorption of a liberal arts education for Robert and his friends. It is a time remembered affectionately by all those who visited or lived in Wellington House.

Honor Wyatt:

"We took in visitors from all over the world, that's how we managed to pay for the house. It's really a lovely house, eighteenth century house and there was plenty of room in it. At one time we had as many as fifteen foreign students I think, so that I was cooking for about twenty people. And then on top of that came Robert's friends, his school friends, sometimes my daughter's friends. It was a free for all, it was lovely."

Ted Bing:

"I used to spend a great many weekends at Wellington House. His parents were very, how shall I put it? Liberal. In every sense of the word. At any rate, for myself and for a good many others that place was like a cultural oasis. I was not a musician myself, so I never played with them at all."

Kevin Ayers:

"At that time, when I first hit Canterbury, I was sixteen or seventeen (1960/1961) and just out of school. I'd had a drug bust in London and they said 'get out of London.' In those days they could say that sort of thing. So I was sent down to live with my mother, which wasn't a very happy arrangement, and I gradually met up with people like Robert. I think we had a girlfriend in common, or certainly the desire for her. In fact I've got a song called 'When Your Parents Go To Sleep' which is about that particular lady, because I used to have to creep in there at night and creep out very early in the morning and then walk to Wellington House, which was about six miles. It was quite a schlep first thing in the morning in the cold. But there was always a welcome for me there, and yes it's true jazz was the thing but it wasn't just jazz. As Ted Bing so aptly put it, it was a cultural oasis. I mean things were happening, people were talking, people had some education and read books. And they looked at paintings and they listened to music, none of which I did. I thought this is fascinating, these are really interesting people. But yes, Wellington House was like a refuge, it was really like another country."

Brian Hopper:

"I came to know Robert basically through associations at school and out of school, at Wellington House. We were all listening to records of various kinds, particularly modern jazz based ones, a few blues based as well, but mostly jazz I would say. That was the prime influence and that was really the background that set the scene if you like. Robert was quite heavily into it, I think I was less into it at that stage but when we got together jazz was always going on. And there were other people around with their own interests as well."

Hugh Hopper:

"He was interested in jazz really and his parents were interested in more modern classical music, so musically I really didn't start getting close to him till virtually when I was about sixteen or seventeen, when we were both leaving school. Robert and his brother had a large jazz record collection so I started hearing music there. I started playing bass about the same time really so I was copying things like Ornette Coleman and Charlie Haden. I really didn't understand what was going on but that was the sort of thing I was listening to and trying to play on the bass."

Brian Hopper:

"Initially I brought around my clarinet and also doing a little bit on guitar, but mostly clarinet at that earlier stage. We were just improvising with Robert on basically tins, the odd sort of drum, cymbals, and things, but no proper drum kit. And also Robert was doing a bit of cornet which he had around, actually quite a lot I seem to recall."

"My hi-hat was one of my mother's old broken typewriters and you'd put your foot on the keys and that's one sound and you'd take your foot away and they'd all clatter back and that's another sound. It sounded a bit like those synthesizer handclap drum things, very nice. For my cymbal, I used a metal clothes rail which was very loose and I just tapped it. And the snare was just an old ammunition box.

"As well, I had my trumpet which in those days I used to carry around on a string. My father was very upset when I swapped my violin for a trumpet because although there is a great classical repertoire for the violin, not even Wynton Marsalis has been able to find a great repertoire of classical music for the trumpet! So he just couldn't see what I was going to do with it. I always used to feel embarrassed about this trumpet, of course I couldn't play it, I just liked tootling on it."

Roger Turner:

"I used to live at the top of Whitstable, just before the roundabout that went up to the number 5 bus route to Canterbury. I'm younger than Robert and all that mob, and they came around a few times to where I lived. I had a little old drum kit that had like a parachute sort of skin on the bass drum that my dad put together. It was a real old beat up wooden kit with odd sounding cymbals, what you could find. There were little jam sessions at my place. There was a guy with a clarinet...Stewart...somebody Stewart, I can't remember, my brother Ian played trumpet, Robert, myself, and whoever. It was actually what I'm doing now, just making music with what is at hand. Robert didn't come round much, I guess because I had such a clapped out drum kit."

In the weeks prior to the Christmas of 1960, a young Australian beat named Daevid Allen is received by Wellington House as a lodger. Daevid's arrival, via taproots through the jazz scenes of Paris and London, was a self exile from Melbourne's small bohemian arts community. During the late fifties Daevid had discovered the world of beat literature while working for Melbourne University press, led a jazz group as poet and guitarist, and acted with radical theatre troupes.

Daevid Allen:

"I put an ad in the paper, for a loft or something for minimal rent, and the most interesting reply was from this family in Kent; rambling old house, mother a broadcaster, father a writer with creeping paralysis, family all actors, and so on. Full board for 2d a week, a good gig, the Wyatt's."

Honor Wyatt:

"He was very freakish, I must say. He dressed oddly, he thought for himself and he didn't care what anybody else thought of him. He drank rather a lot, he smoked pot when it was considered really a dreadful thing to do. At first Robert was dazzled by Daevid and went for everything Daevid said and thought it was wonderful. He was a nice man, I mean there's nothing vicious about Daevid, he was very kind, very friendly."

"When Daevid came I really liked him. Incidentally, I'd heard some third hand thing that he'd advertised in The Times. This is absolutely wrong, my father would wash his hands if he found himself touching The Times by accident left on a train. It was the New Statesman. That may not mean anything on the other side of the Atlantic but The Times was a right wing establishment paper and my dad wouldn't be caught dead with one. Anyway, Daevid came along with his guitar and his records, mainly I remember the records. I just thought he was really good fun. Alfie's got a saying that she got from one of her mystical people that she once read; you either live as part of the dance or as if there's a great weight on you. I think that Daevid seemed to be living life with everything as part of the dance and up until then everything had been like there was a great weight on me. Daevid lessened the gravity somehow, made me feel that you could float free in any direction, that a lot of the prisons you're in are of your own making. I think it was that, which was so welcome with Daevid.

"On a practical level, he wanted to practice guitar but anybody who plays an instrument wants to play with somebody. So he just said to me, cause he'd heard me sing along to records 'I know you can hear it, could you just play a blues chord sequence on the piano.' And I didn't know what it was so he said 'Never mind what it is, just go...' (plays blues motif on piano), etc. So he taught me that and I found the notes. He said 'just play those over and over again' and he'd play over top of it. So that was really very good for me because it was just the opportunity to play something that was useful for somebody else on a keyboard. So I wasn't just playing a rhythmic thing, I was involved in a very humble way harmonically."

Daevid Allen:

"Robert and I became good friends right away, which is unusual for a fifteen year old and a twenty-one year old to have so much in common. I don't know if that says more about Robert as a precocious fifteen year old or for my maturity as a twenty-one year old, but we did have a lot of the same jazz records in our collections."

Mark Ellidge:

"You know the other thing was painting. Robert was painting and so was Daevid Allen and that was a common thing. Robert was doing a lot of painting and sculpturing, on anything really, he'd work on anything."

Daevid Allen:

"It was really a beautiful existence 'cause I was able to do a lot of painting and a lot of writing. I retuned my guitar 'cause I'd been playing jazz up until then with a normal tuning. I decided to experiment with tuning and in particular studied Thelonious Monk's tunes.

'Then on one of my visits up to London, for one reason or another, I found an Ornette Coleman record. The very first one called 'Something Else' in the window of a shop called Doebell's. I brought it back and was very excited by it 'cause they were playing free jazz. I decided that's what I wanted to do so I started woodshedding and playing music like this. And Robert, who was still at school in Canterbury would play drums on boxes and tins and things like this."

Mike Ratledge:

"Daevid had been around a bit and was a fantastic influence in Canterbury at that time. He had moved into Robert's house when we were all fifteen or sixteen, he was a friend of Robert's mother and brought about two hundred jazz records and turned everyone in Canterbury on to them...early Mingus things. I don't know what would have happened without them."

"Daevid also had a dog which he used to take for walks with him. It was actually a tin can on the end of a bit of string which he would trail some yards behind him. To an impressionable lad of my age that was pretty far out."

In October of 1961 Daevid Allen returns from his second visit to Paris bringing a new fellow-traveller in George Niedorf, an American drummer he'd met at a bar. As envisioned, George is welcomed into Wellington House with an agreed arrangement whereby lodging cost would be offset with drum lessons for Robert.

Honor Wyatt:
"This is the sort of thing that would happen; they'd be living on an houseboat on the Paris Seine on their uppers and with very little to eat and so on, and suddenly they'd appear at Wellington House. Oh I can't tell you all the people who came to Wellington House! I can't tell you!"

George Niedorf:
"If you wanted to pick ideal parents, you'd pick Robert's parents. They were fully supportive of everything Robert did. There was great love in the family, great warmth, support for what we did, interaction. I mean there was no generation gap, everything was discussed amongst the parents, the children, whoever was in the house at the time. It was really a very open situation and very intellectually stimulating. Robert's father especially was very interested in music. I mean we would all sit down and listen to everything from Schoenberg and Webern, Stockhausen to Eric Dolphy, to Ornette, to Coltrane. We had a great friendship and a great time. That was a wonderful experience, living in that house."

"I learned from a jazz drummer who taught me to play with my elbows in, using my wrists like Philly Jo Jones. But I never really mastered it, and anyway you can't get the volume or intensity that way, so I rather let it go and started using my forearms more."

George Niedorf:
"Most of the playing in the house took place between Daevid Allen, Robert, and myself on whatever I had as a kit. At that time I think I had a snare drum, a hi-hat, a ride cymbal. Daevid would play guitar and Robert would play various things, trumpet, whatever he had around. We just improvised."

Daevid Allen:
"One night I'd been out drinking with a Gypsy friend of mine who actually lived in a Gypsy's caravan over the hills. And when I came back I was in a pretty merry state of mind, happy to be back, but there had been a crisis in the house and Robert had been rushed to Dover hospital. Apparently Robert had attempted to take his life and swallowed his father's sleeping pills.
"Now the funny thing was for three nights before that we had been sitting up talking and Robert had been talking very intelligently about that he figured life ended at puberty. That there was the innocence of child like vision which ended when one reached puberty so there was no point in going on. He felt he had done all his best work as a painter 'cause he could no longer do it innocently because he'd begun to think and to rationalize it. he decided that there was nothing more to do in life so he decided to kill himself.
"For quite a long time I argued various arguments against this towards him but he was so clever and rationally clear that he almost convinced me! Anyway, in the end I thought, 'Well, he's so hot on the subject I'll just change my tack.' I said

'Alright, Robert, if that's what you believe then kill yourself' and the very next day he tried. And because there had been a couple of people around when I said that, the word got around that I told Robert to kill himself and that he tried and therefore it was my fault. The fact that he passed out on the pills in my room listening to my records didn't help. So I had to leave."

"I did feel that as I wasn't able to become an academic that there wasn't anything I was allowed to be, if it wasn't academic. And I felt very suicidal at my total failure to deal with A levels and go on to university, just finding a place to belong. I always found not so much hating the world, but despair at finding a place where I could fit in and flourish."

Daevid departs immediately to the Belsize Park district of north London and is soon followed by George. In May, with tent, trumpet, and ten pounds, Robert accompanies George and Prue Niedorf on a nomadic journey through France and along the coast towards the Mediterranean island of Majorca, where an extended settlement is offered from poet, author Robert Graves.

"I left school illiterate and unskilled to boot. We drifted off to Majorca where Robert put me up. It was rather a relief to him that I wasn't another academic young poet asking him lots of questions about white goddesses. He had Coltrane records in his collection, we listened together. He had once embraced Cecil Taylor after a set in a New York club. This was the Robert Graves everybody had warned me I was going to be frightened of, with whom I should watch my manners. He said I shouldn't worry about college. He approved of my wanting to be a drummer. He made it feel all right to like the things I liked."

George Niedorf:
"We had built an amphitheatre for Robert Graves up at his house in Deya and to inaugurate the opening a bunch of local artists and musicians played, so Robert joined in that. He had done some modifications to his trumpet. He'd cut the bell off and attached various lengths of hose to it, to get different kinds of sounds and completely different timbres. He was also doing a lot of sculpting in stone and writing. Robert was a very talented young man, it wasn't just music."

Throughout the summer of '62, private musical explorations between George and Robert are undertaken, along with drum instruction from both George and Graves' son-in-law Ramon Farran. By October, the Niedorf's leave for Australia and Robert returns to England, working oddjobs.

Hugh Hopper:
"He did a few weeks as an apprentice for the Forestry Commission (can you imagine that?) I think it was his parents' idea that he should try something like a job. I was working on a farm and Robert was deep in the Lyminge Forest. He stayed with an Alf Garnett styled worker and his family. It was the coldest winter since 1940. Weekends at Wellington House, we compared numb feet."

Around February 1963 Hugh and Robert are invited to move to London where they share Daevid Allen's one room flat at 40 Belsize Park with Ted Bing and Kevin Ayers

1963

"Everybody has had their heroes, mine was Daevid Allen."

For Daevid Allen, Hugh Hopper, and Robert Ellidge, the spring of 1963 brings the formation of a jazz and poetry trio with an eye towards working a proposed three month residency at 'The Establishment Club'. Throughout months of preparation for The Daevid Allen Trio the scene at Belsize Park hosts numerous jams and explorations with visiting friends. As example, Brian Hopper recalls dropping in, playing, and composing one of his earliest songs, 'Hope For Happiness'.

It is at The Establishment Club where the young rhythm section receive their first opportunity to play before a public audience. Various media have since erroneously reported that these gigs were performed in support of The Dudley Moore Trio and that the club was managed by Dudley.

Dudley Moore:

"I was in America with my band from 1962 to 64 actually. I did play there a lot but that would be 60 and 61. The club was on Greek St. or was it Frith St.? It was managed by Peter Cook who was my comedy partner for twenty years, but he brought in someone else, and by the time I'd come back in 64 it had been mismanaged into the ground, more or less."

May (late) — The Daevid Allen Trio, The Establishment Club
supporting The Peter McGurk Trio

Daevid Allen:

"I was playing loud electric guitar, strangely detuned. Ratledge was imitating Cecil Taylor at the piano, Hugh Hopper on electric bass, and Robert...he didn't have a kit, just various tins and things. About the only person who showed any interest was Malcolm Cecil who was playing with Dud at the time. We lasted about a day and a half."

Hugh Hopper:

"The residency swiftly ended after three nights for being too weird for the public; 'Could you just play some nice ballads?'. We were joined on the last night by Mike Ratledge, then studying at Oxford."

Mike Ratledge:

"The group did mostly standard jazz tunes and Daevid's numbers, it varied enormously. It was totally undiscriminating, we played jazz and it didn't matter where we began. It probably sounded like bad imitations of Cecil Taylor to bad imitations of Bill Evans. We tried to play the whole gamut of jazz because we liked so many styles, always switching from one style to another. It got to be more and more of Daevid's tunes with a few minimal standards but it had a short history because you couldn't survive on that type of music. It was everybody's first taste, apart from Daevid, of moving away from home into a big city and it was sort of a failure."

June 3 — The Daevid Allen Trio 'Live New Departures', Marquee (CD Voiceprint 122)
Set consists: a) 'Love Is' b) 'My Head Is A Nightclub' c) 'Capersity Travels (Four Imbalancing Constructions)' d) 'The Song Of The Jazzman' e) 'Little Rootie Tootie' f) 'Your Sun' g) 'Carmen Mouse'
Daevid Allen, guitar/voice/poems; Hugh Hopper, bass; Robert Ellidge, drums; augmented by Mike Ratledge, piano (e, f); Mike Horovitz, voice/poem (g)
e) composed by Thelonious Sphere Monk

Mike Horovitz:

"We first met at a concert at the LSE (London School of Economics) where he was working washing up at the canteen. Pete Brown and I were doing a concert with our jazz and poetry troupe and Robert came up after the concert, it was lunchtime, he had to go back to washing up, and he jumped up to where we were queueing up for food in the canteen saying 'Wow, great gig! Wow, modern jazz! Yea, bebop! Beat poetry, terrific!' He seemed a nice young lad, we were a little bit older than him."

Pete Brown:

"Mike Horovitz and I were the guys who did New Departures, we were the poets at that time; and we had a regular show on Tuesdays at the Marquee. We used to have different guests which meant anybody from Lawrence Ferlinghetti to Richard Rodney-Bennett to different jazz musicians, and the Daevid Allen group were among them."

Summer — Daevid Allen, Institute of Contemporary Arts
also: William Burroughs, Brion Gysin, John Esam, New Departures Quartet, The Machine Poets
Daevid Allen, poems/tapes: augmented by Hugh Hopper, bass, Robert Ellidge, drums: Ted Bing, slide projections.

Daevid Allen:

"Ted Bing was a very important character. He was a tower of strength, a lovely guy. He had a wonderful sense of humour. He shared a particular curious banana humour, what we called banana humour, he shared that very rapidly and easily. He was also into a lot of photography and did the visuals for some of my early shows."

With his plans for The Experimental Music Club in Hampstead now shelved, and no opportunity for work, Daevid dissolves the group and returns to Paris (and represents Australia at the '63 Paris Biennale). Professionally for Robert, Hugh, and Mike, the net effect is a retreat to square one. However Hugh rememebers that 'Robert stayed in London, doing a few gigs'. On Boxing Day 1963, a quartet consisting of Mike, piano; Brian, alto sax; Hugh, bass; and Robert, drums convenes in Canterbury for a private session of jazz, improvised, and Monk music. It's an informal hour as captured by Brian's portable reel to reel tape recorder.

Right: a letter from Robert Graves upon the passing of George Ellidge.
The nickname 'Batty' derives from Batterie, Spanish for drums.
In turn Graves' nickname was Scatty.

CANELLUÑ
DEYA
MALLORCA
SPAIN

Aug 30
1963

Dear Betty :

Thanks a lot, it's an unusual experience for me which makes me the more grateful.

Lucia's bank is :—

Westminster Bank
Bayswater Branch
Westbourne Grove
W.2

Ramon's 'Indigo Club' is fine. & will be even better when he gets permission till 3.am. At the moment it's only 12 pm. Ronnie Scott came for a week; we liked him a lot.

— Married, indeed! Well, I did it too at your age.

— I'm sorry about George; we didn't see eye to eye but Honor loved him so he must have been all right, & anyhow he begot Betty.

— Love from us all

Robert

1964

"I used to live precariously in a kind of reconstructed '40's Harlem in my head and only come out to eat and sleep."

Hugh Hopper:

"Ted Bing and I went to France at the beginning of January. The intention was to groove on down to Tangiers, Morocco with Daevid and Gilly (Smyth) to a club called the Fat Black Pussy Cat, but when we got to Paris plans had changed. We went on to Majorca (Deya) to wait until the Tangiers thing happened. It never did, although Daevid and Gilly did get there eventually. The postcard to Robert from Bourges was written on the way down through France in January (God, it was cold — the shutter of Ted's camera froze). Ted went back to England after a couple of months, and I followed, via Paris around April. I stayed in Paris until (I still remember the date) 21st May. Robert came out to stay at Daevid's in April or May for a couple of weeks, head shaven totally (mine on top). He had a piece from a London paper about him and Mick Jagger 'All hair and no hair' quite by chance."

Daevid Allen:

"That's when Hugh actually constructed quite a lot of the tape loops that I used in my compositions, Robert shaved his head and we listened to lot of Ornette Coleman. He started taking LSD for the first time as well. This woman showed up who had been one of Bob Dylan's girlfriends and brought us LSD, it was very rare before that time."

"In those days I used to make noises on trumpet, I wouldn't call it playing trumpet, with Daevid and people he knew (i.e. Terry Riley), beat exiles and so on. Hugh and I learned a lot there, that was the most exploratory stuff we did. Nobody had gigs there, that was just going around to people's flats and playing with tapes and so on. They were fairly open houses, you couldn't call them gigs, nothing anybody paid to hear.

"Terry Riley and John Esam had recorded some amazing tape of trumpeter Chet Baker using an echo loop, exactly something that I was always trying to develop with my voice. At this time, Terry was doing things with piano rolls that were very funny."

Hugh Hopper:

"I was back in Canterbury by the end of May and Robert was living in London. He went to Deya that summer and his sporadic love, Sandra Morland, went out to join him for a short holiday. Ronnie Scott was also there and Swedish trombonist Eje Thelin and guitarist Julian Bream."

Summer — house trio, Indigo Jazz Club, Palma, Majorca

The club was managed by Robert Graves' son-in-law, Ramon Farran, who offers Robert a stay to gain experience. This took the form of a part-time trio which played between visits from, and occasionally backed, various British and European jazz musicians.

"I was working in the Palma Jazz Club, mainly there putting stickers on car windows telling people to come to the club. I was part of a spare group that could play odd things that had Ron Rubin on bass and a bloke named John Mealing on piano, who's since gone on to become an R&B organist. But I couldn't really play then, it was like an apprentice who could be alongside people who could play."

Kevin Ayers:

"The first time I went to Deya I went because of Robert. He said 'come along and I'll find a place to stay' or something like that. And that's really where the musical side of things gelled. Deya was a starting point. Everybody was doing something, everybody was creative, everybody was intellectually curious. Particularly in music — there were loads of people playing around, writing poems and songs, and painting pictures and talking — it was really zappy. So I went to stay with Robert who was friendly with Robert Graves and he gave us one of his fisherman's cottages. I think we had one stove and two mattresses between us and that was fine.

"I remember going to a jazz club called the Indigo with Robert. We used to go there every week and I used to sit and watch. Robert would occasionally get to play drums, I would occasionally get to play very bad guitar, anything I was capable of. But I was enthusiastic. I think Robert and I may have jammed a couple of blues there occasionally, maybe I'm wrong. It's not terribly significant. The main thing was that Robert Graves took us both in and we became friendly with the Graves family, especially the younger brothers. That was a magical time."

Daevid Allen:

"By the time I got there, George was gone and Robert was just there still. We had brought a kit of drums from Paris that somebody had left in our apartment, and gave him the drums. He left almost immediately and we stayed and that was the beginning of our living in Majorca."

VICTORIA GARDENS---CHATHAM

(for Robert, Hugh, and Ted: 'The Belsize Boys')

Hosanna!—blow yellow string!—children of equinox: sing tangled wire
they pluck for hair...!

(...see Ted: it's real   and small:
blobbed-out with one finger between the blue-
crossed Finnish freighter fromthe midnight
sea————and my squinting eye)

     See your own British tanker: see
     the Midway: see the rat-grey water--

Paint the air with muddy hands!—run in
other people's shoes!—ride the hills of
smoky wind—-ON WHEELS MATE!—-Wwhhheeee!!!

               me-chanical compositions:
                         splinter! grind!
     laugh!

As for me or the sparrows on the twigs or that
yapping puppy over there, Spring is green, heaven sent.

     Forget thanksgiving, the doled-out crumb.

     Good to forget the cold, stone-kneeling prayer.

     Neccessary to forget the fear they've taught us
     as an afterthought.

_____-Look!   Knighted
are we in our muddy rubber boots:
                              Robert's
                                  got a
               stick
          for a sword: it's sharp.

                    OUCH!

                         Hugh's got
     a lid
          for a shield.

Christopher Perret was an American poet who stayed at Wellington House.
He later lived in Deya, where he died of a heart attack.

Hugh Hopper:
     "Just remembered, 1964. Robert telling me about going to a gig in London (with Ron Rubin?) in an open sports car, hanging onto his bass drum as they squealed around corners."

Back home in Canterbury, the Hopper brothers initiate the formation of a contemporary Beat group and forces are soon joined with a young guitarist named Richard Sinclair. Upon re-entry into Canterbury, Robert Ellidge is invited to drum while Kevin Ayers brings his tambourine and poems upon his recruitment as a singer. Around this period, Ayers' book of poetry 'Le Book Bookle' was published. Hugh names the quintet 'Wild Flowers', though Kevin soon adds an 'e' as inspired by his affection for Oscar Wilde. Rehearsals for an eclectic repertoire of Rhythm and Blues, Jazz, Pop, and original song commences at Hugh and Brian's home 'Tanglewood', and periodically at the Sportman's Arms and Friends Cottage in the village of Barnham. Management is under the wing of Peter Gilfillan.

Robert, Hugh, Brian, and Mrs. Hopper

Richard Sinclair:

"Brian and Hugh had started off and their father knew my father so Hugh's father phoned my father to say that Hugh was quite interested in organizing a band. He knew that my father had bought me a guitar and I was playing guitar at school (with the Pulsators). Within about a month I was up there at Tanglewood playing through my fathers old P.A. system which I've still got, crocodile skinned box and all! Anyway, up I went and did these things with Brian and Hugh at their house and sure enough we whacked through some numbers and it went on for some weeks.

"Then suddenly this guy turned up with a drum kit. Well, it wasn't a drum kit, it was a huge bass drum with pedal and a cymbal and a snare drum, that was it. And this chap played drums, Robert Wyatt. He was quite nice and quite hairy too. We needed a singer so we tried a local guy out, who's actually got a house next door to Hugh now, but that didn't work out. So Kevin Ayers turned up. I don't know how they knew Kevin but they did, and he turned up at a forty-five degree angle with a bottle of Mateus Rose and Jane Aspinall, Pye Hastings' sister, but I didn't know Pye then. So we just bashed away."

Hugh Hopper:

"I think Robert moved down to Canterbury around November and by Christmas he was staying at my parents' house. We worked for the post office's Christmas rush for two weeks, he working days, me nights. We hardly saw each other, but I was writing tunes like 'Memories' and 'Have You Ever Been Blue?' etc. and I'd leave them on the table for him and Brian to look at while I was post officing at night.

"Our first gig was at a party in the tiny bungalow in Swalecliffe, a retirement locality on the coast near Canterbury, wherein Kevin lived. Lasted about a half-hour before the stunned retired couple next door raised the alarm."

Richard Sinclair:

"Before our first official gig the band played a bunch of parties in people's living rooms and things. There was one at Theresa and Tracey's place upstairs in Dover St. Canterbury. They were a pair of Art College students."

Brian Hopper:

"My own part in those early years and in later Wilde Flowers years was, besides a playing member and writing member of the group, somewhat unique in that I was slightly older and was the only one with a 'regular' job and thus able to afford transport of sorts. I was able to provide a certain stability and direction to the group as well as move it around for rehearsals and gigs. Most of the earlier (and some later) rehearsing was done at my parents' home: 'Tanglewood', Canterbury, and our collective thanks go to them for their tolerance and encouragement through many years of intrusion of 'strange' people and a lot of noise!"

"It was Hugh who made all the contacts to play. We used to rehearse at his place. His poor parents, they were so nice. They had a very small house and we used to play right behind the main entrance. Nobody could enter the house without banging into the drums. We improvised and tried to play stuff by Cecil Taylor and Ray Charles. Hugh's parents never said anything about our music, so that tells you how nice they were."

Brian Hopper:

"I would suggest that the live gigs were somewhat, almost irrelevant fleeting moments (although obviously important to many who experienced them). Much more important were most of the moments in-between gigs. The real creativity, culture formation and whatever, happened during many long hours, weekends, days spent together in ones and two and sometimes as a group. This would sometimes be spent playing instruments, trying things out, informal recordings, etc. But just as often and just as important from the viewpoint of our total 'education' and formation of ideas, styles, writing, composition, etc. etc. were the many hours spent talking, discussing, listening to records, other bands, introducing new sounds and ideas to the others...the list goes on! From experience I have of other musicians, this is a very common 'evolutionary' process, to a greater or lesser extent, in the formation of the creative spirit. I can't stress more strongly that this was the really important aspect of those early days for all of us — Robert included."

No drinks at the inn for Wilde Flowers

Their hair is too long, says licensee

By Don Packham

CANTERBURY'S latest popbeat group, the five-piece Wilde Flowers (three Rolling Stones' haircuts among them), complained this week that a city publican refused to serve them drinks.

And the licensee confirmed that bass guitarist Hugh Hopper—"I last went to the barber a year ago"—was not welcome and nor were his pals.

THE PUBLIC-HOUSE is the Three Compasses in St. Peter's-st., almost next door to the College of Art.

THE LICENSEE is Mr. Reginald Baxter, who has been mine host of the popular pub for 3 years.

Among those banned is 19-year-old Hugh, ex-grammar school, unemployed, and son of an accountant, from Giles-lane, Canterbury.

Asked to leave

He was with two members of the group and two other friends in the saloon bar on Monday evening when the Three Compasses pointed the way to the door.

Hugh said: "As soon as we walked in the publican said: 'I am sorry. I'm not serving you.'

"We asked him why and he said: 'I am allergic to long hair.' He said this before we had even asked for a drink.

Guitarist Hopper and Hair

"Our drummer tried to talk to him but obviously the publican had his point of view, while we had ours . . .

"There were only about three people in the bar at the time."

When he went into the pub, Hugh wore a ginger suede jacket, green pullover, and brick-coloured neckerchief.

About town, he usually wears a brown corduroy "cheese-cutter" cap as well.

Hugh, who is a former Simon Langton, Canterbury, grammar school pupil, commented: "One is used to being laughed at but we are surprised at the strong reaction. It seemed as though he hated long hair. Mine keeps my ears warm!

"I have my hair trimmed occasionally. When I was working abroad most of last year I had it shaved right off the top.

"We have never been refused service in other pubs and cafes."

Own tunes

Publican Mr. Baxter told me: "It all started a couple of weeks or so ago. He wasn't refused initially but his conduct has proved that I should have done so.

"He is not welcome and nor are his pals."

Other members of the Wilde Flowers turned out of the pub were drummer Robert Ellidge, 19-year-old art school model from Swalecliffe, and vocalist Kevin Ayers (20), who is out of work.

Hugh's bearded brother Brian, 22, a laboratory assistant, is lead guitar and 16-year-old Richard Sinclair, an art student from Downs-rd., Canterbury, performs on the rhythm guitar.

The Wilde Flowers write their own tunes. Unwilting, they make their first big public appearance tonight . . . in another public house, the Bear and Key at Whitstable!

1965

"We were never very good. We didn't get work not because we were too far out, just because we were bad. However, both Kevin and Hugh very early on did start writing what I thought were really good pop songs and it was because of that we did ultimately start doing their stuff. Our friends thought we were mad. They were all jazz fans."

This Canterbury combo really swing

They try for an Indian influence

THEY call themselves the Wilde Flowers and they engender extreme reactions wherever they go. Their Rolling Stones' haircuts make the fans go crazy, as well as the parents—in opposite directions.

But that doesn't detract from their skill. Although they have only been playing for three months, this Canterbury combo really swing together whether they are playing straight R and B or hard, driving, soul jazz.

Lead guitarist Brian Hopper also doubles on alto sax for the jazz numbers and the group write all their own tunes.

"We are trying to get more of an Indian influence in our music," said bass guitarist Hugh Hopper. "We use the group as a unit to say what we want."

Why Wilde Flowers? "Well we were looking through a list of library books for a title and there was this one called British Wild Flowers."

The line-up is: Brian Hopper (alto sax and lead guitar); Robert Ellidge (drums); Kevin Ayres (vocals); Hugh Hopper (bass guitar).

Jan 15 — 'Dance' Bear and Key Hotel, Whitstable (see photo at left)

Richard Sinclair:

"Our first gig came up and Hugh's mum had made all these satin shirts for us to wear. Sure enough I got stuck with the dark green one which I didn't want, you know there were all these nice colours, magenta, red, yellow. It was upstairs at the Bear and Key in Whitstable and there was Robert's girlfriend Pam and Brian's girlfriend Ali on the door and that was the first time I'd met Pye."

Winter — Starlight Ballroom, Herne Bay

Winter — College of Art, Canterbury

Winter — The Beehive, Canterbury

Roger Turner:

"I remember the first time I saw them at the Beehive, and I do remember saying to Robert, like, 'What are you doing? What's all this?' I felt it had really helped the scene, but no doubt being someone with a life he had spotted something else that he wanted to get in on. I was surprised by them, I really was, that it was his musical choice, he was actually promoting it. I remember that very clearly because it seemed like...almost...traitorous."

Kevin Ayers:

"The only thing I can remember about the Wilde Flowers is being beaten up for my long hair when we played. Where? The Beehive."

March 16 — SRS, Broadstairs, demo recording sessions
Released on Wilde Flowers CD (Voiceprint VP123)
a) 'Parchman's Farm' (B. White)
b) 'Memories' (H. Hopper)
c) 'She's Gone' (K Ayers)
d) 'Almost Grown' (C. Berry)

Kevin Ayers, vocals (a, b)/backing vocals (d)/tambourine; Richard Sinclair, rhythm guitar/backing vocals (d); Brian Hopper, guitar/alto sax (a)/vocals (d); Hugh Hopper, bass; Robert Ellidge, drums

SRS is an acronym for Steenhuis Recording Studios, which was owned and operated by the late Dutch musician Wout Steenhuis. For local groups SRS offered an inexpensive opportunity to have their songs recorded and cut directly onto acetate discs for demonstration to prospective record companies and club owners.

Paul Steenhuis:

"My dad did all the recordings and a guy named Clive Taylor was the engineer. I was at most of the sessions and I do remember The Wilde Flowers, but only vaguely. One of them had flowers painted all over his boots though. This was around when the hippies were starting to come in."

"Our first time in a proper studio was at Wout Steenhuis' own. Wout was a successful middle-of-the-road Hawaiian guitarist or something. We quite simply hadn't a clue how to translate our stuff to tape, that I remember!"

Wilde Flowers Have Claim To Fame

From the Beatles to Big Bill Broonzy; from Manfred Mann to Mose Allison—the repertoire of the Wilde Flowers, one of East Kent's newest groups, includes rhythm and blues, rock 'n roll, as well as jazz and original compositions.

The Flowers make their public debut tonight (Friday) at the Bear and Key Hotel, Whitstable. Since they formed three months ago they have played at parties and private functions, but now they hope to make an impact on the local music scene.

Line-up of the Wilde Flowers is: Brian Hopper, 22, (lead guitar and alto sax); his brother Hugh, 19, who plays bass guitar; rhythm guitarist, 16-year-old Richard Sinclair; Robert Wyatt Ellidge, 19, (drums) and vocalist, 20-year-old Kevin Ayers, who says he germinated to the Wilde Flowers.

PUBlicity note: The Flowers already have one claim to fame —on Monday three of the group, Brian, Hugh and Robert were refused drinks at a Canterbury pub because the landlord thought they were "scruffy." Said Hugh, whose hair is nine inches long, "We're used to being stared at, but it's the first time we've been thrown out of a pub."

The Wilde Flowers (left to right): Brian Hopper, Richard Sinclair, Robert Wyatt Ellidge, Hugh Hopper, and Kevin Ayers.

Meet the Wilde Flowers

*The group most likely to turn heads in Canterbury is one made up of five young men who call themselves the Wilde Flowers.

For four months now they have been playing in and around Canterbury, making their name known by their particular style of music and their unconventional appearance.

The group, who chose the name from a book on wild flowers as well as that they all come from the garden of England, Kent, play jazz, rhythm 'n' blues, folk, and pop.

The two brothers in the group, Hugh and Brian Hopper, from Canterbury, write a good many of the group's numbers. Hugh, a 20-year-old garage hand, plays a bass guitar which is decorated by hand-painted flowers. Dark, bearded, Brian, a laboratory assistant aged 22, is on lead guitar, saxophone and vocals.

YOUNGEST PLAYER

Youngest member of the group is 16-year-old Richard Sinclair, from Herne Bay, an industrial design student at the College of Art. He is on rhythm guitar and vocals.

Singer and harmonica player, 19-year-old Graham Flight, a toy maker, is the quiet member of the group with a sound like Bob Dylan.

The drummer, 20-year-old Robert Wyatt, a model at the art school, has no worries that his casual clothes, and shoulder-length hair might raise eye-

brows among the older people, for, as he said: "My appearance is completely irrelevant to me."

Robert used to play in a club with Tubby Hayes, who is recognised as the top tenor player in the country.

He said he used to loathe pop music on the principle that if it was so popular, it must be bad. But when he listened carefully to the songs of pop composers such as Lennon and McCartney, and Burt Bacharach, he realised that good things were being done in music.

It is a possibility though, that the Wilde Flowers will eventually give up pop music and concentrate more on modern jazz.

DIFFERENT TASTES

The members of the group claim to differ from each other in their tastes in music. Graham, for instance, is a firm fan of Bob Dylan, while Richard prefers Nat King Cole.

They believe, too, that they have their own very individual outlooks on life. But life itself, they do not take too seriously, because feeling that way, said Robert, better things come from it.

In the future, the Wilde Flowers, who have played at the Beehive Club, the College of Art, and at Whitstable, hope to record several of their own numbers. They would accept a good offer to turn professional, and as they say, they are keen to make money.

reprinted from Kent Observer, June 8, 1965

Work for the Wilde Flowers proves difficult to obtain and gigs, which total little more than a handful, are often received with indifference. By spring, Kevin Ayers departs and is replaced by a young singer named Graham Flight, who shared a flat in Herne Bay with Robert.

Apr (late) — SRS, Broadstairs, demo recording sessions

Twenty seven years later, only Brian Hopper retains a faint memory of the four songs recorded by the new quintet.

Brian Hopper:

"This Steenhuis session included a Beatles number which I think would have been 'Till There Was You' which Richard used to sing. Although I cannot definitely remember the other songs, I seem to recall that Graham played harmonica on at least one track. It was almost certainly an instrumental, probably either our version of Monk's 'Friday the 13th' or the Adderley Brothers 'Sack of Woe'. The other tracks were, I think, Hugh's songs and or possibly a Dylan song."

Spring — College of Art, Canterbury

Spring — The Beehive, Canterbury

June 5 — Frank Hooker School, Canterbury
supporting The Secrets

June or July — Sellindge, demo recording
sessions (studio unknown) Released on CD Voiceprint 123
a) 'Slow Walkin' Talk' (B. Hopper)
b) 'He's Bad For You' (R. Wyatt)
c) 'Don't Try To Change Me' (H. Hopper)
d) 'It's What I Feel' aka 'A Certain Kind' (H. Hopper)
Graham Flight, vocals (a, b, c)/tambourine (c); Brian Hopper, guitar/alto sax (b)/backing vocals (d); Richard Sinclair, rhythm guitar/vocals (d); Hugh Hopper, bass; RW, drums/vocals (b)/backing vocals (d)

Brian Hopper:

"'He's Bad For You' is a number influenced by John Coltrane and Elvin Jones and has a special atmosphere which was very representative of quite a lot of the early Wilde Flowers sounds—combining jazz, Eastern influences, etc. An interesting sidelight is that the opening drum roll is in fact a coin spun on the tom-tom miked up. We also used to do that trick at live gigs, which meant that we got very expert at spinning coins first time!"

Graham Flight recalls that Hugh had only the first verse for his Bo Diddley-ish 'Don't Try To Change Me' finished in time for the Sellindge sessions. The song was quickly completed with Graham writing the second verse and Robert the third.

'Don't Try To Change Me'

I used to go to school
I always broke the rule
But now I've gone away
I can go back and stay
'Cause that's the way I am
Don't try to change my way
If you can understand
You'd better get away

I used to chase around
Feet never touch the ground
But now I'm on the run
This game has lost its fun
So when I sing this song
You mustn't get me wrong
It's what I said to Susie Wong
This could be two hours long

Baby you would be a fool
To think I'd catch you if you fall
I won't stick with you alone
I just was then skin and bone
I won't always hold your hand
I won't say our love is grand
That's not how it's gonna be
You need a man but it's not me

July 10 — 'Canterbury Jazz and Folk Festival', Kingsmead Stadium, Canterbury

The same evening that the Wilde Flowers play to a near empty Stadium, Daevid Allen hosts an evening of poetry at the Galeria Teix in Deya, Majorca featuring his private recordings of readings by Robert Frost, e.e.cummings, William Burroughs, T. S. Eliot, John Esam, Christopher Perret, Gillian Smyth, Kurt Schwitters, and Robert Graves.

July 31 — The Beehive, Canterbury
augmented by Norman Hale, vocals

Through Norman Hale's performance with the Flowers, Robert is invited by the ex-Tornado singer/pianist to form a fifties styled rock 'n' roll act. With work offered sparingly, Robert floats freely between the two groups. Billing themselves simply as Norman and Robert, the duo perform occasionally at the Beehive club and various Kentish town dances until early 1966.

"Norman was from Liverpool, which was the correct place to be from at the time, which meant he could get gigs. It was good for me because I had to learn to play a lot of classic rock numbers one after the other fairly fast, so it was good for my muscles."

Aug/Sept — Norman and Robert, The Beehive, Canterbury

Aug 31 — Bekesbourne Youth Club, Bekesbourne

Wildeflowers Get Together With Ex-Tornado

Canterbury's Wildeflowers took over a booking at the Beehive at short notice last Saturday . . . and brought with them a surprise for their audience.

Singing with them for the first time ever, was Liverpudlian, Norman Hale, who has been performing among the top names in professional show business for a number of years.

One time member of the Tornadoes (of Telstar fame) and recently with The Lively Set who backed Chris Sanford, Norman, at present in Canterbury visiting his girl friend, was happy to oblige the Wildeflowers in joining the group for the night.

Although they have never played together before, Norman and the Wildeflowers made a good combination.

Norman particularly praised the drummer, Robert Wyatt, whose drumming he said, was " very technical."

Norman's professionalism shone through on Saturday, with a good visual act accompanying his versions of well-known numbers such as "Kansas City" and "Too Much Monkey Business."

Tall, good-looking with a blond Beatle hairstyle, he naturally went down well with the girls.

Heinz, Billy Fury, and John Leyton are some of the names with whom he has worked, but now, Norman is to be launched on a solo career. His act will be based on the Jerry Lee Lewis idom, he himself being a pianist as well as a singer.

Much of his visual stage act, he said, was inspired by Tom (It's Not Unusual) Jones, with whom he used to share a flat in London.

He explained that the audience liked to have something to watch.

Norman, who has started writing song numbers himself, is hoping that his career will lead to solo recording.

Norman and Robert

NORMAN AND ROBERT
—Know-How And Blues Beat

"They're good, aren't they," the girls at the Beehive Club said to each other, nodding towards Norman and Robert.

And some liked them for the way they looked (both fair-haired and green-eyed) and the image they presented, and others for their musical know-how and blues-style beat.

And they are good. Not only do their backgrounds, musical and otherwise, differ greatly from other local musicians, but they each, in spite of being a combined act, project an individuality which most groups, even national ones, fail to acquire.

Pianist Norman Hale, and drummer Robert Wyatt both use music as a means to different ends.

For Norman, music is in itself the most important factor. He enjoys entertaining people, but would be just as happy playing alone.

He said: "Music is my way of expressing myself."

He does not read notes, but has an amazing aptitude for playing by ear. On one impromptu occasion at the Beehive Club, he played to a small audience grouped around the piano pieces such as 'The Dream of Olwyn' . . . pieces which he said he had never played before. Although he feels classical music will win finally, his present style is very much in the fast-moving Jerry Lee Lewis idiom.

He is a true show business professional, believing in his own ability. He will go on until he reaches that maximum ability in himself which he knows he possesses.

Norman said: "If I make records and chart hits, well, God's been good, but most of all I want to be a success for myself."

Robert was educated in Canterbury. His drumming was taught by an American who was lodging at his parents' home.

Later he played in London clubs and then went to Spain, where he was once given the opportunity of playing with Tubby Hayes.

"When in London, I used to go for terribly avant-garde jazz, believing that if anything was really popular, it was not good," he said.

Later, listening to the simplicity of the Beatles' compositions, he realised that things could be good and popular. He thinks very highly of the personality and work of Beatle John Lennon. During the past year he has been with the local Wilde Flowers group, where he was once the drummer, but is now the singer.

Both Norman and Robert believe in the possibilities of their act, but neither considers going to London agents in an attempt to obtain big offers. They would rather build up a strong local following . . . Robert believing staunchly in Provincialism, . . . so that attention comes to them.

Temporarily the act was split by varying offers to both boys, one of which took Norman on a month's tour of German clubs.

Together again, they must now start to rebuild their following, their next Canterbury appearance being at the Beehive Club this Friday.

Although he comes from a musical family, Norman, from Stoneycroft, Liverpool, did not begin his own career until recent years. He has toured the country with top groups like The Tornadoes, and backed artistes such as Billy Fury and John Leyton.

In contrast to Norman's realistic approach to life, Robert lives in his own fantasy world. His dress, outlook and approach give him a second personality and one that can leave quite an impression on the people he meets.

He believes that every person has their own make-believe world, his being different only because it is the minority. He illustrated this point when he said: "Most people have the same sort of reasons for wanting short hair as I have for having mine long.

"I wear the things I think look right on me."

Robert's ambitions alter day by day, and he seems to worry little about the future.

Musically, he contrasts again with Norman in his attitude to his drumming. Like his paintings and poems, it is used not for its own sake but as an instrument to establish contact

September brings the departure of both Graham Flight and Richard Sinclair who returns to college. Robert moves centre stage as lead singer with the drum stool occupied by former Rojeens drummer Richard Coughlan.

Autumn — ABC Cinema, Canterbury

Hugh Hopper:

"Soon after Richard Coughlan joined we did some Saturday morning gigs at the ABC Cinema, playing about four songs in between the children's films. We were paid by having six months of complimentary tickets for Sunday night shows. Coughlan worked Saturday mornings nearby as a dental technician and had to sneak out for fifteen minutes to play."

Brian Hopper:

"We drove around Canterbury in this open Mini Moke (a jeep version of the British BMC Mini) carrying our instruments with posters attached etc. to promote the release of the film 'Catch Us If You Can' starring the Dave Clark Five, which, if you recall, was a reasonably popular pop/rock group of the sixties."

Oct 29 — Norman and Robert, The Beehive, Canterbury

Oct 30 — The Beehive, Canterbury

The above date is taken from the only newspaper notice the Beehive ever placed for a Wilde Flowers appearance. Throughout late '65 and early '66, the group are frequently booked into the club and a popular following begins. This period also brings various dance gigs at surrounding Kentish town halls and youth clubs, where Richard Coughlan recalls deliberate power cutoffs on more than one occasion.

Franco Bevan (owner of the Beehive):

"I'm not a musicologist but I remember that they were very good. They played there often, about every other weekend, and they became very popular, people liked them. They went on to play around Europe and become famous, didn't they? My that was such a long time ago."

Autumn — Baptist's Hall, Whitstable

Autumn (?) — Norman and Robert, Folkestone
(venue unknown)

"In 'Norman and Robert' I did my first ever public drum solo. We had to play a Police Cadets ball in Folkestone and this drunken Police cadet came up and demanded 'Caravan with a drum solo!' Norman, scouse trooper that he was, knew some quaint two chorded version of 'Caravan' and I just hammered away. They were all so drunk they thought it was a great solo. That was the start of something or other. Basically, all Norman did was play Jerry Lee Lewis songs, about twice as fast as any punk record."

Dec 31 — Norman and Robert, The Beehive, Canterbury

An all night New Year's Eve dance; "added attraction will be the Miss Beehive 1966 competition."

WILDE FLOWERS ARE GROWING

original artist/composer (if different)	song title	singer
Cannonball Adderley	Sack Of Woe	instr.
Mose Allison/Booker White	Parchman Farm	KA
Mose Allison/Willie Dixon	Seventh Son	KA
Mose Allison/Willie Dixon	I Live The Life I Love	KA
Mose Allison	If You Live Your Time Will Come	KA
The Beatles/Lennon—McCartney	All My Loving	RS
The Beatles/Lennon—McCartney	I Saw Her Standing There	RS
The Beatles/Lennon—McCartney	I'll Get You In The End	RS
Chuck Berry/Bobby Troup	Route 66	BH
Chuck Berry	Almost Grown	BH
Chuck Berry	Johnny B. Goode	BH
Chuck Berry	Little Queenie	BH
Chuck Berry	Talkin' Bout You	BH
Chuck Berry	Too Much Monkey Business	BH
Chuck Berry	Memphis Tennessee	BH
Chuck Berry	Sweet Little Sixteen	BH
Chuck Berry	Around And Around	BH
Chuck Berry	No Particular Place To Go	BH
Big Bill Broonzy	My Babe	BH
The Birds/Ron Wood	You're On My Mind	RW
The Birds/Holland—Dozier—Holland	Leaving Here	RW
Booker T and the MGs	Green Onions	instr.
Booker T and the MGs	Red Beans And Rice	instr.
James Brown	I Feel Good	RW
James Brown	Papa's Got A Brand New Bag	RW
Solomon Burke	Down In The Valley	?
The Byrds/Bob Dylan	Mr. Tambourine Man	KA
The Byrds/Clark—McGuinn—Crosby	Eight Miles High	KA
The Coasters/Leiber—Stoller	Poison Ivy	?
Eddie Cochrane	Twenty-Flight Rock	BH
John Coltrane	Mr. Syms	instr.
Ray Charles/Percy Mayfield	Hit The Road Jack	RW
Ray Charles	Hallelujah, I Love Her So	BH
Spencer Davis Group/Jackie Edwards	Keep On Running	RW
Bo Diddley	Bo Diddley	?
Lee Dorsey	Get Out Of My Life Woman	RW
Lee Dorsey	Working In A Coalmine	RW
Bob Dylan	Maggie's Farm	?
Bob Dylan	Motorpsycho Nightmare	HH
Bob Dylan	Rainy Day Women	RW
Duke Ellington	Don't Get Around Much Anymore	KA
Marvin Gaye/Holland—Dozier—Holland	Can I Get A Witness	RW
Herbie Hancock	Watermelon Man	RW
Wilbert Harrison/Leiber—Stoller	Kansas City	BH
Roy Head	Treat Her Right	KA
The Hollies	(titles unknown)	RW
John Lee Hooker	Dimples	GF
The Kinks/Ray Davies	You Really Got Me	KA
The Kinks/D. Covey—H. Abramson	Long Tall Shorty	RW
Manfred Mann/Barkin	Pretty Flamingo	?
Martha And The Vandellas/ Holland—Dozier—Holland	Nowhere To Run	RW
The Merseys/ Feldman—Goldstein—Gottehrer	Sorrow	RW
Thelonious Monk	Friday The 13th	instr.

Wilson Pickett/Pickett—S. Cropper	Midnight Hour	RW
Otis Redding/Redding—S. Cropper	Mr. Pitiful	RW
Jimmy Reid	Big Boss Man	BH
The Rolling Stones/Rufus Thomas	Walkin' The Dog	BH
The Rolling Stones/Willie Dixon	Little Red Rooster	KA
The Rolling Stones/Willie Dixon	Satisfaction	RW
The Rolling Stones	Get Off My Cloud	RW/BH
The Rolling Stones	Paint It Black	RW
The Rolling Stones	19th Nervous Breakdown	RW
Nina Simone/Screamin' Jay Hawkins	I Put A Spell On You	RW
The Small Faces/Samwell—Potter	Whatcha Gonna Do About It	RW
Dusty Springfield/Verdi—Kaye—Gin	Little By Little	?
Temptations/S. Robinson—R. White	My Girl	RW
Bobby Timmons	Moanin'	RW
The Velvelettes/Whitfield—Stevenson	Needle In A Haystack	RW
The Who/P. Townshend	Substitute	RW/BH
The Who/P. Townshend	My Generation	RW/BH
The Who/P. Townshend	I Can't Explain	RW/BH
The Yardbirds/Graham Gouldman	For Your Love	RW
The Yardbirds	(titles unknown)	RW

WILDE FLOWERS originals

composer	song title	singer
Kevin Ayers	She's Gone	KA
Kevin Ayers	Television Dreaming	KA
Robert Wyatt	He's Bad For You	RW/GF
Brian Hopper	Hope For Happiness	RW
Brian Hopper	Slow Walkin' Talk	RW/GF
Brian Hopper	Those Words They Say	RW/BH
Brian Hopper	How Many Tears	BH
Hugh Hopper	Memories	RW
Hugh Hopper	When I Don't Want You	KA/RW
Hugh Hopper	It's What I Feel	RS/RW
Hugh Hopper	Have You Ever Been Green	RW
Hugh Hopper	I Should Have Known	RW
Hugh Hopper	Never Leave Me	RW/BH
Hugh Hopper	I Am Glad (Glad I Am)	RW
Hugh Hopper	Don't Try To Change Me	GF
Hugh Hopper	Just Where I Want	RW
Hugh Hopper	No Game When You Lose	RW
Hugh Hopper	Time After Time	RW

Brian Hopper:

"It was necessary to have that many songs in our repertoire for some of the extended gigs we did. I think you'll find that most bands on the 'semi-pro' circuit had a similar extensive repertoire just to satisfy the requests of the punters! Where we were unusual was in our doing so many of our own numbers. Most of the other local bands just played other people's stuff and never wrote any of their own material.

"We also pioneered the continuous set idea early-on, playing continuously for up to an hour non-stop, merging one song into the next or including linking numbers and instrumentals. the concept was quite revolutionary at that time. It sure tested the keenness of the dancers!"

Hugh Hopper:

"I think what it was is that we were open to different influences from outside. Evenings of Indian music and ethnic music, so it wasn't just...I think most other bands that were actually playing then in Canterbury were just doing one sort of music. They were playing Rock or pop or Country or Western, whereas we were interested in lots of different things."

Gilli Smyth:

"My first book of poems, that came out in 1966, 'The Nitrogen Dreams of a Wilde Girl', was dedicated to the Wilde Flowers."

1966

"We did the experimental type stuff with Daevid and his friends for years, then we tried pop music and we couldn't really do that properly either. So we had to make up our own sort of music...sometimes I wonder why we even bothered!"

Winter or Spring — SRS, Broadstairs, demo recording sessions.
Released on CD Voiceprint VP123
a) 'Memories'
b) 'Never Leave Me'
c) 'Time After Time'
d) 'Just Where I Want'
e) 'No Game When You Lose'
f) 'Those Words They Say'
g) 'Impotence'
Brian Hopper, guitar/backing vocals (b, f); Hugh Hopper, bass; Richard Coughlan, drums; RW, vocals/tambourine (b, e)
All compositions Hugh Hopper except f) Brian Hopper

Hugh Hopper:
"I remember playing 'Never Leave Me' to Mike Ratledge, who was just down from Oxford and I also sent a copy to Eric Burdon, because 'Never Leave Me' was a bit like the Animals, 'We Gotta Get Out Of This Place.'"

Feb 19 — 'Big Beat Night' St Thomas Hall, Burgate
supporting the Turnarounds

Mar 12 — 'City Youth Dance' Canterbury Technical College
The Others supporting

Apr 2 — 'Dance' St Thomas Hall, Canterbury
supporting The Turnarounds

Apr 9 — 'Youth Dance' Prince of Wales Youth Club, Canterbury
supporting The Secrets

Spring — Christchurch College, Canterbury

Brian Hopper:
"We had done a gig someplace and we had packed up and there was this guy who kept hustling around and he was some sort of manager type guy and we weren't quite sure what was going on. What transpired was that there was this other guy hanging around in the background, a typical 1950's R & R look a like with a big quiffed hair and this sort of thing. What this manager wanted was for us to be his backing band, he was doing typical 50's Rock and Roll type things. We tried to do things with him but this guy, well he really couldn't sing! It was most embarrassing. This manager wanted this guy to go on the record and needed a backing band since he could see this guy had the look but that was about it!"

Hugh blows a bass amp during Richard and Robert's drum duet

TOFT'S

35 to 39 GRACE HILL, FOLKESTONE   TEL. 38173

Established 10 years

E OF THE COUNTRY'S LEADING AND MOST FAMOUS CLUBS

Fridays & Sundays 8 - 11   **Saturdays 8 - 11.45**

FOR ALL BLUE BEAT AND SKA FANS

PRINCE BUSTER'S

WEST INDIAN BAND

THE BEES

also

THE WILDE FLOWERS

Saturday, April 1st   Admission 7/6

Prince Buster who arrives in this country later will be appearing here with **The Bees** on ~~With~~ Saturday, May ~~13th~~ 6th

---

ZOOT MONEY

and his

BIG ROLL BAND

Saturday, April 8th   Admission 10/-

John Mayall

and his

Blues Breakers

Saturday, April 15th   Admission 8/-

THE MIKE COTTON SOUND

with

LUCAS

Saturday, April 22nd   Admission 8/-

THE SQUARE DEAL SOUL SHOW

JAMAICAN BLUE BEAT AND SKA SPECIALISTS

Saturday, April 29th   Admission 6/6

Resident Bands

THE EARL GUTHERIDGE EXPLOSION

THE WILDE FLOWERS

Fridays 2/6   Sundays 3/-

Why not arrange to meet your friends in our Fabulous

BEACHCOMBER Coffee Bar

Members Only   **Membership 1/- per year**

Meanwhile back in Majorca...Deya becomes the backdrop for an LSD inspired confluence of individual ambition and collective lunacy. Here Daevid Allen and Kevin Ayers meet Wes Brunson and spend three sleepless days on a tour of happening bars and parties around the island. If the instigative circumstances border on the mythical, by contrast the professed intention was clear: to start a pop group in pursuit of fortune and fame.

Lady June:

"I met a tall, gangly Texan who was looking for 'the scene'. Deya was really wild at that time, rather like a Fellini movie really. I used to go up to Deya at weekends and I told the guy I'd meet him at the bus and take him up, but had second thoughts about it as I got weird vibes from him. So I arrived late, by which time Daevid had got him tripped out and he was putting up the money for Daevid and Kevin's band. He subsequently went quite mad, thought he was the 7th incarnation of Jesus Christ and ultimately became violent — the story is too lengthy to tell here but quite hysterically funny at times."

Gilli Smyth:

"It was Easter Sunday. The village was alive with preparations for the Easter procession, celebration of the day that, to Catholics, Jesus rose again. There was an atmosphere of expectation, of unusualness, waiting for something to happen. The first visitor was Robert Graves with the Easter blessing. He was extraordinarily psychic and always appeared at important moments. Kevin Ayers was staying with Daevid and I and we were just abandoning ourselves to the unexpectedness of the day when other visitors appeared, Blind George and Tom Fu the painter with Wes Brunson in tow.

"Wes was a wealthy night club owner from Tulsa, Oklahoma and had had a vision that to serve God he must give a lot of his money to people who would broadcast the New Age. To him this vision was ultimately of a great white boat which would sail round the world with Daevid, Kevin and other elite males in psychic charge. At the time his fanaticism was not apparent, apart from a paranoid streak which manifested in having a knife and a gun down each sock. However this was only a tiny note of foreboding among an atmosphere of excitement. He wanted to put his money into flying us all to London, renting a house and getting the group that Daevid and Kevin had been fantasizing about actually on the road. It all had an air of complete unreality about it, Wes lost in his own religious vision of a born again Christian, Daevid and Kevin enthused by the fact that the music they had been playing together for weeks was magically going to be transported to a real life situation of gigs and audiences."

Daevid Allen:

"I was living in Majorca and actually on the full moon of Easter Sunday a bunch of people showed up. Kevin Ayers arrived, a guy named Wes Brunson arrived and Kevin talked Wes into financing a band saying 'We have got to start a band as soon as possible!' He then went back to America and sold his business. He brought the money back to England and that is what we used to buy guitars, amplifiers, and rent Jane Aspinall's house in Kent to prepare the band."

Hugh Hopper:

"Rent is a euphemism for 'descend upon and fill with 1966 weirdness'."

Gilli Smyth:

"Daevid and Kevin went first to set up a house where the group could live and rehearse, which turned out to be the Old Coach House in Sturry near Canterbury. I flew to London a few weeks later and arrived to find the house full of the P.A. and equipment that Wes had bought, and rehearsals going full swing. Larry Nolan, an American guitarist from Palma was there, we had met and spent time with him and Janey Alexander. The air of unreality continued during the months of rehearsal — every day Wes would fill the basket on the kitchen table with money for shopping and things. Meantime there was a great shifting around of musicians."

Brian Hopper:

"Robert was really wanting to change direction but he didn't know which way to go. He had his bit in the Wilde Flowers but also was being pulled by the others to form something new and open up completely new avenues. I think it created quite a bit of tension at that time and the rest of us in the Wilde Flowers didn't quite know what was going on or what we wanted to do. It was a strange sort of time, but things resolved themselves of course. However we still did things. We had a few jam sessions and things with other people, Kevin and Daevid Allen and so forth. We were doing things, free form things on another level as it were. I mean that was the peculiar thing, there were several different sorts of music, and we all participated in them to a greater or lesser extent. Then obviously the whole thing resolved and Mister Head went off in its own directions."

Mister Head is Daevid's name for the new quartet comprising Daevid Allen, bass/vocals; Kevin Ayers, rhythm guitar/vocals; Larry Nolan, guitar; Robert Wyatt, drums/vocals. Throughout the formative months of May and June, Robert fluctuates freely between gigs with the Wilde Flowers and rehearsals for Mister Head, who quickly adopt several Hugh and Brian Hopper songs into their repertoire.

May 14 — 'City Youth Dance' Frank Hooker School, Canterbury
The Secrets supporting

On May 23rd, Pam Howard and Robert Wyatt Ellidge welcome the arrival of their newborn son Sam Wyatt. For mother and child domestic stability is found through an invitation to stay with Honor Wyatt in her London home.

May 29 — 'Melody Maker Beat Contest' Regent Ballroom, Brighton
Set consists entirely of original songs - lost to The Pathfinders

Brian Hopper:
"We had a support team in the audience and I remember it was a particularly good performance. I know Robert agreed by his saying that it was probably one of the best performances that the Wilde Flowers had ever done. We didn't actually win it but we did reasonably well and certainly had some very good comments afterwards. At that time also, one or two agents that were there were particularly interested in Robert's singing and approached him afterwards. Nothing specific came of it but he was certainly noticed at the time."

June — Mister Head, Jazz Club, Herne Bay
augmented by Dave Stewart, soprano sax

June — Mister Head, The Beehive, Canterbury

June 24 — 'Radio London Beat Competition' Dreamland Ballroom, Margate
also : The Soul, The Runarounds, Ways and Means, The Chaos
With Richard Coughlan unable to make the gig, Robert takes over the drum kit for a performance that nets the trio a shared first prize placement with The Runarounds.

Richard Coughlan:
"The trouble was that we'd all got rather fed up with having to play soul music in order to keep ourselves earning money. What we really enjoyed playing at that time were Mose Allison numbers and stuff like that, even some material written by Hugh and Robert. Almost everyone who was in the Wilde Flowers felt basically the same at the time, about the sort of stuff they wanted to play. It was a period of groundwork for all of us."

Hugh Hopper:
"The legend is that Canterbury was sort of a great hotbed of music, but in fact it wasn't. I mean things didn't really happen until people left Canterbury to work in London, or wherever, or Paris. It just happens that about a half dozen musicians who came from Canterbury at one point then went on to make other bands. Canterbury has always been a very conservative place and it still is. It's a very hard place to do any music, a coincidence maybe. Or maybe not, maybe it's because it is a conservative place that it's kind of forced people to think in different ways, if they had that tendency anyways."

Upon the onset of summer, the zeitgeist of the Old Coach House was, from all accounts, becoming quite bizarre. The local police were making surprise visits to search for Wes Brunson's daughters, whom he had abducted and kept in hiding from both the authorities and the band. With Wes under arrest and facing deportation to America, and Jane preparing to sell the property, Mister Head are bound for London. Curiously, Larry Nolan remains in Canterbury, preferring to travel for future gigs and rehearsals. In London, Kevin Ayers is quickly signed to the management of the Animals as a songwriter.

Daevid Allen:
"We were picked up by a woman (Willow Morel), who managed us briefly, who lived near Chelsea, and we stayed in and around Chelsea in their apartment for a little bit. Then we were picked up by Henri Henroid who was Mike Jefferies Cockney offsider. His famous phrase was 'the boys were really great tonight' and 'aggravation' and all these terms from the Cockney world."

Kevin Ayers:
"We used to call him Henri Hemorrhoid. He was just the gopher. It was Jefferies who held the real power."

"Kevin Ayers was important in that he knew the Animals office, where Hilton Valentine and Chas Chandler were already starting to manage, and they signed us up really on the basis of Kevin's songs. They were looking for something commercial. Chas was always looking for Slade, and eventually he found them, meanwhile he had to put up with people like us and Jimi Hendrix."

Summer — sessions for Kevin Ayers Anim Publishing demos (studio unknown)
a) 'Contusions' (K. Ayers)
b) 'Another Lover Has Gone' (K. Ayers)
Kevin Ayers, rhythm guitar; Larry Nolan, guitar; Daevid Allen, bass/vocals; RW, drums/harmony vocal (b)
In August, the group obliged Mike Ratledge with his

offer 'if you ever need a keyboard player, call me.' Mike dropped into the scene from Oxford where he had studied classical music, worked with avant-garde musicians (including improvisors Mal Dean and Rab Spall) and gained impeccable academic credentials from the University College. A mink coat which a friend gave to Kevin Ayers was promptly sold and in return Mike bought his first electric organ, a Vox Continental, and a fuzz box.

Mike Ratledge:

"There were a lot of fuzz boxes around and the sound of a Vox Continental was so abysmal, you try anything to make it more aggressive. Guitarists had begun using them a great deal then, trying to alter the sound of their guitar, and I didn't see why guitarists had to have a monopoly on fuzz boxes. Using it changed my style, it can do that, it's an aggressive sound and henceforth made my playing more aggressive."

"At the time one of the characteristics of pop music that I didn't like is the fact that it was based on guitar. I found this extremely limiting. I wanted to work with instruments that could give you uninterrupted sounds, totally sustained. I wanted to work with a keyboard player, except all the keyboard players at this time were some bad imitation of Jimmy Smith or Booker T. But that wasn't the case with Mike. He was using his knowledge as a keyboard player, who were generally speaking more technically competent than the guitar players of the time. Mike was a very important element in my development."

Having now decided to drop the name Mister Head,

suggestions for a replacement vacillate between the members of the new quintet to the degree where a booklet of considerations builds. Included are The Bishops of Canterbury, Dingo Virgin and the Four Skins, and Nova Express after the William Burroughs novel. The compromise is found upon agreeing to adopt a name from outside the group.

Mike Ratledge:

"It came second hand through a book by William Burroughs called 'The Soft Machine'. He in turn had taken it from a lecture by a physiologist in America, I can't remember what his name was. Soft Machine is a generic term for the whole of humanity and we were all Soft Machines. At that time being I guess what we hoped to be was a pop group i.e. we hope to appeal to as...well our basic assumption is what we like everybody else is going to like as well, you know, that we all have things in common, and therefore we all are Soft Machines and we're all going to like Soft Machine music. It might have been a false assumption but I hope it's true."

Jimmy Hastings:

"I've got the actual copy of that book 'Soft Machine' at home, the one they named themselves after. I don't know how I came to get it, maybe it was left behind somewhere. I've never read it."

Aug — 'Midsummer Revels' Coombe Springs

The Soft Machine's first photo session, on the streets of West Dulwich. No photos of the original quintet are known to exist. L-R: Ayers, Ratledge, Wyatt, Allen

The Soft Machine's first concert.

Daevid Allen:

"Under very weird circumstances J. G. Bennett and disciples of Gurdjieff the philosopher decided to sell their house, which they'd had for ages, to Idries Shah of the Sufi's for a smallish sum of money. It was an inauguration for the Sufi's taking over the house. Idries was a friend of Robert Graves who was a friend of Honor so that's the connection. So we played there, we met Idries Shah and we met all these guys and of course I was interested in that whole thing. But what was really strange was that the Sufi's then promised not to sell it, but they did about six months later for a huge profit."

Bill MacCormick:

"They were the first rock band I'd ever seen in my life. The whole circumstances of the party were very very weird. Apart from going in there and staring at them and wandering around the building and the garden checking things out...I was still a very innocent fifteen year old in those days and the whole thing was quite bizarre for me."

Aug — Star Club, Hamburg, Germany

Daevid Allen:

"We were booked into the Star Club for a week's residency but after about a half hour into the first night the manager pulled the plug. I think the audience had never experienced psychedelic music before and we were getting equal amounts of boos and applause. It seemed pretty well balanced, I mean half the audience loved us and the other half hated us so shouting and scuffles broke out. We did tend to create mass schizophrenia in audiences and to that extent I suppose we were quite successful, in a revolutionary sort of way."

Gilli Smyth:

"I suppose the Star Club was the toughest of all the strange gigs. Organized by Henry in London with an uncertain contract in Hamburg, we arrived to find a very tough scene in this smoky club in the middle of the red light district. The management did not like the music, refused to pay, awkward since we had no return tickets or food, and now no money. Meantime, Mike had got to know some strippers in a nearby club who, touched by our predicament, gave us money to travel and a basket of food, and came to see us off at the railway station, a memorable parting."

Kevin Ayers:

"I wrote 'Love Makes Sweet Music' in Hamburg when we were all staying in toilets. And I got really excited about it and said to everybody 'listen to this, we've got a big hit here.' I thought suddenly everything was going to change, that this song was going to do it."

Behind the scenes significant support for the Soft Machine arrived from two members of Robert's family. Mark Ellidge took responsibility for driving the band to their gigs, maintaining their van and became their exclusive photographer. Honor Wyatt opened the doors of her home in West Dulwich, London to care for family and friends.

"We swamped my mother's life, we just took it over. We lived on her house, I mean all of us, girlfriends, wives, children, guitars, road managers, we just packed ourselves in."

Honor Wyatt:

"They rang me up from Canterbury 'Mommy, we're comin' in', so I thought 'they're coming to London, that means they're coming to my house.' And of course they did, the whole group! Now I was brought up on Cole Porter, Irving Berlin and people like that, but when he started I didn't know what Robert was on about, I could not understand it at all. I listened to what they had to say on their instruments and I thought 'well, I don't know, I don't get it at all.' But of course hearing this day after day because they'd rehearse, and rehearse, and rehearse, and fortunately I'm not a very nervy person, so that although to me it was quite frankly a noise to start with, nevertheless it was a noise with a purpose, they knew what they were doing. Well gradually I got used to it and I began to like it and grew quite fond of it!"

Bill MacCormick:

"Robert's mother and my mother worked in the same school through the mid-sixties. We were invited around for dinner one night and it sort of went on from there. There was an interesting culture clash between my parents then and the Soft Machine, well not quite the Soft Machine, the whole house being decorated on the outside and inside with all sorts of exotic murals. It happened to be on the way to school for me, so I'd stop off on the way back and drink a cup of tea, listen to music and chat."

Ian MacDonald (nee MacCormick):

"My brother and I lived near the group's house in Dalmore Road, Dulwich, London and got to know them around late '66. We used to hang out there alot, being total pains and getting in everyone's way, but fascinated by their music and hippie lifestyle. Even though we lived so close, I used to write letters to Robert and he'd write postcards back by return, telling me what was going on and carrying on discussions about this and that. He and Mike would talk entertainingly and informatively for hours on everything from modern art to politics and free jazz. They were by far the most intelligent and educated people on the English rock scene and I learned a lot from them. Daevid was equally amenable and happy to talk, though his interests were more mystic and esoteric, over my head at the time, though I've come to share them since. I remember him mystifying me with long discourses on prana and sex-magic. Kevin was the cool, aloof one, always disappearing off to his room with another woman, smiling enigmatically. Some members of Caravan dropped by now and then, though I have no particular memories."

Daevid Allen:

"I can remember we were all living as if we were great pop stars, in our heads at least."

Sept — 'Spontaneous Underground' Marquee

also: Donovan, AMMusic

"Mickie Most came to us saying 'I can put you in the charts but you're going to have to do the songs I want.' We said no. Our management was furious because Mickie Most had already made Lulu, Donovan, Jeff Beck and he wasn't making offers to just anybody. What was crazy for us in the beginning was that we were ready to make LP's and the record company was telling us 'You can't do an album, you don't have a hit single.'"

Sept 30 — All Saints Hall, London Free School
supporting Pink Floyd Sound

After his fourth gig, guitarist Larry Nolan decides to leave the Soft Machine and the music business entirely. Gilli Smyth remembers Larry as "an excellent guitarist who never quite fit in."

Oct 15 — 'All-Night Rave' Roundhouse
also: Pink Floyd Steel Band
A party organized by Daevid's friends, John Hopkins (owner of Indica Books) and Barry Miles to launch International Times, Britain's first underground newspaper.

John Platt (author/archivist):
"The IT party was a memorable event. Some 200 people turned up and were greeted by Miles handing out sugar-cubes (which turned out not to be of the LSD-coated variety). What took place set the style for later events — people in bizarre fancy dress rolling in huge jellies, dancing, revelling, tripping and watching films; a Bacchanal of the first order. Paul McCartney showed up dressed as an Arab. Italian film director Michelangelo Antonioni was there to take a break from shooting 'Blow Up' and Marianne Faithfull, wearing a nun's habit, won the prize for the 'shortest/barest' costume."

Daevid Allen:
"That was our first gig as a quartet. Yoko Ono came on stage and created a giant happening by getting everybody to touch each other in the dark, right in the middle of the set. We also had a motorcycle brought onto the stage and would put a microphone against the cylinder head for a good noise."

Oct 27 — Tiles
supporting The Toggery Five

Nov 2 — De Lane Lea, sessions for Jimi Hendrix Experience 'Stone Free' demo (unreleased)
Jimi Hendrix, Guitar/vocal; Noel Redding, bass; Mitch Mitchell, drums; Kevin Ayers, RW, backing vocals

Autumn — unnamed collective, 'Spontaneous Underground' Marquee
Mal Dean, trumpet; Rab Spall, violin; John Surman, soprano sax; RW, drums; other musicians unknown

Throughout the month of December, the Soft Machine

hold a weekly residency at the Zebra club and it is at a rehearsal session here that Mike Ratledge meets Marsha Hunt, an American singer who had just left Long John Baldry's group. To relieve Robert's frustration at synchronizing his drumming and singing roles, Marsha begins rehearsing with the group but after a week decided not to join.

Marsha Hunt:
"My singing with the Soft Machine didn't come to fruition but marrying Michael did."

"I've listened to tapes of concerts (1969) where I'm trying to do this (simultaneous drumming, singing) and the result is a complete fuck-up on both fronts. It's not just difficult, it's impossible. All the sixties reminds me of is trying to ride two horses which want to go in different directions at the same time. I think that's why only when I was drunk and everything is double and facing the other way, eyes and brain also, is it possible to even try these things. But I started in a group called the Wilde Flowers in Canterbury, we did some James Brown stuff 'I Feel Good' which is great. But that I used to sing and play at the same time, but you'll notice that with James Brown maybe it's possible because the words and the rhythm are kind of truncated (sings vocal then drum parts of 'I Feel Good'). You can put down the sticks for the little bit of voice."

Dec 10 — The Zebra

Dec 17 — The Zebra

Dec 24 — The Zebra

Gilli Smyth:
"The personal manager was Henri Henroid, an East End wise guy who had sold many products before this band; who put them on for a disastrous gig at Tiles, and whose pithy rock-bottom saying became legend ('The boys were great tonight' et. al.). It did not seem as if the management cared at all about the personal well-being of the musicians, only their percentage. I remember waiting every Friday afternoon for the weekly pay in the Animals office, one Friday on the eve of Christmas they forgot and went away, so we all found ourselves penniless. Fortunately, the band was always surrounded by very supportive fans, family, and friends, which rescued us several times."

Dec 31 — The Zebra

Dec — CBS Studios, sessions for 'Fred The Fish'/'Feelin, Reelin, Squeelin" 45

below: Pam, Robert, Daevid, Vox Continental, Kevin, Michelle at Zebra Club

Music or Noise?

The older generation are adamant. "Call it what you will," they say, "but it's not music."

They find it difficult to appreciate the mass acceptance by young people towards the revolution in sound. What was once considered too 'way-out' for the general public has been made popular and acceptable in the last couple of years by top groups such as "The Yardbirds" and "The Who."

Locally, most of the groups have remained in the general beat idiom, but a couple have themselves experimented with the trend that uses electronics as a means in itself of sound.

The Methods are one group, now professional, who, to their success, have used the feedback style of music of The Who.

More concerned with the actual experimenting in this field, without the hampering concern of an audience is Robert Wyatt Ellidge, who, with some of his equally involved friends, records on tape their experimental numbers.

Robert, a drummer, and knowledgeable on music in its various forms, has written several jazz articles. The following in his own words, is his opinion on the debatable question:

"Is this trend music or just noise?"

"People hate noise; there are laws against it; cafes, theatres, restaurants, churches and neighbours throw people out for making it.

"It's not that simple; there are two kinds; incidental noise and noise made on purpose to attract attention, communicate and 'please the ear.' Music is supposedly in the second category. The trouble is a lot of people claim that modern music should belong to the first. It sounds both useless and meaningless.

"Personally I call music conveying a state of mind purely in terms of sound. Sure, pretty melodies, consonant harmonies and easy flowing rhythms are part of it, but there is a lot more.

"The use of electricity in music has exaggerated the situation.

"Now, strong microphones allow musicians to be heard for miles, and transistor radios and juke-boxes tell everybody the good news whether they want it or not. As most serious composers are way beyond their audiences, the public tends to feel deserted by its own entertainers.

"And now, to make matters 'worse,' electrical devices themselves are being considered musical instruments in their own right.

"Recently the pop musician has been using 'unmusical' electronic devices as well.

'I am thinking particularly of guitarists Jeff Beck (The Yardbirds) and Peter Townshend (The Who).

"To me this is the important part where new musical ideas and general public meet face to face, and sympathetic teenagers in their millions actually involve themselves with new exciting ideas.

"Jazz too left the masses (to the mercy of rock 'n' roll) as it developed harmonies and rhythms to about the most sophisticated possible in an improvised art.

"And the jazz musicians are now using the accidental effects of tape-recorders and microphones as an integral part of the music.

"Now the closing gap between advanced musical ideas and mass acceptance is possible for the first time in many years. Young people are realising how many different sounds can make music, and how true art can grow from the most unexpected sources."

R. WYATT ELLIDGE

First published in Kent Observer and Canterbury Times, Feb 1, 1966

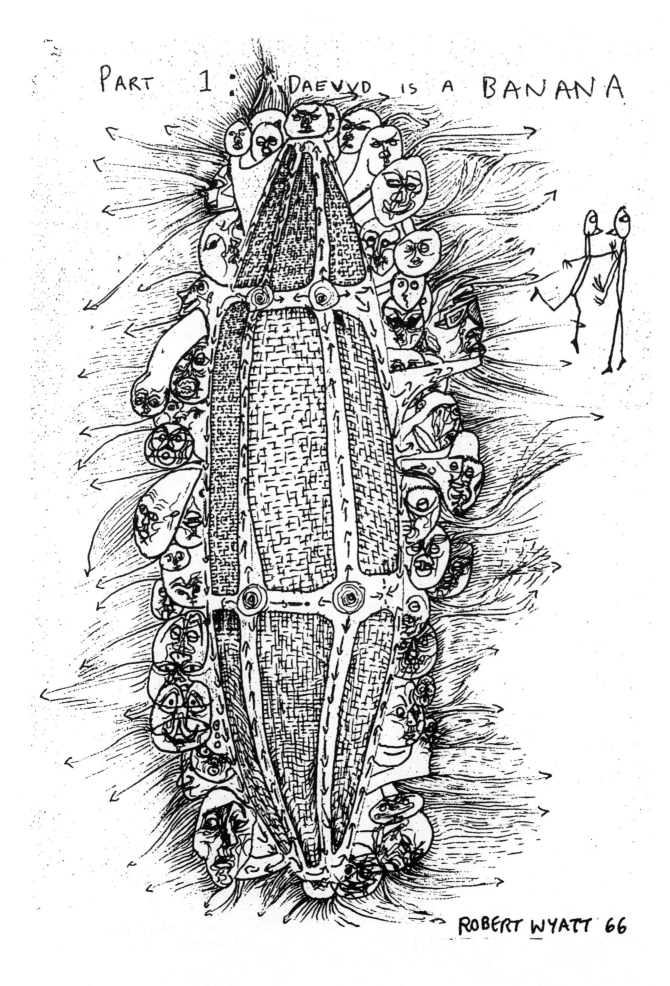

1967

"In terms of how we amplified our music we were a rock group, but what we heard in our heads wasn't pop music. We never looked to other groups for inspiration, in fact we were listening to Coltrane records. We got booed a lot in England at these dances where people were waiting for Jimmy James & The Vagabonds and instead got us — not a tune they recognized, just a row of stony faces. I thought the worst part of it was the break between numbers when there'd be this silence. So I suggested we link all our tunes up together so that the end of one was the beginning of the next. So the only time we stopped was when we left the stage, and that was how we developed the Soft Machine style of sustained continuous sets. Because of this brilliant compositional device, I never really had a clue what the audiences really thought of us."

Throughout the early months of 1967, the Soft Machine quartet are placed by their management on the pop/dance circuit of universities and colleges across Britain. Here the group's "version" of pop music proves too esoteric for the provincial teenagers who commonly respond with bewilderment, indifference, or violent protest (see histories of The Pink Floyd, Jimi Hendrix Experience). Short of researching all regional U.K. newspapers for public notice, these concert dates are lost and probably best forgotten. Similarly numerous London area concerts were performed with no advance notice. These include venues such as Electric Garden, ICA, Blaises, Happening 44, the London School of Economics, and an East End boxing arena where Gilli Smyth first performed a set of poems and voice sounds accompanied by the quartet. Additionally, Mike Ratledge recalls live New Departures gigs at the Marquee with poets Daevid Allen and Mike Horovitz and musicians Ratledge, Wyatt, Mal Dean, and Rab Spall. No one can remember any further details.

It is patently impossible to rehear a live concert performance of the Soft Machine with Daevid Allen as no single concert recording from this epoch is known to exist. This is confirmed by group members, associates, and private archivists, although AMM's Eddie Prevost suggests that Bob Woolford often made reel to reel recordings at U.F.O.

What has been attested to is that wherever possible the group would play for up to two hours, and at an extremely high volume. This sheer sonic intensity would cause Mike's new Lowry Holiday Deluxe organ to feedback during pauses, thereby prompting a style of continuous playing. Primitive electronics also forced Daevid to abandon the practice of integrating his tape recordings with performance after several early concerts. By group policy their expansive repertoire consisted entirely of original compositions and songs penned by the Hopper brothers. Set lists could draw upon the following titles as listed by composer:

Kevin Ayers — 'Another Lover Has Gone', 'She's Gone', 'Love Makes Sweet Music', 'Vaguely', 'We Did It Again', 'Feelin' Reelin' Squeelin'', 'Why Are We Sleeping?', 'We Know What You Mean', 'Lullabye Letter'

Daevid Allen — 'What's The Use?', 'Fred The Fish', 'Multiprayer To The Millionaires' (this being a poem set to intense improvisation)
Robert Wyatt — 'Save Yourself', 'You Don't Remember', 'That's How Much I Need You Now'
Brian Hopper — 'Hope for Happiness'
Hugh Hopper — 'Memories', 'Impotence', 'I Should Have Known'

Kevin Ayers:
"We couldn't play well enough and we were too white. So we invented our own white music by pooling our resources, which ended up sounding rather wacky. Sometimes what we did was really exciting; on occasion, the music seemed to play itself, an experience I've never had since the Soft Machine — I've never had the freedom of expression since then. I think we had more fun than the audience. There was a 'fuck you' element to the Soft Machine. We weren't underestimating the audience, but we didn't mind if they didn't like it. I think Robert was much more conscious about getting across to audiences."

Daevid Allen:
"From my point of view we were coming at it from the point of view of jazz, and yet we were playing Kevin and Robert's pop tunes with a sort of jazz flavour. It was a bit of an uneasy marriage in some respects, but it had a strange effect because no one was really doing it. I would say it was probably the first crossover, what you would say fusion, in the history of pop music. I don't know, maybe the Doors were doing their little bit, and Arthur Brown was doing his bit, but not many people were using those sorts of jazz things."

"Daevid Allen was a crazy guitar player, the only guitarist back then who wasn't imitating the blues. Around Daevid, his raga structures, his songs, his rhythmic conception, we decided to do long improvisations and so on. There is no doubt to me that the most important member of the band at this time was Daevid.
"Our music didn't fit into an already existing format. Pop music didn't offer enough open space for improvisation. And also when you have a hit record you always have to play it the same way and for us there was no way we were going to play a tune the same way twice."

Mark Ellidge:
"Mike Ratledge would never repeat his solo. You'd say 'can't you play that particular bit again, it worked so well' and he'd pretend he couldn't remember. They never played to the crowd, you know this thing of not introducing songs and playing long sets...they never took bows. In those days pop groups made little three minute songs to sell and they weren't comfortable with that, so nothing fit in."

Jan 28 — Roundhouse

Jan 28 — The Electric Poets, Roundhouse
Daevid Allen, guitar/voice/tapes; Gilli Smyth, voice; RW, drums

Jan — CBS Studios, sessions for 'Fred The Fish'/'Feelin', Reelin', Squeelin'' 45

Rejected A side performed by Daevid Allen, vocals; Mike Ratledge, piano; Kevin Ayers, bass; RW, drums/homemade trumpet/backing vocals. Released on CD (Voiceprint VP122).

Kim Fowley (producer):

"I met them at the Roundhouse and then we went into the studio. Chas Chandler didn't like the A-side and made them re-record it, but they kept the same B-side. That was great wasn't it? You should have heard the A-side we did, much better than the one which came out."

"The first time that I saw Kim Fowley's name was on the cover of the first album by the Mothers of Invention where it says he's playing hypophone, which means nothing. He's a freak from Hollywood, a fantastic guy. He was at the first Roundhouse gig we did with Pink Floyd and he was more conscious of our possibilities than the British were back then. He managed to convince our manager to allow us to record. He came to our place, gave us money, and made Kevin sing his songs all night long. It's thanks to him for 'Feelin', Reelin', Squeelin''."

Kevin Ayers:

"Of course I remember Kim Fowley. His favorite expression was 'Teenage Dogshit'."

Jan (?) — sessions for Jimi Hendrix 'Fluffy Turkeys' demo (studio unknown)

Jimi Hendrix, guitar/bass (?)/vocal (?); RW, drums/vocal (?) Song composed, session produced by Kim Fowley.

Jan — Advision, sessions for 'Love Makes Sweet Music'

Feb 4 — Roundhouse

Feb 5 — Olympic Sound, sessions for 'Love Makes Sweet Music'/'Feelin', Reelin', Squeelin'' 45

released Feb 17 (Polydor 56151)

A-side — Kevin Ayers, guitar; Mike Ratledge, organ; Daevid Allen, guitar; RW, drums/vocal

B-side — Kevin Ayers, bass/vocal; Mike Ratledge, piano/organ; Daevid Allen, guitar/whistle/backing vocal; RW, drums/vocal

Contrary to old rumour, Jimi Hendrix does not play rhythm guitar on this single.

Daevid Allen:

"Jimi Hendrix and us were both signed to the same management so we found ourselves following each other in and out of various studios throughout various stages of recording and mixing. Yea, Jimi did some things with us, although nothing was ever used. We just tried out different things together. We didn't record that single in just one sitting."

Feb 17 — 'Love Festival' UFO
also: Mark Boyle, Disney Cartoons, Indian Music, Feature Movie

UFO was located in an Irish dance hall called the Blarney Club in the basement of 31 Tottenham Court Road, opposite the Dominion Theatre, and was opened by The Pink Floyd on December 23rd 1966. It was an unconventional club that bypassed a daily "entertainment" schedule towards hosting all night events each Friday, as organized by managers Joe Boyd and John Hopkins.

Joe Boyd:

"The object of the club is to provide a place for experimental pop music and also for the mixing of medias, light shows and theatrical happenings. We also show New York avant garde films. There is a very laissez faire attitude at the club. There is no attempt made to make people fit into a format, and this attracts the further out kids of London. If they want to lie on the floor they can, or if they want to jump on the stage they can, as long as they don't interfere with the group of course."

John Platt:

"It certainly wasn't just a club in the entertainment sense; it was a genuine meeting/market place for the underground. For the first couple of months virtually everyone knew everyone else who was packed inside and sniffed the overpowering aroma of sweat and dope. Deals were made and projects planned. One could buy hippie paraphernalia from the 'head' shop or frilly shirt from John Pearce's Granny Takes A Trip stall. It was a remarkably relaxed environment, in which the likes of Mick Jagger or John Lennon could sit all night without being pestered for autographs."

"We felt like suburban fakes dressed up on Saturday and visiting the city. I never dared take LSD. I was in total awe of the audience at UFO, people like the OZ crowd. We used to come in the train and pretend we were like them. Just because we played long solos people assumed we were stoned, which was great for our credibility. I didn't know much about it. Daevid had connections with a whole generation of people there, all these people with very advanced ideas. Daevid was the internationalist of the group, he got us into all of that. The rest of us were all provincial."

Feb 18 — Corn Exchange, Chelmsford (photo left)
The Mooche supporting

Daevid Allen:

"We very nearly got killed at that gig."

"We had such terrible times in the early days if we ventured outside UFO. We'd get microphones and gear bashed up. Six times out of ten we'd come off stage in tears."

Feb 22 (afternoon)— Speakeasy (photo below)
augmented for a blues jam by Jimi Hendrix, bass
A press reception for the release of the 'Love Makes Sweet Music' single.

Though supported by promotional interviews with Radio Caroline, the BBC's Dave Lee Travis, and the Speakeasy reception, the commercial success of the Soft Machine's debut single is marginal, peaking at number twenty-eight on the Radio London pop charts. But serendipitous success is found with a weekly Wednesday night residency at the Speakeasy club, which runs through until June.

Gilli Smyth:

"The residency at the Speakeasy was a good showcase for the 'fashionable' on the rock scene. Other interesting musicians, like Brian Auger or The Beach Boys played there and you never knew who you would see, at three o'clock in the morning, talking business over a bottle of wine (e.g. when Daevid met John Lennon in the toilet). Robert hated the fashion part of it."

Feb 22 — Roundhouse
supporting The Jimi Hendrix Experience

Mar 1 — Speakeasy

Mar 3 — UFO
AMMusic supporting

Mar 5 — Padworth Hall, near Reading

Mar 8 — Speakeasy

Mar 9 — Polydor Studios, sessions for demos
Further details unknown.

Mar 15 — Speakeasy

Mar 22 — Speakeasy

Mar 24 — UFO

Mar 29 — Speakeasy

Mar — unnamed collective, 'Destruction in Arts Symposium' Institute of Contemporary Arts
Mal Dean, trumpet; Rab Spall, violin; Dave Tomlin, Evan Parker, George Khan, saxophones; Kevin Ayers, bass; John Stevens, Laurie Allen, Glenn Sweeney, RW, drums

Mal Dean:

"We played a gig at the ICA, which was a kind of free jazz day with an audience of about fifteen people in eighteen hours. And we met George Khan and Kevin Ayers and Evan Parker and Laurie Allen and John Stevens and it was a terrible mangle; all drums and a few bleating sounds."

Evan Parker:

"One of the artists involved in Destruction in Arts Symposium was arrested for something. I'm not sure who it was, it might have been the German guy, but somebody wanted to dynamite donkeys on the beach somewhere. I think it was a kinda joke that the police misunderstood. Anyways somebody got arrested and this was a benefit gig to pay the fine. It was at the old ICA on Dover Street. I'll never forget Glenn Sweeney saying to me during the gig 'Jazz is dead! and we are the pall-bearers.' It was the only time I ever played with four drummers. Yea, it was nice, a very nice evening."

Apr 5 — Speakeasy

Apr 7 — UFO (photo right)
augmented by Mal Dean, trumpet; Rab Spall, violin

Apr 12 — Speakeasy

Apr 13 — Middle Earth

Apr 15 — Roundhouse
The Block, Sam Gopal Indian Group supporting

By spring, if not earlier, the Soft Machine begin working in tandem with Mark Boyle, a twenty-eight year old artist/sculptor hailing from Scotland. In 1966 Mark obtained sophisticated projectors and created the visual/audio experiences 'Bodily Fluids and Functions' and the award winning 'Earth, Air, Fire and Water'. Donning goggles and gloves Mark performs as Soft Machine's fifth member from a rigged scaffold using an array of coloured acids and slide materials to develop and chance projections. Throughout 1967 most all of Soft Machine's concerts are enveloped with projections from Mark Boyle's Sensual Laboratory.

Mark Boyle:
"The most complete change an individual can effect in his environment, short of destroying it, is to change the attitudes to it. This is my objective. I am certain that, as a result, we will go about so alert that we will discover the excitement of continually digging our environment as an object/experience/drama from which we can extract an aesthetic experience so brilliant and strong that the environment itself is transformed."

"The Roundhouse then was a wonderful place, it was before the Arts Council had discovered it and tidied it up, it was just a great warehouse. You could project anything you like onto it and people did and Mark Boyle took ideas from there for his light show. He did most of the lightshows in UFO afterwards. And it wasn't just onto the groups, I mean he used to play tricks with groups, like he used to project moving bubbles coming out of the flies of the lead guitarist and stuff like that. He used to project stuff onto the group and they didn't even know what was happening to them."

Apr 19 — Speakeasy

Apr 22 — Roundhouse
The Creation, Sam Gopal Indian Group supporting

Apr 26 — Speakeasy

Apr 29 — '14 Hour Technicolor Dream' Alexandra Palace
also: Alexis Korner, Champion Jack Dupree, Alex Harvey, Graham Bond, Move, Pink Floyd, Purple Gang, Pretty Things, Pete Townshend, Social Deviants, Ron Geesin, Mike Horovitz, Yoko Ono, Allen Ginsberg, Jean Jacques Libel, Andy Warhol, Mothers of Invention, Velvet Underground.

John Platt:
"At the beginning of April 67 the police raided the offices of IT in a calculated attempt to close the paper down. In order to raise money a benefit event was put together and it turned out to be the biggest single underground event, though it is a curious paradox that something that attracted over ten thousand people could be described as 'underground'. This immense crowd turned up to watch forty-one bands, listen to poetry, see films and ride the helter-skelter. There were two stages with bands playing simultaneously, which with the various light shows was almost too much to take in. In retrospect, the Technicolor Dream was not only the biggest and best underground event but also the last genuine one."

Daevid Allen:
"As I recall, The Floyd played at Alexandra Palace in 67, at four in the morning. It must have been one of the greatest gigs they ever did, and Syd played with a slide and it completely blew my mind, because I was hearing echoes of all the music I'd ever heard with bits of Bartok and God-knows-what. I don't understand why nobody else has ever attempted to do it since. Anyway I thought I'd better investigate it."

l to r, Theatre Royal, Stratford East, UFO

Apr — College of Technology, Leicester

Apr — De Lane Lea, sessions for lp demos
released 1971 on 'Rock Generation Volume 7 and 8' (France BYG 529 707 and 708)
a) 'Thats How Much I Need You Now' (R. Wyatt)
b) 'Save Yourself' (R. Wyatt)
c) 'I Should've Known' (H. Hopper)
d) 'Jet Propelled Photograph' (K. Ayers)
e) 'When I Don't Want You' (H. Hopper)
f) 'Memories' (H. Hopper)
g) 'You Don't Remember' (R. Wyatt/D. Allen)
h) 'She's Gone' (H. Hopper)
i) 'I'd Rather Be With You' (K. Ayers)
Daevid Allen, guitar; Mike Ratledge, piano/organ; Kevin Ayers, bass/vocals (d); RW, drums/vocals
After the third day of recording producer Giorgio Gomelsky stopped the sessions and kept the studio masters when manager Mike Jefferies refused to pay the studio costs.

Also in April, Soft Machine were invited to play in a soccer match at London's Regent Park. This event was either promotional or charitable in purpose, but it is remembered that the team which included Kevin, Mike and Robert played against a Radio Luxembourg, FAB 208 Magazine team which included celebrity DJ's such as Alan Freeman.

Spring — sessions for 'Television Dream'/ 'What's The Use Of Tryin' 45
(unreleased)
Both of these songs were composed by Kevin Ayers and were considered for the A-side. The B-side was to be a recording of Daevid Allen reading a John Hopkins poem at UFO but extraneous audience noise shelved this performance. Further details unknown.

May 3 — Speakeasy

May 5 — UFO
The Crazy World of Arthur Brown supporting augmented by Graham Bond, alto sax

"One of the biggest influences was the atmosphere at UFO. In keeping with the general ersatz orientalism of the social set-up you'd have an audience sitting down. I mean everything was done sitting down, peaceful protests were all done sitting down in those days, some sort of Ghandish principle of passive resistance to everything, and you'd listen to music sitting down. Just the atmosphere created by an audience sitting down was very inducive to playing, as in Indian classical music, a long gentle droning introduction to a tune. It's quite impossible if you've got a room full of beer swigging people standing up waiting for action, it's very hard starting with a drone. But if you've got a floor full of people, even the few that are listening, they're quite happy to wait for a half hour for the first tune to get off the ground. So that was a wonderful influence, or a terrible one according to your taste, but it was an influence on what the musicians played."

May 6 — 'Rag Ball' Technical College, Canterbury
supporting Graham Bond Organisation, also: Wilde Flowers Hugh Hopper filmed this concert with his 8mm camera, but the film reel has since been lost.

May 10 — Speakeasy

May 17 — Speakeasy

May 24 — Speakeasy

May 31 — Speakeasy

May — Theatre Royal, Stratford East

June 16 — UFO
The Crazy World of Arthur Brown supporting

June 24 — 'A Midsummer Nights Dream' London School of Economics

June — Sound Techniques, sessions for 'She's Gone'/'I Should've Known' 45 (unreleased)
A-side released Mar/77 'Triple Echo' (Harvest SHTW 800)
Daevid Allen, guitar; Mike Ratledge, piano/organ; Kevin Ayers, bass; RW, drums/vocal
'She's Gone' includes a fragment of spoken word from Daevid's recording of William Burroughs.

Through their friend Giorgio Gomelsky, the members of Soft Machine, their roadie Ted Bing, Mark Boyle, Gilli Smyth and Mark Ellidge, with panel truck, equipment and cameras in tow, depart to the south of France on July 1 for a two month odyssey of freelance work and bohemian living. The groups initial engagement is at a portable discotheque designed by Ian Knight and Keith Albarn to house a variety of 'Happenings', though it is also remembered that they played at parties for Barclay Records, J. J. Lebel, and the actress Carroll Baker.

Mark Ellidge:
"At the Carroll Baker party they played 'We Did It Again'. That's all they played that night, it went on for about an hour with everybody dancing."

Kevin Ayers:
"The time we did it in the St. Tropez, with all of us going da-da-da-da-da for twenty minutes non-stop was the nearest I got to doing what I wanted with that song".

Mike Ratledge:
"It was his idea that if you find something boring, a basic Zen concept, then in the end you find it interesting. And there is something in that if you listen to something repeated in the same way your mind changes the structure of it each time, the ear either habituates or forces a change on it itself, which is similar in a way to the stuff Terry Riley's doing. I saw it mainly as an irritant source. I saw it directed at the audience. And the only times I wanted to use it was when I felt like saying fuck you to the audience. But Kevin wanted to use it at any time possible. And Robert saw it as a gesture too. Kevin saw it half way between this spiritual liberation thing, and showing how hip we were. These ostinato techniques. I saw it as an irritant source though mainly."

July — 'Beer Festival' Discotheque Interplay, Saint-Aygulf Beach, France

Cramdom Bentley (Hit Parade writer):
"The club designed by Keith Albarn, was especially created around the music and the light show. When the building was completed, it looked like a vision from space, iglooed with four wings rising at the center in a concentric stack, with four shoulders jutting out at the base. Inside the building, at the center was a stage, seven feet off the ground where the Soft Machine played and the light show was given. The skin of the building was only an inch thick, so the sound coruscated off the exterior, carrying across the bay to the neighboring inlets, causing concern to the bourgeois campers. It was a total experience. Of course, the inevitable happened. Crowds came in the daytime to hear rehearsals and in the night time to leap out of their encapsuled selves, dancing to exhaustion, then running to the water some twenty yards away immersing themselves sauna style; then creeping from the water's edge into the darkness of the moon."

Daevid Allen:
"We only played there about five times. They found that the music was too loud and there were a lot of complaints from people around and alot of unfavorable publicity."

The beer festival was banished by the mayor of Saint Tropez, Mr. Lescudier, who proclaimed "It's the tourists who pay but the Tropeziens who vote. I do not want that pigstye in my house." The Happenings banned were such things as: tearing chickens to pieces in the middle of the audience, and "Total Theatre Ben" who played Russian Roulette on stage, or advanced into the audience with a bag over his head while swinging an axe. A dozen artists and writers such as Nadeau, Ionesco, Prevert, Lapasiade protested "energetically against such an unqualifiable measure." J. J. Lebel pressed the mayor, "The theatre is free in France. You have no right to censor." Replied the mayor, "Very well, it is for reasons of safety that I forbid the presentation of your spectacle."

Aug (early) — 'Festival of Free Theatre' (Expression) Cogolin

For two weeks Soft Machine are given half the evening to reduce the audience by "transmissions hallucinatoires" in opening J. J. Lebel and filmmaker Allen Zion's production of Pablo Picasso's play 'Desire Caught By The Tail' (1941). The play was intended for the Papagayo, which gives onto the harbour of St. Tropez, but was moved to a nearby field site despite a threat from the Catholic Archbishop of Darguinan not to consecrate a new chapel at Gassin unless the play was removed.

Gilli Smyth:
"This was staged in a huge marquee, and drew big crowds. It was here that a local farmer, enraged by the sound of the music, stood up with a shotgun aimed at the musicians, and said he would shoot if they did not stop. They did not stop, and he fired, but a roadie knocked his arm at the crucial moment and the bullet lodged in the generator at the back of the stage, occasioning panic in the audience and disbelief among the musicians in the pitch black silence as to whether or not they were still alive."

Aug — Cafe des Arts, St. Tropez

Aug — Town Square, St. Tropez

Daevid Allen:
"It was the big event, it was like we were supposed to be the big psychedelic band and we did right in the middle of St. Tropez. People like Bridget Bardot were there and lots of film producers and directors. It was that event that really gave us the standing in Paris that led to Soft Machine being that favourite band in the land after about six months."

Aug — Voom Voom Club, St. Tropez

Daevid Allen:
"That's when we had this lady who wanted to get us onto video. The latest thing at that time was called 'Scorpitone' and it was like video jukebox, except it was movies or something. She took us into her big pad and had us stay there in the hope of doing that with us, but she never did quite get it together. Meanwhile she put us into the Voom Voom Club, that I now remember as being with a big swimming pool in the middle of it. We were high above this pool, an exotic French thing."

"I don't really remember what we did in the south of France. What I remember is playing a gig in the nude for Jean Jacques Label's 'Happening' around a swimming pool. I was OK because I had the drum kit but the others were very self conscious, I think."

Discotheque Interplay outside (left) and inside (below)

State Of Mind

A DIFFERENT DRUMMER

By MICHAEL ZWERIN

ROBERT AND I are lost in Frejus, driving around in circles. We are looking for the Autoroute to Juan-Les-Pins and the Antibes Jazz Festival. Finally, we ask a cop standing in front of a gendarmerie. He points the way politely.

"That's the building they took us to—looks like it at least," Robert says.

"Who took you?"

"The cops. They picked us up, man."

"What for?"

"For being in the south of France. We were sitting in a cafe in Cogolin having coffee. Two cops pulled up and said to come with them. We told them we had an important date in a half-hour to see about a gig. They didn't care, though. We had our passports, and they let us go after two hours.

"Long hair can be a hangup. I cut mine a couple of times—couldn't decide which way I wanted to go. Finally, I let it grow long after I saw the Stones for the first time. I like that look. But you get put in a bag. We are known as a psychedelic group so everybody looks at us like we are some kind of side show. People say, 'Boy, it must be wild to play on acid.' Man, I do my thing myself. I don't need acid to play the drums."

As we chug along in my little old French car, Robert starts singing *Donna Lee,* and Bird's solo on it. "Man, for a 21-year-old rock-and-roll drummer, you sure know a lot about jazz," I shout over the unmuffled motor.

Robert is hugging his crumpled shirt and shaking his blond hair rhythmically as he talks.

"I spent a lot of time listening to jazz," he says. "That's all I did when I wasn't in school. I even wrote some criticism once."

"Really? About what?"

"Sonny Rollins and Cecil Taylor. But it was mostly teenage fan stuff. I was pretty star-struck. Still am, I guess. It's a drag, too, because—well, I know that most of the guys I like don't dig what I'm doing. Categories are a drag. But I guess I'm just a rock-and-roll drummer. Funny. . . ."

He talks about Robert Graves, the poet and novelist, and the two summers he spent in his house on Majorca. I think about the Soft Machine, the pop group from London with which Robert Wyatt is drummer and lead singer. They are pretty freaky-looking on stage, wearing their weird hats, long hair, shades, and their funky, bizarre garb. It is odd that young people who look that way are familiar with *Donna Lee,* Robert Graves, or Cecil Taylor. But things are not always as they appear.

The Soft Machine has been playing around St. Tropez a lot since I've been here, and I've heard them a lot. There is no doubt that the music they play is jazz. Of course, there are vocals, but when Ray Charles or Jack Teagarden sing, it is still jazz, isn't it?

In between the vocals, the Soft Machine improvises, and they swing. It's not simple-minded either. They do it all on electronic instruments, though, and this throws many people off. The sound is as new, as strange—and as fresh—to jazz as bebop seemed at first. And as the older cats laughed at the boppers in the '40s, the establishment of jazz laughs at the music of the flower children in the '60s.

The Soft Machine's members have a cloudy sound. They use vocal sound effects close in on microphones. Robert sings with plenty of soul, in tune, swinging, reminiscent of Wilson Pickett or Otis Redding. Mike Ratledge on organ is a very exciting cat. He is obviously influenced by Cecil Taylor as he flies around the keyboard, often atonally, over the hard rock beat.

And rock is stretching out. The time moves from slow to fast and back again. They have a number in 7/4, subdivided 1,2,3,—1—1,2,3. Robert swings hard in a style I've never heard before, a combination of Ringo Starr and Elvin Jones.

The tunes are very long, perhaps too long. They sometimes lose the dancers and even the listeners. But the Soft Machine is exploring in lonely territory, not accepted by its heroes and yet not commercial enough to make heavy bread. If it should eventually have a hit, it may be because it has sold out, whatever that means. The temptations of the market place can be overwhelming. Right now, though, you really have to listen to the Soft Machine to understand it. And it is music really worth listening to, truly avant-garde. All you have to do is throw away all your prejudices.

In Juan-Les-Pins, Robert and I take a walk before the concert. Robert talks about drummers. Elvin is his favorite but "Jimmy Cobb is very underrated. When everybody was driving that two-and-four high-hat thing into the ground, Jimmy was doing something entirely different. Tching, tching, tching, tching, on the ride cymbal, way on top of the beat. Man, that's a groovy way to keep the time. And when he plays in another meter, like six, he just keeps doing it instead of subdividing into two threes, like so many other drummers."

Later, we have dinner with Paul Desmond. I wonder, at the beginning, how these two generations of jazz musicians will relate to each other. It is immediately clear that Robert has great respect for Paul and is rather flattered to be with him.

Like so many of his peers, he is extremely mature and knowledgeable for his age. He talks and listens in the proper places. He talks about the musicians he likes—Mingus, Monk, Trane, Ornette. He knows details about the life and music of Steve Lacy and even about more obscure players such as Clarence Shaw.

As the evening progresses I can see that Paul is becoming more interested in Robert, less concerned with his long hair or image.

The next night, the Soft Machine is working. They are covered with moving, multicolored polka dots. Lights are flashing. Dancers, bodies are jumping, twirling, shaking. The place is alive and swinging with the Soft Machine in gear, and there is no category.

"There is just a great tradition to France of listening to music and dealing with the arts that is completely conducive to the creation of and the appreciation of, the sort of avant-garde set ups that we dealt in. Plus a whole avant-garde theatre tradition, Jarry was French after all. It's quite different from here, there's no sense of having to deal with the hit parade or anything like that, just didn't arise. You could really stretch out in front of a French audience, you almost had to apologize for it in England. There was also the whole American expatriate thing that centred on the Shakespeare bookshop on the Left Bank and bars like the Chat Qui Peche, where they had racks of jazz albums behind the bar that you could request if you bought a drink. Fucking paradise as far as I was concerned."

DEAR MELODY MAKER. <u>SOFT MACHINE BULLETIN</u>

SOFT MACHINE - LONDONS MYSTICAL DISAPPEARING
NEW MUSICAL TRAVELLING CIRCUS IS HAPPENING NR ST. TROPEZ
EVERY NIGHT UNDER A KALEIDOSCOPIC SKY WHICH 2
SOME MEN CALL A TENT. TO QUOTE RITA RENOIR
MOST FAMOUS OF ALL FRENCH STRIP TEASE
ARTISTES -"THE SOFT MACHINE IS THE ONLY INTERSTING
HAPPENING ON THE SOUTH OF FRANCE - I LOVE
THEM". UNDER THE PSEUDONYM OF 'PICASSO'
THE SOFT MACHINE HAVE ALSO NOT PRODUCED A
PUPPET SHOW CALLED "DESIRE CAUGHT BY
THE TAIL" STARRING ULTRA VIOLET WHO IS
ALSO THE SOFT MACHINE AND 'TAYLOR' BRIGITTE
MEAD" THE RENOWNED AMERICAN DOG WHO
FEATURES AS THE UNFORTUNATE TAIL.
SOFT MACHINE LEAVE ~~FOR~~ S.T. TROPEZ FOR
AMSTERDAM WHERE THEY WILL FEATURE IN
THE FIRST DUTCH BE-IN 'SPONSORED' BY
THE PROVOS AND SEVERAL CHEESES.
THE SOFT MACHINE WILL RETURN TO
ENGLAND ON AUGUST THE 16TH.
          LOVE ♡ ST TROPEZ. 3/8/67

Kevin Ayers' letter home

With Dutch gig bookings now on hold "The Machine" returns home form France and faces obstruction from British customs at Dover.

Mike Ratledge:

"It was purely by chance. We had been working quite a bit in France and when we came back Daevid couldn't get back into the country because he was working illegally in England with no work permit or other necessary papers to work here. You need visas for a period of time and he had been staying here for God knows how long without one, so he wasn't allowed back in the country, so we became a trio."

Gilli Smyth:

"As an Australian he had overstayed his visa by a few days only. The customs took one look at him, put on his form that he had no money when in fact he had one hundred pounds and marked his passport with a life long refusal enter U.K. I had to go to Dulwich and pick up our stuff and sadly leave Honor and the home we had experienced so much intensity in. After this we went to Paris and started the band Gong."

Aug 27 — Middle Earth

Sep 1 — 'Edinburgh Festival' Barrie Hall, Edinburgh, Scotland

This performance was titled 'Lullaby For Catatonics' and augmented by the dancing of Graziella Martinez from the visiting Argentinian ballet company 'Epileptic Flowers'

"It was the first time I had taken an aeroplane across England, and what I remember was looking out the window and thinking for the first time 'How could anybody be talking about an immigration problem?' cause I looked down and I couldn't see anybody! It just looked like a load of empty fields and I thought 'This is an empty island!' I mean you'd come up to a town from an aeroplane and it's so fucking small! And you think 'they're stupid if they think this is crowded because they're only crowded in their own tiny huddle!'"

Sep 3 — 'Edinburgh Festival' Traverse Theatre Company's 'Ubu In Chains', Barrie Hall

"That really was incidental music at the point of a finger from a director, almost. Including an introductory thing but then kind of filling in for scene shifting or 'wow, this is a really funny link coming up, we want a drum roll.' Almost a kind of circus role."

left, 'Lullaby For Catatonics'; above, 'Ubu In Chains'

From Allen Wright's review for the Scotsman:

"Jarry was writing about abuse of freedom — and that is borne out by the production, which resorts to all kinds of crude devices to create a sense of anarchy. A group that calls themselves 'The Soft Machine' blast away on electronic organs and guitars, enormously amplified so that the hall vibrates. Transparencies are projected on to a screen behind the screen behind the stage, including some pretty pictures of the Tattoo which are allowed to melt in the heat of the arc lamp. The relevance of this tattoo-phobia quite escapes me."

From David Buchan's review for the Edinburgh Evening News:

"Why the Travers Theatre Club have chosen to put it on, I do not know. It displays no development of character, presents no telling argument and is a further example of the contemporary theatre's fixation about ugliness. A sense of grotesque figures are paraded before the audience, to the accompaniment of a hideously loud and out of tune beat group."

Sep 9 — 'U.F.O. Festival' Roundhouse
also: Denny Laine, The Pink Floyd, The Move

Sep 15 — Roundhouse
The Family supporting

Sep 16 — Middle Earth

Sep 22 — Vitus Studio, Bussum, Holland, Hoepla T.V. filming
broadcast Oct 9, rebroadast Sep 22/91
'I Should've Known', 'We Know What You Mean' performed released 92 on 'Psychomania! 20 Golden Greats' video (Australia GEMV 474)

Sep 23 and 24 — The Birds, Amsterdam, Holland
John Mayall supporting

Mark Boyle:

"We were supposed to open for The Mothers Of Invention at the Concertgebouw but Frank Zappa wouldn't let us, saying 'Anyone can open for The Mothers...except The Soft Machine.' It worked out though because we were asked to open a new club called The Birds or The Bird Cage...I can't remember...anyway I do remember something strange with Robert. He became convinced that the vibrations from his drum kit was causing the synchronicity of the images projected behind him. Of course it wasn't, since things happened when there was silence. But to test this Robert would bang his drum then look at the projection which was a visual explosion. He did this a few times and naturally the crowd went crazy. The next night I played a movie behind them."

Oct (early) — 'Biennale des Jeunes Artistes', Museum of Modern Art, Paris, France (two nights)
augmented by dancer Graziella Martinez
Mark Boyle was awarded first prize for his sculpture at this bi-annual international arts festival.

Oct (early) — O.R.T.F. Studios (?), Paris, France, Dim, Dam, Dum T.V. filming

Oct (early) — Theatre des Champs Elysees, 'Ste - Geneviève sur le Tobogan', Paris, France
augmented by dancer Graziella Martinez for this avant-garde and dada festival.

These are the only confirmable gigs for Soft Machine's brief European tour of early October. All were performed in conjunction with Mark Boyle's Sensual Laboratory and sequenced here in chance order. While in Paris the group are awarded 'Ordre De La Grand Gidouille' by France's Pataphysical Society. This certifies Soft Machine as the official group to lead the pataphysical parade, though this event never occurred.

Mike Ratledge:

"Pataphysics is the science of imagining solutions, theory of exceptions, it still exists. It's very complex, it covers a vast amount of knowledge, religion, art. There are numerous philosophies that belong to that school of thought, such as false science and artistic science, dealing with imagining machines, just dealing wholly with ideas, the artistic possibilities of science. We were all heavily into it."

left, Graziella Martinez; above, feeding Sam in Dulwich Park

Oct 13 — Middle Earth

Oct 14 and 15 — Friar's Hall

Nov 10 — Middle Earth

This gig is the first for Soft Machine's new roadie, Hugh Hopper.

set consists: 'Clarence In Wonderland/We Know What You Mean/untitled instrumental/That's How Much I Need You Now/I Should've Known/solo organ/We Did It Again/Why Are We Sleeping?/Save Yourself/Lullaby Letter/A Certain Kind

The untitled instrumental is a vamp on the chords from the middle section of Kevin Ayers' 'May I?' (1970).

Nov 12 — ' Hippy Happy Beurs Voor Tiener en Twens', Ahoy Hallen, Rotterdam, Holland

Tomorrow, 9' 65 supporting

Nov (mid) — Heliport, Rotterdam, Holland

Nov (mid) — Theatre 140, Bruxelles, Belgium

Nov (mid) — Golf - Drouot, Paris, France

This could possibly be the gig where Daevid Allen remembers "dancing on stage with them in Paris when they came back." The French press report that director Jean-Luc Godard attended.

"The way Daevid Allen moved on stage—the only thing I've seen since like it is the way Bob Marley dances about. Daevid was also the first pothead I knew and I used to think 'Is this the pothead dance?' But I don't know, I still don't know."

Nov 18 — 'L'Fenetre Rose', Palais des Sports, Paris, France

also: Tomorrow, Cat Stevens, Dantalion's Chariot
Filmed by French T.V.
A four minute excerpt (end of 'Clarence In Wonderland', beginning of 'We Know What You Mean') was broadcast on the T.V. programme 'Bouton Rouge' December 9th.

These are the only confirmable gigs for Soft Machine's brief European tour of mid-November. All were performed in conjunction with Mark Boyle's Sensual Laboratory and sequenced here in chance order.

Dec 5 — Aeolian Hall, BBC Top Gear recording

broadcast Dec 17
a) 'Clarence In Wonderland' b) 'We Know What You Mean'
c) 'Hope For Happiness' d) 'A Certain Kind' e) 'Strangest Scene' performed
Mike Ratledge, organ; Kevin Ayers, vocals (a, b)/guitar (a, b)/bass (c, d); RW, drums/vocals/piano (e)
Details for 'Strangest Scene' remain unknown as it was not broadcast and no recording exists. The instrumental credits submitted to the BBC's review panel states that Robert plays piano on this session, therefore it was on 'Strangest Scene'.

Dec 8 — The City University

Dec 10 — Concertgebouw, Amsterdam, Holland

supporting Electric Prunes, also Zipps

Ron de Bruyn (concertgoer):
    "They used the giant Zipps lightshow screen to project their bubblin' lights. In fact, Zeta lightshow man Han Elzerman also joined the Softs lightshow and it was as psychedelic as psychedelia could be!"

Dec (mid) — L'Olympia, Paris, France

Dec 15 — The Jimi Hendrix Experience, Playhouse Theatre, BBC Top Gear recording broadcast Dec 24.

Released early 89 (Castle Communications CCSLP 212)
a) 'Day Tripper' b) 'Spanish Castle Magic' c) 'Radio One Jingle' d) 'Getting My Heart Back Together Again' e) 'Wait Until Tomorrow' performed by Jimi Hendrix, guitar/vocals; Noel Redding, bass/backing vocals (a,b,e); Mitch Mitchell, drums/ backing vocals (b,e); augmented by RW, backing vocals (a)

Note: The probability of Robert's participation as studio guest (with tambourine?) during d) is speculative. Hendrix biographer Caesar Glebbeek states that Mitch played the tambourine.

Dec 16 — Middle Earth

Dec 22 — 'Christmas On Earth Continued' Grand and National Halls, Olympia

(afternoon photo shoot, right)

Dec (mid) — O.R.T.F. Studios, Paris, France, sessions for Francois Bayle 'The Acousical Experience' tape

Played at 'Currents: Electronic Music From France', Theatre Vanguard, Los Angeles, USA. Dec 6/74 (US Premiere)
Francois Bayle, all instruments/electronics; RW, vocal on 'It' (based on the ostinato 'We Did It Again')

As roadie, Hugh Hopper seems to recall this recording project utilising The Soft Machine trio.

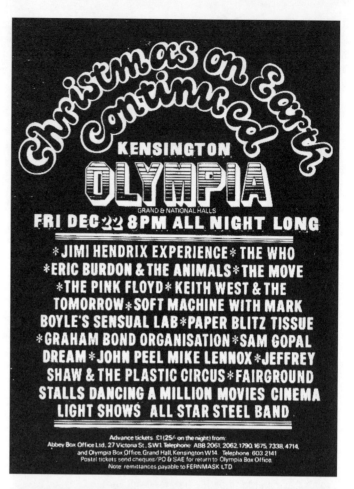

ITEMS: "Clarence In Wonderland"; "We Know What You Mean";

INSTRUMENTATION: Kevin Ayers — Vocals/Bass Guitar   Robert Wyatt — Voc/Drums/Piano
Michael Ratledge — Organ/Piano;

A strangely professional 'nothing' group. It's rather
uninteresting — and different for difference sake. I don't
see too much future.

NO

Sounds rather unexceptional new wave group. Not very in tune
but rather difficult to assess. Only likely to be booked by a
programme specialising in this type of sound.

YES

Nothing special to offer. Started as a rather cute sound, but
interest flagged almost immediately. Uninteresting material,
indifferently performed.

NO

The two singers had a very limited vocal range and little or
no personality, the accompaniment was pretentious rubbish.

NO

Quite unusual little group. I found it fairly 'nothing' but
fairly appealing. it will, as a group, have limited exposure,
but it's neat,pretty, and charming. Musicianship good with
nice attack.

YES

Very 'twee' sound and lyrics, it all adds up to nothing.
Probably appeals to the pseudo pop intellectual.

NO

ITEMS: same as above plus
"Certain Kind"; "Hope For Happiness";
"Strangest Scene";

The majority of the material I don't find entertaining for
myself. One or two of the things have something to offer, but
the arrangements and performance lack lustre - and,I suspect
integrity — meaning they may be weird for weird's sake, rather
than through genuine interpretation. They probably satisfy a
minority thirst for the abstruse, but are definitely not for
majority listening. the vocals in particular are not strictly
speaking up to standard. Nevertheless, since both supply and
demand are small in this field, I don't fail them, in the hope
that those few who may wish to book them may be aware of what
they are letting themselves in for.

YES

Difficult to work up much enthusiasm for this group. I think
the basic fault here is that their musical ability is barely
up to the standard required for this sort of advanced pop
material. Their singing is very suspect on the first number,
particularly and I find the overall result somewhat pretentious.
On the third number there does seem to be a little evidence of
worthwhile in inventiveness but judging the performance as a whole
I could only give them a borderline pass and then only for use on
'Top Gear'

YES

BBC production panel comments regarding the Dec 5/67 session

1968

"What pulled us together musically was not audiences as such, but being on the road with the Hendrix trio in 1968. They were so nice to us. At the end of the tour Mitch Mitchell gave me this custom built Maplewood drum kit. They knew we hadn't much money, but without being condescending they kind of just helped us along. They never tried to pull rank on you, they just wanted to encourage us by not saying anything about the duff bits in our set and helping us with the good bits. All three of them Jimi, Noel and Mitch."

Jan 12 — Drury Lane Arts Lab

Jan 13 — Middle Earth

On January 30th the Soft Machine, along with Mark Boyle's Sensual Laboratory and road manager Hugh Hopper, depart for San Francisco via New York City, to embark on a gruelling nine week tour throughout the United States and Canada as support for the Jimi Hendrix Experience. A cumulative schedule is set up by manager Mike Jefferies although the Softs occasionally obtain gigs independent of the Experience itinerary. These dates are denoted by an asterisk. Readers are advised to refer to Harry Shapiro and Caesar Glebbeek's biography of Jimi Hendrix 'Electric Gypsy' (Mandarin ISBN 07493 0544 4) for a detailed account of the various additional support acts and the numerous fiascoes encountered throughout the '68 tours.

Hugh Hopper:
"The miracle about the Jimi Hendrix tour of 68 was not that he brought wonderful music to people all over the States and became a legend within two months; it was that any single one of the concerts happened at all."

"You've gotta remember we're talking about a continuous period of total drunkenness."

Feb 1 — Fillmore Auditorium, San Francisco, California (two shows)

Feb 2 — Winterland, San Francisco, California (two shows)

An intemperate dispute between Robert and promoter Bill Graham removes Soft Machine from the Experience's next two Winterland dates.

Feb 5 — Sun Devils Gym, Arizona State University, Tempe, Arizona

Feb 6 — V.I.P. Club, Tucson, Arizona

Feb 8 — Men's Gym, Sacramento State College, Sacramento, California

Feb 9 — Anaheim Convention Centre, Anaheim, California

Feb 10 — Shrine Auditorium, Los Angeles, California

Feb 11 — Robertson Gym, Santa Barbara, California

Feb 12 — Center Arena, Seattle, Washington

Feb 13 — Ackerman Union Grand Ballroom, UCLA, Los Angeles, California

Feb 14 — Regis College, Fieldhouse, Denver, Colorado

Feb 15 — Municipal Auditorium, San Antonio, Texas

Feb 16 — State Fair Music Hall, Dallas, Texas

Feb 17 — Will Rogers Auditorium, Fort Worth, Texas

Feb 18 — Music Hall, Houston, Texas (two shows)

The Soft Machine are unable to perform at the Feb 21st Electric Factory gig in Philadelphia as the organ doesn't arrive in time.

Feb 22 — Electric Factory, Philadelphia, Pennsylvania (two shows)

Feb 23 — Masonic Temple, Detroit, Michigan

Feb 24 — CNE Coliseum, Toronto, Ontario, Canada

Feb 25 — Chicago Civic Opera House , Chicago, Illinois (two shows)

Feb 27 — The Factory, Madison, Wisconsin (two shows)

Feb 28 — The Scene, Milwaukee, Wisconsin (two shows)

Feb 29 — The Scene, Milwaukee, Wisconsin (two shows)

Mar 2 — Hunter College, New York City

Mar 3 — Vets Memorial Auditorium, Columbus, Ohio

Mar 4, 5, 6 — The Scene, New York City *

Mar 9 — **State University of New York, Stony Brook, Long Island, New York**

Mar 10 — **International Ballroom, Washington Hilton Hotel, Washington, DC** (two shows)

Mar 11 — **The Scene, New York City** *

Mar 14 — **The Scene, New York City** *
This performance is part of a press reception party held for Soft Machine. A photo collage of the group and party were published in the March 21 issue of the Village Voice (Scene At The Scene, page 38 entire).

Mar 15 — **Atwood Hall, Clark University, Worchester, Massachusetts** (two shows)

Mar 19 — **Capital Theatre, Ottawa, Ontario, Canada** (two shows)

Mar 21 — **Community War Memorial, Rochester, New York**

Mar 22 — **Bushnell Memorial Hall, Hartford, Connecticut**

Mar 23 — **Buffalo Memorial Auditorium, Buffalo, New York**

Mar 24 — **IMA Auditorium, Flint, Michigan**

Mar 26 — **Public Music Hall, Cleveland, Ohio** (two shows)

Mar 27 — **Teen America Building, Lion's Delaware Co. Fairgrounds, Muncie, Indiana**

Mar 28 — **Xavier University Fieldhouse, Cincinnati, Ohio** (two shows)

Mar 29 — **Chicago University, Chicago, Illinois**

Mar 30 — **University of Toledo Fieldhouse, Cincinnati, Ohio** (two shows)

Mar 31 — **Arena, Philadelphia, Pennsylvania**

Apr 2 — **Paul Sauve Arena, Montreal, Quebec, Canada**

Apr 6 — **Westchester County Center, White Plains, New York**

Hugh Hopper:
"Mike once suggested on the Hendrix tour that I should play bass when Kevin had too much to drink before the gig. But I reckoned that Kevin sounded better drunk, so I never played with them."

Apr (mid) — **Record Plant, New York City, sessions for 'The Soft Machine' lp**
released Nov (US Probe CPLP 4500)
a) 'Hope For Happiness' (B. Hopper, K. Ayers, M. Ratledge)
b) 'Joy Of A Toy' (K. Ayers, M. Ratledge)
c) 'Hope For Happiness' (reprise)
d) 'Why Am I So Short?' (H. Hopper, K. Ayers, M. Ratledge)
e) 'So Boot If At All' (K. Ayers, M. Ratledge, R. Wyatt)
f) 'A Certain Kind' (H. Hopper)
g) 'Save Yourself' (R. Wyatt)
h) 'Priscilla' (M. Ratledge, K. Ayers, R. Wyatt)
i) 'Lullabye Letter' (K. Ayers)
j) 'We Did It Again' (K. Ayers)
k) 'Plus Belle Qu'une Poubelle' (K. Ayers, M. Ratledge, R. Wyatt)
l) 'Why Are We Sleeping?' (K. Ayers)
m) 'Box 25/4 Lid' (M. Ratledge, H. Hopper)
Kevin Ayers, bass (except m)/vocals (j, k)/backing vocals (g, i)/piano (e); Mike Ratledge, organ (except m)/piano (m)/piano strings (e); RW, drums (except m)/vocals (except b, e, h, k, l); augmented by Hugh Hopper, bass (m); Cake, backing vocals (l) both uncredited.

Notes:
    1. 'So Boot If At All' is Hugh's 'I Should Have Known' with Robert's new lyric, and is a first take.
    2 'Box 25/4 Lid' was composed by Mike Ratledge and Hugh Hopper in their New York City hotel room just prior to the four days of sessions.

Kevin Ayers:
"I think it was a shame that it wasn't better produced. We had one of the top guys, Tom Wilson (Bob Dylan, Cecil Taylor, Velvets) working on it, but I don't think he was interested at all. All I can remember about him was that he sat on the phone and called his girlfriends all day long. We just played the live set, and they said, 'That's a take.' There was very little dubbed on. Had there been a more sensitive or more efficient producer, it could have been much better."

Apr 19 — **Troy Armory, Troy, New York**

Apr (?) — **'Jazz Series' Museum of Modern Art, New York City***

Mike Zwerin (journalist):
"Enveloped in Mark Boyle's moving, abstract projections, floating in many colors on top of them, the Soft Machine presents quite a sight onstage, though not an unusual one in our time. They wear the accoutrements expected of the prototype shoulder length hair, hats from thrift shops, tiny dark glasses, paisley shirts, beads and bells. Drummer Robert Wyatt sometimes plays dressed only in a bikini bottom. In short, they look like three freaky dropouts."

"The memory of some of the concerts with trio of Mike and Kevin are really fantastic, much better than the record. Kevin was truly amazing."

Upon the band's return to London, concert dates are quickly acquired, then cancelled when it is learned that a second American tour with the Experience is being set up. On May 4th a jam session with Andy Summers, Brian, Hugh Hopper, and Robert takes place at Andy's flat which leads to Andy Summers joining the Soft Machine as their guitarist. Rehearsals for the new quartet commence in Gravenay and Canterbury.

Andy Summers:

"I was in this band called Dantalions Chariot and we were out there playing for about a year, and it was difficult, sort of acid rock. It was great in London where everybody loved it but when we went up north or anywhere outside of London it was too freaky. But there was a fantastic scene in London. We were all playing in these clubs, Middle Earth, UFO, the Roundhouse, going on stage at midnight, blah blah blah and we'd play all night. Those were amazing times.

"Anyway the Dantalions Chariot band came to an end mostly because of a terrible car crash which happened one night on the way back from Yorkshire. I got the worst of it unfortunately. I'd broken my nose and had this plastic cast around my head. I remember playing on stage with this mask like thing and Robert thought it was really cool. He must have come round to see us or something. But whereas I was feeling very embarrassed about this whole thing, you know appearing on stage looking like the invisible man, Robert was very complimentary about it.

"I can't remember how I joined them but they must have asked me. So I moved out of my flat in West Kensington and went to live with Robert in Dulwich. There were quite a few people living in this house, kind of floating around. Anyway it was a very interesting time. Robert and I would jam late into the night most nights. It was just him and I, we'd get really stoned and just play until four in the morning."

July 30 — Independence Hall, Lakeshore Auditorium, Baton Rouge, Louisiana

Aug 2 — Municipal Auditorium, San Antonio, Texas

Aug 3 — Moody Coliseum, Southern Methodist University, Dallas, Texas

Aug 8 — jam session, The Scene, New York City
Larry Coryell, guitar; Jeremy Steig, flute; Noel Redding, bass; RW, drums

Larry Coryell:

"I don't remember that jam session cause there were so many jams around that time. I had moved to New York City and didn't have a dime to my name, and I wanted to be a jazz musician. But there was so much else happening, I mean you just couldn't see everything and everybody. Hendrix always seemed to be around. So I began to use rock and blues ideas so that I could play with different musicians. But I do remember Robert though. I think it was my wife who introduced me and I liked him, I mean he was a bubbly, bouncy, chatty guy. So yeah we played, but to be honest I just wanted to play with anyone who was English."

"I was very honoured to be asked. Mitch introduced us and I thought it was a bit out of my league, but we did a blues I think. We got away with it."

Aug 9 — Record Plant, New York City, sessions for Noel Redding demos
further details unknown

From Noel Redding's diary:

"It (Linda Eastman photo session) goes a lot better than the recording sessions I organize the next day to try to get some of my newer songs down. The drummer was terrible and we had to call it off. Then took some acid and headed off with The Who to the Scene where I had a blow with Robert Wyatt and Larry Coryell. It went well, so the next day I asked Robert to do the demos with me and we succeeded in getting two songs down."

Aug 10 — Auditorium Theatre, Chicago, Illinois
(two shows)

Aug 11 — Col Ballroom, Davenport, Iowa
Thirty eight minute set consists: 'Lullaby Letter/Priscilla/Lullaby Letter Reprise/We Did It Again/Why Are We Sleeping/Joy Of A Toy/Hope For Happiness/Clarence In Wonderland/You Don't Remember/organ solo/collective improvisations/10.30 Returns To the Bedroom' (inc. 'Plus Belle Qu'une Poubelle')

Aug 16 — Merriweather Post Pavilion, Columbia, Maryland

Aug 17 — Atlanta Municipal Auditorium, Atlanta, Georgia
(two shows)

Aug 20 — The Mosque, Richmond, Virginia
(two shows)

Aug 23 — The New York Rock Festival, Singer Bowl, Flushing Meadow Park, Queens, New York

Andy Summers:

"There was a problem between Kevin Ayers and myself. Kevin really wanted the band to be a three piece. He didn't like having a guitar or he didn't like me or whatever it was. So when we finally got to New York City he got me out of the band. It was an interesting tour, we were basically being booed off everywhere we went because it was too freaky."

Kevin Ayers:

"He joined for part of the American tour, but it didn't work. Andy Summers is a very good jazz guitarist, but I could hear Robert and Mike getting very carried away. And I thought this isn't what I want to do, partly because I couldn't keep up."

Aug 25 — Carousel Theatre, Framington, Massachusetts (two shows)

Aug 26 — Kennedy Stadium, Bridgeport, Connecticut

Aug 30 — Lagoon Opera House, Salt Lake City, Utah

Sep 1 — Red Rocks Park, Denver, Colorado

Sep 3 — Balboa Stadium, San Diego, California

Sep 4 — Memorial Coliseum, Phoenix, Arizona

Sep 5 — Swing Auditorium, San Bernardino, California

Sep 6 — Centre Coliseum, Seattle, Washington

Sep 7 — Pacific Coliseum, Vancouver, Canada

Sep 8 — Coliseum, Spokane, Washington

Sep 9 — Memorial Coliseum, Portland Oregon

Sep 13 — Oakland Coliseum, Oakland, California

Sep 14 — Hollywood Bowl, Hollywood, California

With the trans-America treadmill now ground to a halt, the exhausted group members immediately part ways. Kevin sells his bass to Mitch Mitchell, collects a royalty advance, and escapes to Ibiza, while Mike returns to London and further refines his compositional concepts. Robert remains in the Los Angeles area staying with Jimi Hendrix and Eric Burdon who have homes in Laurel Canyon.

Kevin Ayers:
"The first tour I was completely drunk with the life. Girls lining up outside the door, free drink everywhere, so I was drunk every night, with enormous quantities of girls at my disposal. By the second tour, I had changed completely. I went on a very strict macrobiotic diet so my whole body slowed down. I didn't go to any night clubs. I just stayed in my room in the Chelsea Hotel or wherever, with Mike Ratledge. I used to lie on the floor and stare at the ceiling, while he read books. It was mainly because I had gone so far into macrobiotic thinking and eating that I was so alienated from everything that was going on around me because of the violence and extremity of it. When it was at its worst it was literally hotel—plane—gig, hotel—plane—gig. Mike and I used to go around banging on doors shouting 'I'm cracking up, I'm cracking up.'"

Mike Ratledge:
"Travel in the States with a pop group is like a luxury purgatory. You stay in Hiltons, then a Cadillac Fleetwood takes you to the airport first thing in the morning. Another Cadillac Fleetwood meets you, takes you to the hotel. You wash, the Cadillac Fleetwood takes to the gig and back to the Hilton. You sleep. In the end it completely destroys your sense of geography. You're manipulated like a piece of baggage. You have no control over the direction your life takes. It's like those experiments where they deprive rats of control over their bodies. In the end you suffer from depersonalization, loss of identity. It sounds heavy but it does happen like that. There is no longer any 'I' that travels, the travel subsumes you, there is no such thing as place because air destroys that as a form of travel. And America is constructed in such a way that it denies any individual differences from place to place."

"1968 wasn't an easy time to be in America, I saw a lot of horrible things which make you think a bit. You read articles here sometimes about racism and of course we have a right to talk about it, but unless you've spent some time in the States where the streets smell of racism, you really have no idea. I saw the kinds of things that a sheltered English lad had never seen, the hostility between the police and any kids with hair...the police would ride through crowds on motorcycles without even waiting for them to clear. I saw them pick up one kid, hold him horizontally and run him into the wall like a battering ram. We were pretty much sheltered as a group going from hotel to hotel, but you could see that life on the streets was sticky."

DEAR PaM   2850
FirSt   BENEDICT

thank you for yer letter
and addressessess and lovely
SAM drawing (poem?) (diagram of a Soft Machine)

A N Y W A Y

a. bicycle? Yes Hey Jude number 1 here saw a
lovely film of them doing it on the lovely Smothers Brothers. Please say
hello Mart for me. a bicycle?
There's a fantastic group from Chicago I think called C.T.A
playing at the Whisky this week - a sort of small big band Soft Machine
Also Buddy Miles new group is very strong (the Buddy Miles Express) but
he's such a big head and a maddening Jimmy Hendrix groupie so the
band has lost its appeal for me in a way So is José Feliciano big
yet in England? ooh and Larry Coryell is on a lovely double album
by Mike Mantler featuring Cecil Taylor and Gato Barbieri and
I think Pharaoh Sanders Also Miles Davis "Miles in the Sky"
.i.to... mus   not to mention Brian Hopper's "slow walkingtalk"

he's such "lost it" appeal for me in a way So is José Feliciano big
band has lost its appeal for me in a way So is José Feliciano big
yet in England? ooh and Larry Coryell is on a lovely double album
by Mike Mantler featuring Cecil Taylor and Gato Barbieri and
I think Pharaoh Sanders Also Miles Davis "Miles in the Sky"
is a complete rave not to mention Brian Hopper's "slow walkingtalk"
which I played everything on except the bass which is played by Jimmy
Hendrix. (I believe I already mentioned in some previous boast
about me and Zoot doing most of the higher harmony parts on
the recent Animal recording) (The Animals are the nicest people in the world)

I'M SO GLad To hear that (ARAFAN seem .
to be on their feet at last as I've said before I have no doubts
at all as to their eventual success considering the Kave Dave can
play better than Zoot Money Mike Ratledge and Keith Emerson rolled into one
(what?) which reminds me a) Another record company has offered me
the musical services of Grahame Bond - at his suggestion - and b)
Some reforming members of the old Buffalo Springfield were going
to offer me a job drumming but then but then they heard some
of my new tapes and offered me a job doing organ and piano!
Forget it I replied strongly but nicely who needs another folk-rock group?
which is almost certainly what they had in mind. God how boring as Andy would say.
Pat Paulsen for President and hows old Harold Wilson then? / (N+love) Robert
         P.S. You should hear me playing vibes. (✱ big-head)

On several occasions during his seven week stay in California friends invite Robert along to T.T.G. Inc. Sunset — Highland Recording Studios in Hollywood. For sessions recorded here the studio will be referred to as T.T.G.

Oct 3 — T.T.G., Hollywood, sessions for Eire Apparent 'Sunrise' lp
released May/69 (Buddah 203 021)
Ernie Graham, rhythm guitar/vocals; Eric Stewart, bass; David Lutton, drums; Jimi Hendrix, guitar; Noel Redding and RW, backing vocals (uncredited) on 'The Clown'

Oct — T.T.G., Hollywood, sessions for Eric Burdon and the Animals 'Love Is' lp
released 69 (MGM Standard 2619 002)
Eric Burdon, vocals; Zoot Money, keyboards/backing vocals; Andy Summers, guitar; John Weider, bass; Barry Jenkins, drums; RW, backing vocals (uncredited) on 'River Deep Mountain High'

Oct — T.T.G., Hollywood, sessions for Robert Wyatt 'Moon In June', 'Rivmic Melodies' demos

Oct — T.T.G., Hollywood, sessions for Robert Wyatt 'Slow Walkin' Talk' demo
released Nov 27/92 on Jimi Hendrix 'Calling Long Distance' CD (UniVibes UV 1001)
RW, drums/vocal/piano/organ; Jimi Hendrix, bass
A remake of Brian Hopper's 1965 composition for the Wilde Flowers.

"It's a kind of Mose Allison kind of thing, Jimi came in and listened and whispered, 'I could try the bass line on that, you wouldn't have to use it.' And he got Noel's bass, and you have to remember he's left handed, so he's playing bass the wrong way around. Puts down the first take, a fucking Larry Graham [of Sly and the Family Stone fame] bass line. He heard it once, including the changes, the breaks and all that, and it was staggering."

Nov 10 — Larry Coryell, The Village Vanguard, New York City
Larry Coryell, guitar; Miroslav Vitous, double bass; RW, drums

Larry Coryell:
"I had a trio around that time with Miroslav Vitous and Bob Moses on drums. But I think that night we had two gigs, another at the Scene so we were really rushed. So if you say that Robert played with me that night then I guess Bob must have asked him to sit in. I do know that we used to get com plaints at the Vanguard cause we weren't playing just standard fare jazz."

Nov — Record Plant (?) New York City, sessions for Robert Wyatt 'Moon In June', 'Rivmic Melodies' demos
RW, vocals/drums/organ/piano/electric piano/flexitones

Notes:
1. 'Moon In June' is a ten minute set including the thematic motifs of 'That's How Much I Need You Now' and 'You Don't Remember' (Gomelsky demos 4/67)
2. 'Rivmic Melodies' is a suite including several dormant Hugh Hopper compositions (inc. 'Have You Ever Been Blue') with new arrangements and lyrics. This set may not have been known as 'Rivmic Melodies' at this point.

"The record company didn't know we'd broken up. Their first album wasn't released yet, though it was six months since we'd recorded it, and there seemed no obligation to carry on. And I'd got various things I'd been wanting to do that I couldn't do with the group as it then was. It was a great relief to get into the studio and play all the instruments myself and do it along without having to be democratic about it, that's all. There were two sets, See, I went to the record company and said 'Look, Mike's gone back to London, I dunno'...I mean, it was winter, 1968, and I'd just got back to New York and I'd been approached to do some film music and I was quite happy. But they said 'No, listen, this record's amazing, we want to put it out, the group should go on the road.' So I said, 'Is it? Should it?' And I phoned up Mike in London and said, 'Do you want to start up a new version of the group?' And he said 'No, yes, no, yes. Yes.'"

When attempts to contact Kevin Ayers in Spain to relaunch the Soft Machine prove unsuccessful, an invitation for Hugh Hopper is sent. On the eve of selling his bass in favour of buying a motorbike for travelling through France, Hugh receives the SOS and on December 21st leaves Canterbury to join Robert at Honor Wyatt's home in West Dulwich where the new trio begin rehearsing.

Meanwhile the groups eponymous debut has been issued in America where it climbs to number thirty-eight on the Billboard charts. Various legal problems prevent a British release and limited import copies vanish quickly. The albums gatefold jacket presents photos of the musicians within a dadaist collage that rotates through a pinwheel design, a landmark design which inspired the jacket for 'Led Zeppelin III' two years later.

George Niedorf:
"I was in a record store one day, I had heard about Soft Machine, and I picked up an album that turned out to be the first album where it credited me with teaching Robert all those instruments and I laughed to myself cause I certainly didn't do that. I mean I don't know why my name got on the cover. They spelled it wrong though, I did notice that. They called me George Niedori, I thought maybe I was some famous Italian drummer!"

Dec 28 — 'Super Star Jam Session', Roundhouse
George "Zoot" Money, organ/electric piano/vocals; Andy Summers, guitar; Hugh Hopper, bass; RW, drums
set includes 'Dear Mr. Fantasy', 'Why Don't We Do It In The Road'.

1969

"For me, the element of magical presence, individually within Soft Machine, the one who really captivated my imagination, was Hugh."

Hugh Hopper:

"By no means was I the first person to use fuzz bass. I mean the first fuzz bass I ever heard was on 'Rubber Soul' by The Beatles, Paul McCartney was using it. I can't remember now but I think it was Mike Ratledge who suggested I use fuzz on bass, 'cause he was already using it on organ. And when we were rehearsing to do 'Volume Two' there were lots of unison lines where the bass had to be as strong as the lead thing to actually sound good. After that it became a habit."

Feb 18 — Royal Albert Hall

Twenty-four minute set consists: 'Pataphysical Introduction Pt 1/A Concise British Alphabet Pt 1 and 2/ Hulloder/Dada Was Here/Thank You Pierre Lunaire/Have You Ever Bean Green/Pataphysical Introduction Pt 2/As Long As He Lies Perfectly Still/Fire Engine Passing With Bells Clanging/ Pig/Orange Skin Food/A Door Opens and Closes/10.30 Returns To The Bedroom'

Hugh Hopper:

"At soundcheck in the afternoon, spontaneous outbreak of applause from all surrounding musicians, roadies, etc. from other bands at the end of short impressive run-through by Softs. This is not to be sniffed at. From then on, it's all downhill."

Feb and Mar — Olympic Sound, sessions for 'Volume Two' lp

released Sep (Probe SPB 1002)
Side I
Rivmic Melodies
a) Pataphysical Introduction—Pt. I (R. Wyatt)
b) A Concise British Alphabet—Pt. I (H. Hopper—arr. R. Wyatt)
c) Hibou, Anemone, And Bear (M. Ratledge-R. Wyatt)
d) A Concise British Alphabet—Pt. II (H. Hopper—arr. R. Wyatt)
e) Hulloder (H. Hopper—arr. R. Wyatt)
f) Dada Was Here (H. Hopper—arr. R. Wyatt)
g) Thank You Pierrot Lunaire (H. Hopper—arr. R. Wyatt)
h) Have You Ever Bean Green? (H. Hopper—arr. R. Wyatt)
i) Pataphysical Introduction—Pt. II (R. Wyatt)
j) Out Of Tunes (M. Ratledge-H. Hopper-R.Wyatt)
Side II
Esther's Nose Job
k) As Long As He Lies Perfectly Still (M. Ratledge-R. Wyatt)
l) Dedicated To You But You Weren't Listening (H. Hopper)
m) Fire Engine Passing With Bells Clanging (M. Ratledge)
n) Pig (M. Ratledge)
o) Orange Skin Food (M. Ratledge)
p) A Door Opens And Closes (M. Ratledge)
q) 10:30 Returns To The Bedroom (M. Ratledge-H. Hopper-R.Wyatt)
Mike Ratledge, piano (except l, m, o, p)/organ (c, g, k, m—q)/harpsichord (l)/flute (c, j); Hugh Hopper, bass (except l)/acoustic guitar (l)/ alto sax (c, n, o, p); RW, drums (except l)/vocals (except m, o); augmented by Brian Hopper, tenor sax (c, i, j, n, o, p), soprano sax (o, p);
Notes:
1. The Spanish 'Dada Was Here' is a lament for a lost lover.
2. The horn sections of c, n, o, p were co-written and arranged by Brian Hopper.
3. Chapter four of Thomas Pynchon's 1963 novel "V" is entitled 'In which Esther gets a nose job'.
4. The album's final four tracks will comprise the concert suite 'Esther's Nose Job'.

Mike Ratledge:

"We had to fulfill our record contract so we had to get back together again. We didn't anticipate remaining as a group any longer. So we wrote material and did the record, pretty quickly. We did take the album seriously but we just didn't want to tour anymore, we were so sick of it. It was strange because the record company required that we break up our long pieces into small titled themes, even though they were heard as one long piece. So we had to put all of these ridiculous titles on segments of pieces."

"I never considered the Soft Machine recorded in any kind of intelligent relationship to our progress, what we actually sounded like. We'd take new compositions into the studio, record them, two months later learn how to play them, six months later discard them, and then a month after that go back into the studio again with more new things we hadn't learned to play properly. The Soft Machine at its best is hardly on record. At best, those records are only an indication of what the group was all about."

The Soft Machine: Hugh Hopper, Mike Ratledge, Robert Wyatt

Mar 1 — The Royalty Theatre
Egg, Arcadium supporting

Mar 14 — 'Rag Ball' Bedford College
also: Timebox, Steve Miller's Delivery

Mar 27 — 100 Club
Jody Grind, Spirit Level, Forest supporting
Augmented by Brian Hopper, tenor sax.

Mar 29 — Paradiso, Amsterdam, Holland
Recorded by Captain Haddock for consideration towards release as a live album. The group declines consent and were later met with betrayal when the bootleg album 'Soft Machine 69' appeared (Priscilla Records P.R.L.P. 4505, edition of 100). The master reel appeared again in 1989 on the German bootleg CD 'Turns On'.

Mar 30 — King's Theatre
supporting Roland Kirk

Mar or Apr — York University, York

Apr 12 — Mothers, Birmingham
Deviants supporting

Apr 13 — Country Club
set consists: 'Moon In June/collective improvisation/Eamonn Andrews/Mousetrap/Backwards/Mousetrap Reprise/Esther's Nose Job', 'Hibou, Anemone And Bear' (as encore)

"Eamonn Andrews was a TV personality (host of Thames TV program 'Today') years ago, known for his improbable links between items e.g. 'and speaking of fish, I was in an aeroplane last Tuesday...' I had suggested the piece as a link because it didn't have a complete structure on it's own, and offered the title."

Apr 19 — Geneva, Switzerland (venue unknown)

Apr 20 — Fribourg, Switzerland, TV filming

Inside the SOFT MACHINE from whence come those incredible sounds, lives a surprisingly content and home-loving hobbit, in the shape of group drummer and vocalist, Robert Wyatt:

"I'm not a revolutionary at all. I'm really a homebody, an average middle-class bourgeois. I'm married, I have a son, I live with my mother and our new bass-player Hugh and his girl-friend and a few others. I like to get on well with the neighbours, you know, we get the odd moan about how I paint up the front of the house, but it's all very domestic and friendly. I enjoy getting on with the grocer and the dentist etc., and try to roughly contribute in return for what I take. I'm just very much part of the bourgeois set-up. But the trouble with most of the bourgeoisie is that they are very bad at being bourgeois. You can't be bourgeois and then carry on about immigrants, for instance. I mean, if you're going to be a good bourgeois you should be a conventional Christian. So I try to be my idea of a good bourgeois.

"The revolutionary notion to me is a kind of romantic notion; it's not an original thought. I just don't see things in terms of revolution, even when it appears to be, close up. Nearly everything I see is *evolution* in the changes happening around. And to deny that you and your community is part of an evolutionary process, which is constantly trying to return to the same values, in a very lovely combination of adapting and staying the same, strikes me as bad thinking. And it's also rather cheating to yourself to make life easier by saying everything on that side is wrong and everything on this side is right.

"We were asked recently to do a benefit for a revolutionary left-wing paper and refused, on the grounds that if anybody needed the money to make the world a more beautiful place, we did, more than they did, doing what we are doing, rather than what they claimed to be doing. We don't consider ourselves as tools of the revolutionary left-wing or anything else; not a trivial thing that people can dance to while having their ideological discussions. So I am afraid we lost a few friends there and we don't like to do that.

"But I always think you are on dangerous ground when you begin to think you can tell other people what to do. You can point out things you've come across in the hope that other people can enjoy the things that you've enjoyed. And I can't see that you can go any further than that.

"Obviously I'm talking from a very privileged position, since life for my equivalent in say, Chicago, is a lot tougher, let alone my equivalent in Czechoslovakia, so I'm very lucky. My word, I've got friends, I've got food, wife and son, mother, and I'm earning money enjoying myself. Of course, people stop you doing things. It's maddening when friends get busted for drug offences, or when Apple have to whitewash the beautiful painting on the side of their building—things like that do hurt. But on the other hand, I think when you're young, things *should* be a little uphill. I don't think it does any harm to have to struggle a bit to preserve your identity. And I don't know anybody who doesn't have that trouble.

"I don't really expect anything of the community around me, which is not involved in what I'm doing, except that they should leave me alone to drink my milk and wheel a pram around, and let me play my records. I try and get on with my particular job in the community. I play drums and the man at the station collects tickets and I don't see that I'm any more outside the community than he is. I have an uninvolved view as far as the *Scene* goes. I consider myself, as I suppose everybody does, to be not quite part of the *Scene*, you know, partly of it and partly an onlooker.

"But whatever activity you take upon yourself, it balances out. You find that within certain disciplines you find freedom, and within freedoms you find disciplines. We all know that's true. And musically it helps us to sort out the constant values from the passing, ever-changing values, so we are very keen on musically disciplining each other.

"We find that the group now, (Mike Ratledge on Lowry organ, Hugh Hopper on bass-guitar and myself on drums and microphone), is the only *Soft Machine* where our intentions and motives have really come out strong in the end product—where I've felt when we got off stage: '*Well, that was what we wanted to do when we got on it.*' I suppose that I have a more theatrical consciousness than the other two as I work from outside stimulus. As far as I'm concerned, our music is really only relevant while we are playing it to people. But Mike can work entirely on his own and his music is self-sufficient for him; and it's the same way with Hugh who used to write for us before we became a trio.

"We didn't choose to become a trio—but we find we can work with each other—whereas other people have found us difficult to work with and obscure in our references. It's just that we know a lot of non-verbal things about each other and make enough sense to each other to cause *Soft Machine* music to come out the other end.

"Unlike a lot of the contemporary rock groups we're not

really close to jazz, which many of them are. We find it rather like performing in a simple, loud, classical orchestra, where you bring the score to life—that sort of situation—where your creative powers are to do with the dynamics and shading on a particular occasion. I tend to sit down in front of people and try to change the pace and pressure, the length of the set and the dynamics of it, which is virtually what a drummer's job is anyway. It's really rock music's version of a conductor. But I need what you call 'vibes' in the Underground business, or in other words, reactions.

"For us, each set is like performing a well-known ritual which we have worked out—like a prayer, for instance, which you might say every day or night, word for word, and takes the right length of time, but has new and different meanings each time it's used. As we launch into a number our horizons are very clear. We can see where the end is. It's been worked out beforehand, note by note, and it's just a matter of the exact way in which we phrase it in getting there. I can think ten minutes or more ahead to what I shall do when a bit comes up as a result of something I just did, I think: '*Well, if I'm going to do that on that bit, then I'll tie it up with something that's coming about a quarter of an hour later.*'

"The discipline of the musical life, when seriously done, is in itself a totally satisfying and absorbing lifestyle. It's only if you are a musician to the reasonably shallow extent say, that the Beatles or the Stones (with all due respect) are musicians, then you have to supplement your way of life, which is not self-disciplining or satisfactory enough, by looking around for other things. They do play music, but they are essentially folk-musicians. In other words, they are people who eat and drink and live—and also play music. None of them, I think, claim to be any more than that. And because of this they have had

such phenomenal success, because they produce music of the people by the people. As Paul McCartney once said: '*I don't want to be one of those blokes who's a brilliant bass-player who nobody listens to.*' But that's exactly the opposite of Hugh who would be perfectly happy to be a brilliant bass-player. He has great facility and doesn't accept the traditional role of the bass, choosing to work on the whole alternative world of sound the bass has to offer. But he doesn't talk about it much. In fact, he hardly talks at all anyway. But he puts so much into a piece that he's very exciting to work with for a drummer. You can't coast, you can't lay back and let it all happen. It's hard work but worth it.

"I want to completely submerge myself in the work of learning to play three or four drums and my lifestyle is beginning to go through this mill now. I haven't by any means got there yet and I've only just realised that that's what I want to do. Mike says that most musicians have somewhere at the back of their heads, a perfect magical sound which they can almost see and hear, which they carry around with them all their lives wanting it manifested. And I became a musician when I realised that nobody else was going to play this sound if I didn't.

"So I don't need to look outside me for different taste thrills in the world. I just want a deeper understanding of the things I have chosen to do. Rather than surround myself with the impacts of a various dozen ways and paths of life and end up with an imperfect half-knowledge of any of them.

"The important things for me at this time, are things like whether we should have an accelerated number just before our last number, or a slower heavier number which leads up to a faster one. These are the only really serious problems which are going on in my head. The rest are just musings."

Apr 25 — London
Filmed by French crew. Further details unknown.

Apr or May — 'Festival' Parliament Hill Fields

Spring (?) — sessions for 'Moon In June' demo
At an unknown studio the second half of 'Moon' is recorded
by the trio and edited with Robert's autumn 1968 demo.

May 3 — Abbey Road, sessions for Syd Barrett 'The Madcap Laughs'lp
released Jan/70 (Harvest SHVL 765)
a) 'No Good Trying' b) 'Love You' c) 'Clowns and Jugglers'
Syd Barrett, guitars, vocals; Mike Ratledge, organ/piano (b);
Hugh Hopper, bass; RW, drums, tambourine (c)
c) appears on the 'Opel' compilation lp of Syd's outtakes.
Released Oct/88 (Harvest SHSP 4126)

Hugh Hopper :
"I didn't really know Syd at all, in fact that session came
about because we were playing the 100 Club, Syd Barrett just
happened to come along and see the gig and in his very, very
oblique way said 'Would you like to come along and record?'.
He had most of the tracks just put down, the guitar and voice.
He just said 'I'd like you to play on these two tracks and do
what you can.' He didn't even tell us how it went, we just had
to listen to it until we had some idea. His music is not very sym-
metrical, you have to really listen and then it changes suddenly."

*"I thought they were rehearsals! We'd say 'What key is
that in Syd?' and he'd say 'Yeah.' Or 'That's funny Syd,
there's a bar of two and a half beats and then it seems to slow
up and then there's five beats there' and he'd go 'Oh, really?'.
And we just sat there with the tape running, trying to work it
out, when he stood up and said 'Right, thank you very much.'"*

May 9 — Royal College of Art
Eire Apparent, 12/6 supporting

May 10 — 'East Anglia Rag Barbecue', Earlham Park, Norwich
also: Hollies, Spooky Tooth, Gun, Marmalade

In an effort to expand their instrumentation, the group enlist the tenor and soprano saxophones of Brian Hopper for a series of concert appearances. Although Brian was asked by Robert to join full time he preferred to associate on a freelance basis. All British dates until September feature the trio augmented by Brian Hopper.

May 23 — 'Midnight Court' Lyceum
also: Procol Harum, McKenna Mendelsohn Mainline, Mighty Baby, Harvey Matasow's Jew's Harp Band

May 31 — Roundhouse
also: Laine, Dankworth, Hendricks, and others

June 1 — Mothers, Birmingham
Babylon supporting

June 10 — Maida Vale, BBC Top Gear recording
broadcast June 21
a) 'Facelift/Mousetrap/Backwards/Mousetrap Reprise'
b) 'The Moon In June' performed
Mike Ratledge, organ/electric piano (a)/flute (a); Hugh Hopper, bass/alto sax (a); Brian Hopper, soprano sax (a); RW, drums/vocal and rewritten lyric (b)
a) released 'Peel Sessions' lp Oct/90 (Strange Fruit SFRLP 201) and identified erroneously as 'Facelift'
b) released 'Triple Echo' lp Mar/77 (Harvest SHTW 800)

"I got fed up with songs where the main accents would make you emphasize the words in a way you wouldn't if you were just saying them, and I got interested in the technique of writing songs where the melody line fits the way you'd say the words if you were just talking. I'd say things you'd say in conversation, not even serious conversation, just things you'd say to make a noise. And that meant singing about things that were true as far as I understood it. And if you're muddled, the only things you're certain are true are that there's a tea machine in the corridor and it works or it doesn't. This is true, it's not wishy-washy bullshit. It may be low profile, but it's true."

June 15 — Country Club
Jody Grind supporting

June 21 — Van Dike, Plymouth

June (late) — Bataclan Theatre, Paris

June (late) — Les Halles, Paris

For this brief visit to France (June 25 to 29) the Soft Machine is a trio as Brian Hopper remains in England. Further details unknown.

July 8 — Marquee

July 11 — 'Midnight Rave No. 3' Classic Theatre
Blodwyn Pyg, Aardvark, Good Earth supporting

July 18 — Oxford (venue unknown)

July 18 — 'Midnight Court' Lyceum
Circus, East Of Eden, Made In Sweden supporting

July 24 — Caravan and Friends, Institute Of Contemporary Arts
The friends segment includes a jam session between Jimmy Hastings, sax/flute; Dave Arbus, violin; RW, drums

Jimmy Hastings:
"I remember that my wife danced with Caravan and that we brought our young son, but did we jam? I don't remember that."

Richard Sinclair:
"That was incredible! There's this bloke on his knees and playing a snare that's placed right on the stage, and he's playing this snare for about twenty minutes by himself. I've never seen anything like it, I mean what's he doing? But that's the thing about Robert that people who didn't get to see him much would miss. He didn't always play just drums. He would do all kinds of things, walking around his kit and playing parts of it."

Aug 6 — Regent Sound, sessions for Hugh and Brian Hopper publishing demos
Released on CD (Voiceprint VP123)
a) 'The Big Show' (B. Hopper)
b) 'Memories' (H. Hopper)
c) 'She Loves To Hurt' (H. Hopper)
d) 'Impotence' (H. Hopper)
Brian Hopper, guitars/soprano sax (a); Pye Hastings, guitars (c, d)/vocal (c); Kevin Ayers, organ (a); Mike Ratledge, organ (a,b)/piano (b)/flute (a); Hugh Hopper, bass; RW, drums/vocals/lyrics (d)

Aug 8 — '9th National Jazz Pop Ballads and Blues Festival', Plumpton Race Course, Lewes
Eight minutes into the set opener, "Moon In June", the festival's power generator suffers a breakdown. Although power is soon restored, a second failure shuts down the performance.

Aug 9 — Mothers, Birmingham

Summer — Abbey Road, sessions for Kevin Ayers 'Joy Of A Toy' lp

released Nov (Harvest SHVL 763)
Kevin Ayers, vocals/guitars/bass/piano; David Bedford, piano/arrangements; Rob Tait, drums; Mike Ratledge, organ/piano/flute; Hugh Hopper, bass; RW, drums/tambourine

Sep (early) — 'Bilzen Jazz and Pop Festival', Bilzen, Belgium

also: Bonzo Dog Band, Blossom Toes, Humble Pie
A rainstorm prevails throughout the entire Soft Machine set.

Sep 7 — Concertgebouw, Amsterdam, Holland

set consists: 'Moon In June/Facelift/Eamonn Andrews/Mousetrap/Backwards/Mousetrap Reprise/Esther's Nose Job/collective improvisation/Did It Again/Noisette', 'Hibou, Anemone, And Bear' (as encore)

Sep 20 — 'Free Concert' Hyde Park

Sep 28 — Cook's Ferry Inn

Sep — Abbey Road, sessions for Kevin Ayers 'Soon, Soon, Soon' 45

unreleased until 'Odd Ditties' compilation lp released Feb/76 (Harvest SHSM 2005)
Kevin Ayers, vocals/guitar/bass; David Bedford, piano; The Ladybirds, backing vocals; Whack Skins, drums
'Soon, Soon, Soon' was composed by Kevin in 1967 for Soft Machine and was originally titled 'We Know What You Mean'. Robert's pseudonym is the result of contractual complications at the time of this release.

On October 1st the groups equipment is stolen, but is recovered later.

Oct 2 — Marquee

Oct 5 — Lyceum

also: Chicken Shack, Van Der Graaf Generator

In the autumn of 1969, the Soft Machine trio expands to a septet upon the recruitment of a four piece brass and woodwind section. Lifted and loaned directly from Keith Tippett's ensemble were: Marc Charig, flugelhorn; Nick Evans, trombone; Elton Dean, alto sax. Elton in turn recommends Lyn Dobson, tenor sax/flute. Lyn's dossier includes a cross-section of group and session work though at the time he was leading a jazz trio.

Mike Ratledge:
"The idea of expanding the group was simply that we were more and more into writing, spending more time writing than playing. Every time we'd write something we had to cut it down to limit it, because there's a definite amount three people can handle. So we felt the need to have other instruments be able to carry out the lines, to give sufficient complexity to what we'd originally written. I was also interested in getting a harmonic support for the organ while soloing."

Hugh Hopper:
"It gives us a chance to bring out certain things in our music that we have been thinking about for some time, apart from having four extra solo voices. We had some nice powerful sounds with the trio but when playing for an hour on stage it gets a bit boring. We had begun to feel rather restricted."

Oct (late) — Liverpool (venue unknown)

Oct 28 — 'Actuel Music Festival', Amougies, Belgium

also: Pink Floyd, Caravan, Blossom Toes, Daevid Allen Quartet, Steve Lacy, The Nice, East Of Eden, Captain Beefheart, Pretty Things, Art Ensemble Of Chicago, Frank Zappa, Archie Shepp
This three day festival organized by Actuel record label owners Jean George Karakos and Jean Luc Young was originally intended for Paris until a police filed court injunction moved the event to a field site just outside a small Belgium village. A seventy-five minute film document of the festival 'Amougies Music Power', produced by Pierre Lattes, begins with the opening three minutes of Soft Machine's set ('Moon In June') and ends with the closing five minutes ('Hibou, Anemone, And Bear'). For this performance, the microphone line for Robert's snare drum was fed through an Echoplex.

Nov 8 — Regent St. Polytechnic

Nov 10 — Maida Vale, BBC Top Gear recording

broadcast Nov 29
a) 'Instant Pussy' b) 'Mousetrap/Noisette/Backwards/Mousetrap Reprise/drumlink/Esther's Nose Job' performed
a) composed and performed by RW, vocal/piano/electronic bleeps
b) released 'Triple Echo' lp Mar 77 (Harvest SHTW 800)

'Instant Pussy'

And later we had coffee and the cream spilled on the sheets
and you said leave it I can clean when you've gone and
underneath the chaos of your hair around your pretty face
and shoulders you were thinking 'bastard you bastard'.

And I get up in the morning, saw your face upon the pillow
where you dribble in the night like a baby in the womb
and you flip the sheets around your head above your soft
and fragile body, then I wanted to stay with you forever.

And I plucked your naked eyelid and the makeup off your
mouth and then the cheeks around your mouth and then you
stretched your legs and arms and closed them up again
tucked up inside the bed clothes and the frontman gave
a dirty little smile.

So wherever peeled off sheets and blankets and you slowly
turn until your bare toe captified them put you on the neck
you slid your fingers down my back and could be only you and
I knew then I'd be picked up to be with you forever.

Nov 11 — Ronnie Scott's
supporting Thelonious Monk Quartet

Nov 15 — The Village Roundhouse, Dagenham
Keith Tippett supporting
Performed on drums and hi-hat as cymbals were forgotten at home.

Nov 17 — Civic Hall, Dunstable
Forever More supporting

Nov 18 — Ronnie Scott's
supporting Thelonious Monk Quartet

Nov 22 — Alhambra Theatre, Bordeaux, France

Nov 26 — Liège, Belgium (venue unknown)

Nov 27 — Theatre 140, Bruxelles, Belgium

Nov (late) — Europe 1 studios, Paris, France, radio recording

Nick Evans:
"Yes, I know that photo in Triple Echo (see below) but I couldn't tell you anything about where it was. We just didn't take notice of things like that. Seriously, I could tell you more about the shirt I was wearing."

Nov 29 — Coventry (venue unknown)

During the month of December, Soft Machine undertakes an extensive tour of France, where 'Volume 2' receives the Meilleur Disque award for best record of the year from the Leisure For Youth department of the French government. A new Hugh Hopper composition '12/8 Theme' is now included in the repertoire. Upon completion of the tour, Nick Evans and Marc Charig leave, reducing the band to a quintet.

Mike Ratledge:
"With seven musicians it was really becoming too much. Technically speaking, we didn't have the experience to control such a sound volume. But it was really tiring because with seven people it was either conceptually too rigid or totally chaotic."

"There were amazing difficulties on all levels, not excluding the practical one of not having the equipment or the money for seven people. Eventually it cracked completely. Poor old Nick got really screwed up. You know, there was a lot of happiness, a lot of new things, a lot of problems, a lot of neuroses, added to which it was incredibly cold in the van and we were all a bit disorientated. The cracks just started to appear. The identity of the group became like a memory after that...for me."

ROBERT WYATT *Drum + Vocal*
MIKE RATLEDGE *Organ + Piano*
HUGH HOPPER *Bass Guitar*

Elton DEAN, *alto sax*   **Lynne DOBSON,** *soprano + ténor sax*
Nick EVANS, *trombonne*   **Mark CHARIG,** *flugelhorn*

FRANCE / DÉCEMBRE 1969

1"	STRASBOURG	Théâtre National
2	NANCY	Salle Poirel
4	THONON-LES-BAINS	Maison des Arts et Loisirs
5 et 6	LYON	Théâtre du 8ᵉ
8	PARIS	Salle de la Mutualité
9	PARIS	Théâtre de l'Est Parisien
10	MULHOUSE	Rallye Drouot
11	SOCHAUX	Salle de l'Hôtel de Ville
13	MARSEILLE	Nouveau Gymnase two shows
15	DIJON	Amphithéâtre Aristote
16	BEAUNE	Sous les Halles
17	TOURS	Grand Théâtre
18	BOURGES	Maison de la Culture
19	AMIENS	Maison de la Culture
20	LE HAVRE	Théâtre de l'Hôtel de Ville

FÉVRIER / MARS 1970

**PARIS - NANTERRE - GRENOBLE - CHALON -
PETIT-QUEVILLY - RENNES - BREST - LE HAVRE - CAEN - etc.**

Soft Machine Management : SEAN MURPHY

France : N. GAMSOHN - **Promotion Artistique Internationale,** 24, rue du Dragon, Paris-6

In the afternoon of December 8 the septet gather in front of the Paris train station where they mime to a recorded extract from 'Volume II' for a television film crew. This is broadcast on the evening news to promote the concert. In fact the Dec 16 Beaune concert was cancelled due to Hugh Hopper contracting food poisoning.

1970

"We don't spend enough time in rehearsals for Mike, and we spend too much time there for me, because I can only discover things in the act of playing the piece, in a performing situation. It's like painting in a way. Some painters do sketches first, but often the whole thing is the work itself. I use time like a painter, putting layers on; the first set starts out casually, and then I build it up as I get into it. It's really very elastic. The basic thing is to find the right people to work with, and after that you commit yourself to working round whatever they're doing. If I thought there was anybody playing something really fantastic, I'd want to work with them — and for me that's Mike, Hugh, Elton, and Lyn."

Jan 4 — Fairfield Hall, Croydon

Jan 10 — University College
with Sam Apple Pie Hugh Hopper's bass guitar is stolen.

Jan 11 — Mothers Club, Birmingham

Jan 16 — Doelen, Rotterdam, Holland
Filmed by VPRO TV.

Jan 17 — Concertgebouw Amsterdam, Holland

Jan 18 — Groningen, Holland (venue unknown)

Jan 20 — Radio Bremen TV Studio 4, Bremen, Germany, Beat Club T.V. filming

Jan 21 — Kiel, Germany (venue unknown)

Jan 23 — Hamburg, Germany (venue unknown)

Jan 24 and 25 — Berlin University, Germany

Jan 28 — Ghent, Belgium (venue unknown)

Jan 30 — Antwerp, Belgium (venue unknown)

Jan 31 — Turfschip, Breda, Holland

Feb 6 — sessions for demos (Further details unknown).

Feb 10 — Kevin Ayers, Maida Vale, BBC Top Gear recording broadcast Feb 28
a) 'Stop This Train' b) 'Clarence In Wonderland' c) 'Why Are We Sleeping?' d) 'The Oyster and the Flying Fish' e) 'Hat Song' performed
Kevin Ayers, vocals/guitar; augmented by David Bedford, electric piano (b)/piano (a, c); Mike Ratledge, organ (a, c); Lol Coxhill, soprano sax (a, b, c); Elton Dean, alto sax (a, c) Lyn Dobson, flute (c)/soprano sax (a)/harmonica (a); Nick Evans, trombone (a, c); Hugh Hopper, bass (a, c); RW, drums (a, c)/ piano (b)/trumpet (e)/ harmony vocals (b, c, e)

Feb 13 — Swansea (venue unknown) This and Feb 14 performed as a quartet since Elton was stranded in Belgium.

Feb 14 — London School of Economics

Rehearsing in Paris, March/70

ROBERT WYATT *Drum · Vocal*
MIKE RATLEDGE *Organ · Piano*
HUGH HOPPER *Bass Guitar*

Elton DEAN, *alto sax*
Lynne DOBSON, *soprano · ténor sax*

FRANCE 1970

21 Février	NANTERRE	Théâtre des Amandiers
22 ”	NANTERRE	Théâtre des Amandiers
24 ”	ANNECY	Théâtre Municipal
25 ”	BEAUNE	Sous les Halles
26 ”	GRENOBLE	Maison de la Culture
27 ”	GRENOBLE	Maison de la Culture
28 ”	LYON	Salle Rameau
2 Mars	PARIS	Théâtre de la Musique
3 ”	ORLEANS	Théâtre Municipal
4 ”	REIMS	Maison de la Culture
5 ”	PETIT-QUEVILLY	Centre Maxime Gorki
10 ”	NANTES	Cinéma Le Paris
11 ”	BREST	Palais des Arts et de Culture
12 ”	LE MANS	Théâtre Municipal
13 ”	CAEN	Comédie de Caen
14 ”	PARIS	Conciergerie

Additional gig played in Rheims on 15th (venue unknown)
Paris gig broadcast on Europe 1 radio

Soft Machine Management : SEAN MURPHY

France : N. GAMSOHN - **Promotion Artistique Internationale,** 24, rue du Dragon, Paris-6

Upon completion of the French tour, saxophonist Lyn Dobson leaves the Soft Machine, who carry on working as a quartet. The sole occasion whereby Lyn recalls an ad hoc performance during his tenure was 'after a concert in Paris, members of Soft Machine, Chicago, and Zoo (both support groups) joined in for a jam of sorts.'

Hugh Hopper:
"I don't remember that, but quite likely it happened. I probably would have already been back at the hotel playing Ping-pong by then."

Lyn Dobson:
"I have great memories of being in Soft Machine. They were fantastic musicians, I mean I just loved their music."

Apr 4 — 'Kölner Festival' Sporthalle, Köln, Germany
also: The Nice, Procol Harum, The Kinks, Colosseum, T. Rex, Chicken Shack

Apr 10 — I.B.C. Recording Studio, sessions for 'Third' lp (photo below) Hazel Mew suggested the title.

Apr 20 to 25 — Ronnie Scott's
supporting John Williams
First set consists: '11/8 Theme/Out-Bloody-Rageous/Eamonn Andrews/Mousetrap/Backwards/Mousetrap Reprise/Hibou, Anemone, And Bear'. Second set consists: 'Facelift/Moon In June (coda)/vocal improvisation/Esther's Nose Job'

Mike Ratledge:

"The way it (the 6 day residency) stretched our repertoire was very challenging, and we had to push ourselves into areas of freedom where we wouldn't normally need to go. We had to improvise more than we usually do because we didn't have enough material. In that sense it certainly taught us something. Our sets are an amalgamation of different tunes by different people, and when you string them together into a 45 minute entity there's bound to be a somewhat ad hoc quality about the arrangement. You try to make the transitions as organic as possible, but it's not the total piece of music that I'd like it to be at the moment."

Apr 26 — Fairfield Hall, Croydon

May 4 — Maida Vale , BBC Top Gear recording
broadcast May 16
'Slightly All The Time/Out-Bloody-Rageous/Eamonn Andrews' performed
Released Mar/77 'Triple Echo' lp (Harvest SHTW 800)
This release excludes the last four minutes of 'Eamonn Andrews' by a fadeout.

May 6 — I.B.C. Recording Studio, sessions for 'Third' lp
released June 6 (CBS 66246)
Side a) 'Facelift' (H. Hopper)
Side b) 'Slightly All The Time' (M. Ratledge)
Side c) 'The Moon In June' (R. Wyatt)
Side d) 'Out-Bloody-Rageous' (M. Ratledge)
Mike Ratledge, organ/piano/electric piano; Elton Dean, alto sax/saxello; Hugh Hopper, bass; RW, drums/vocals, piano, organ, bass (c); augmented by Lyn Dobson, flute/soprano sax (a); Nick Evans, trombone (b); Jimmy Hastings, flute/bass clarinet (b); Rab Spall, electric violin (c)
Notes:
   1. Hugh's 'Facelift' is a tape patchwork of excerpts from performances of the composition recorded in January at Fairfield Hall and Mothers Club. The final minute of the tape is played backwards then speeded up into the fadeout.
   2. A CBS Records employee suggested the title 'Slightly All the Time' for the composition formally known as '11/8 Theme'. 'Slightly All the Time' concludes with Hugh's motif 'Noisette' bookending Mike's 'Backwards'.
   3. 'Moon In June' is performed solo until the audible edit to the second half. Beneath the coda of violin tape manipulations Robert quotes Kevin Ayers' 'Singing A Song In The Morning'.
   4. The inside gatefold photo was taken at the apartment of journalist Winfried Trenkler and Ingrid Blum. That's Winfried's leg and Ingrid's feet in the photo.

Mike Ratledge:

"The long organ thing at the beginning of 'Out-Bloody-Rageous' is actually the first bass phrase played backwards. The end is the same thing done on piano only at different speeds and various other things we could do to it. It seemed like the right thing to do at the time...I don't know what was going on in my mind."

May 21 — Paris Theatre, BBC In Concert recording
broadcast May 31
'Facelift/Esther's Nose Job' performed
Mike Ratledge, organ/electric piano; Elton dean, alto sax; Hugh Hopper, bass; RW, drums/vocals

May 24 — Queen Elizabeth Hall (two shows)

May 31 — Robert Wyatt and Friends, Country Club (further details unknown)

June — Abbey Road, sessions for Kevin Ayers and The Whole World 'Shooting At The Moon' lp
released Oct (Harvest SHSP 4004)
Kevin Ayers, guitar/vocals; David Bedford, organ/electric piano; Lol Coxhill, soprano sax/zoblophone; Mike Oldfield, bass; Mick Fincher, drums/percussion; The Whole World Girly Chorus; RW, backing vocals (uncredited) on 'Colores Para Dolores' and 'Clarence In Wonderland'

During the spring of 1970, Robert Wyatt takes the opportunity to sit in with the improvising ensemble Amazing Band on a temporary basis. The septet is comprised of Mal Dean, trumpet; Rab Spall, violin; Miriam Spall, voice; Mick Brannan, alto sax; 'Top' Topham, guitar; Jim Mullen, double bass with Robert on drums for a few gigs until Ken Hyder joins as full time drummer.

Mick Brannan:

"Basically we weren't into conceptual crap, we just played jazz. We'd heard Ornette Coleman and liked what we'd heard. Other English players just about into bebop thought 'shit, I've just got it together ('All The Things You Are', etc., etc.) and now comes along this geezer that's got nothing to do with chord progressions, standards, playing straight.' Fucked them up. Not us. Anyway, as far as I remember, we could all play but made no pretense to play a tune, unless it was ours. Most of the time we removed the distinction between 'head' and solos by cutting out the 'middle man'. It worked. Can't say it does today. Most people I work alongside are heavily into recipes. We weren't virtuosos, but neither was Thelonious Monk. We were not puritanical."

June 25 — Amazing Band, Mercury Theatre
supporting Piblokto

June (?) — Amazing Band, The Crypt

Mick Brannan:

"We played at this place called The Crypt. Yes, I remember that because that was the first time I realized just how natural Robert was as a drummer. He was running around the room playing on everything, coatracks, tables, all kinds of things. Playing the room basically but everything he did sounded so right."

Jim Mullen:

"Usually, nobody knew what the hell was going on. We'd show up at the gig and we really didn't know what was coming next. I mean these guys walked around looking like something out of a strolling carnival most of the time! With their neon boots with stars, it really freaked me out. But they had a great sense of humour. Mal was really running the band and it was on his enthusiasm, because Mal was an incredible enthusiast, apart from being a great cartoonist and graphic artist, he had wonderful humour. He would come up and tell me he had just heard some jazz record with these guys doing really crazy, nutty things on it and he would immediately picture a scene of what this music was suggesting. He really saw music in a quite impressionistic way so he was quite happy to get this thing together.

"It was just improvised music. There were no heads or any kind of preplanning, it was just get out there and blow. But they did have certain kinds of motifs. You know the ambulance horns that they have here in England? They're a two note kind of thing da-da, da-da. That was one of their themes. And as the audience comes past you the air flow makes the tone change and trailoff. Well that would be the whole set, based on that. It was pretty out there!

"Mal would also say to us 'Okay, I want the next piece to be the national anthem of a brand new African state.' So you know if you've ever heard any of those anthems they're absolutely hilarious, because they're all kind of based on Western marching music harmonically and the standard of playing can be quite dissonant. So they would come up with some quasi-military theme with Robert clattering about approximating a march rhythm and it would end up with something that would sound like almost free jazz. It was wonderfully funny and amusing, and the audience would be smiling and laughing. You don't get too much of that with free jazz."

The Amazing Band, from left: Robert Wyatt, Mick Brannan, Mal Dean, Rab Spall, Top Topham, Jim Mullen, Miriam Spall

June (?) — Pathway Studios, sessions for Amazing Band 'Roar' lp (unreleased)
side a) 'Roar Pt I' side b) 'Roar Pt II'
Mal Dean, trumpet; Veleroy (Rab) Spall, violin/accordion (a)/flute (a); Mick Brannan, alto sax/piano (b); Miriam Spall, voice; Jim Mullen, double bass/harmonica (a); RW, percussion/voicce/synthesizer (b)

June 26 — Town Hall, Leeds

June 28 — 'Holland Pop Festival' Kralingen Park, Rotterdam, Holland
also: Pink Floyd, Art Ensemble Of Chicago, John Surman, Han Bennink, Caravan, Fairport Convention, Fotheringay
Six minutes of 'Esther's Nose Job' appears in the European edition of 'Stamping Ground', a film document of the festival.

Soft Machine man's switch

by RICHARD WILLIAMS

ROBERT WYATT, drummer with the Soft Machine, is joining Kevin Ayers' band, The Whole World — but he will not be leaving the Softs.

"The Soft Machine is a lovely group, and it will be carrying on," Robert told the MM on Monday. "But the fact is that the others don't like life on the road, and that's what I exist on.

"They're perfectly happy sitting at home and writing music, and they don't like to play one piece of music night after night. Being on the road brings them down.

"That's what gets me going, the whole trip of playing the same music night after night, so I'm going to play regularly with some mates, and the most convenient mate happens to be Kevin."

Ayers was a member of the Soft Machine until last year.

"I don't want to do anything very ambitious: just little gigs that the Softs are too big to do now.

"I'm not killing off the Softs — I'm just letting the group breathe, and this is the next stage in the development."

Robert makes his debut with The Whole World in this Saturday's free concert in London's Hyde Park, and he will next be seen with the Soft Machine in their Proms concert next month.

July 18 — The Whole World, 'Blackhill's Garden Party', Hyde Park
also: Pink Floyd, Roy Harper, Edgar Broughton Band, Formerly Fat Harry
A short excerpt from this performance appears as 'A Collective Improvisation' on Lol Coxhill's debut lp 'Ear Of The Beholder' released June/71 (Dandelion DSD 8008). Due to contractual snags the credit reads 'robert of dulwich'.

July 19 — The Whole World, Roundhouse
also: Pink Fairies, Curved Air, Gracious

July 25 — The Whole World, 'Phun City' Ecclesden Common, Patching
Phun City was a three day event that billed itself as Rock Festival, Poetry Gathering, Guerilla Theatre, Sci-Fi Convention, Bikers Grand Run, Electric Cinema, National Pinball Championships, and Giant Rip-Off Market. According to Lol Coxhill, scheduling complications forced organizers to request that either Edgar Broughton or Kevin Ayers forego their set. The dilemma was solved when Edgar and Kevin agreed to combine their groups and sing each other's songs.
Kevin Ayers, Edgar Broughton, guitar/vocals; Mike Oldfield, Arthur Grant, bass; Lol Coxhill, soprano sax/tenor sax/Gibson Maestro; David Bedford, organ/electric piano; Steve Broughton, RW, drums

July 30 — The Whole World, 'VPRO Piknik' Gemeendecentrum, Drijbergen, Holland
set consists: a) 'If You've Got Money' b) 'The Oyster And The Flying Fish' c) 'Lady Rachel' d) 'We Did It Again' e) 'Hat Song' f) 'Clarence In Wonderland' g) 'Colores Para Dolores' h) 'Why Are We Sleeping?'
augmented by Bridget St. John, vocals (a, b); unidentified audience member, flute/vocals (g, h)
Piknik was a free countryside concert series (with picnic) presented by VPRO. Filmed by VPRO TV (a, f, g, h) and recorded by VPRO Radio (a—h). Both broadcast July 30. Audio rebroadcast 1990.

Aug 1 (afternoon) — The Whole World, Vondelpark, Amsterdam, Holland

Aug 5 — The Whole World, 'Le Corps de Pops' Bitot, France
also: Pink Floyd, Keith Tippett, Derek and the Dominoes, Joan Baez, Alan Price, Spencer Davis, Country Joe, East Of Eden, Edgar Broughton, MC5, Champion Jack Dupree, Arrival, Chris Barber, and Balls.

Aug 7 — Lloret De Mar, Barcelona, Spain

Aug 8 — The Whole World, Paradiso, Amsterdam, Holland
These are the only confirmed concerts of this one week tour of Europe.

'The thing I remember most about that (The Whole World) is Lol Coxhill's incredible solos and travelling around Holland. It was only really temporary, the group was put together solely to perform Kevin's songs. It's always pleasant to work with him and things always happen around him. It was more like a holiday really...actually, the only reason that whole thing is worth mentioning is that despite my methodist left wing puritanical image I love having a good time, sex, and getting drunk and loud music."

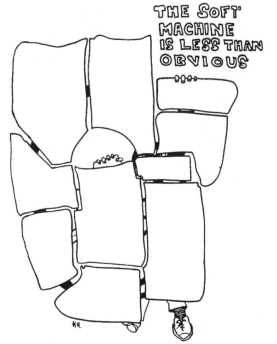

THE SOFT MACHINE IS LESS THAN OBVIOUS

Aug 13 — 'Henry Wood Promenade Concert' Royal Albert Hall

released Oct/88 (Reckless Reck 5)
also: Intermodulation (Terry Riley's 'Keyboard Studies')
Filmed by BBC TV for 'Omnibus At the Proms' (broadcast Aug 23) and recorded for BBC Radio 3 (broadcast Aug 13)

"I don't honestly think the BBC had too much say in it. It was down to Tim Souster, who managed to get into the sort of position of respect where he was allowed to present his own evening, and as he was interested in our music he asked us to be part of it. I don't suppose the powers-that-be at the BBC knew what they were getting at all. There was also the whole thing of playing to a deadline. It was very frustrating having to finish at exactly four minutes before 12 o'clock because if you run over that the engineers will pull out the plugs. But I can also see that it seems to have been important in terms of public relation...for a start, the little old ladies round our way used to think we were a load of nasty, dirty hairies, but now they all say 'Good morning, Robert' very nicely."

Aug 17 — BBC Radiophonic Workshop, Radio 3 Study Session recording

The Soft Machine and producer David Ipps discuss and experiment with the Radiophonic Workshop's VCS3 (Voltage Controlled Synthesizer) for a Radio 3 series on the Pop Scene entitled 'Study Session'.

Aug 21 — The Whole World, Lyceum

Edgar Broughton Band supporting

Aug 27 — Olympic Sound, Radio 3 Study Session recording

Aug — Sound Techniques, sessions for Robert Wyatt 'The End Of An Ear' lp

released Dec 4 (CBS 64189)
The individual(s) to whom the tracks are dedicated are indicated in parentheses.
a) Las Vegas Tango Part 1
b) To Mark Everywhere (Ellidge)
c) To Saintly Bridget (St. John)
d) To Oz Alien Daevyd And Gilly (Allen, Smyth)
e) To Nick Everyone (Evans)
f) To Caravan And Brother Jim (Hastings)
g) To The Old World (The Whole World)
h) To Carla, Marsha, And Caroline (Bley, Hunt, Coon)
i) Las Vegas Tango Part 2
Marc Charig, cornet (b, d, e); Elton Dean, alto sax/saxello (b, d, e)/mouthpiece (g); Neville Whitehead, double bass (b, d, e); David Sinclair, organ (f, h); Mark Ellidge, piano; Cyril Ayers, assorted percussion; RW, drums/mouth/piano/organ/composition except a, i (Gil Evans)

"I was really depressed after we had done 'Third'. I was really into what Mike and Hugh had done and I'd tried to get it right and they hated 'Moon In June' and refused to play on it, and I had to play it all myself except they came in and did a little organ solo with bass accompaniment. I felt really lonely and rejected. So I decided to do a solo album. They let me do one because they thought it was all going to be 'Moon In June' stuff, what I did was to stretch out. It was supposed to include Mongezi Feza but ended up with Elton Dean plus Marc Charig and my brother Mark played a little piano. It gave a taste of what I could do. What was nice about that was I gave myself a chance to play piano, which I wouldn't have dared do in public, in front of real people.

"I like a touch of madness, it's one of my favourite human characteristics. The basic thing that I always end up going back to is not really related to rock or jazz at all. It's related to strange tapes and voice things — more influenced by the Goons."

Sep 1 — BBC Radiophonic Workshop, Radio 3 Study Session recording

broadcast Oct 6
'Analysis Of A Session With Soft Machine' is a thirty minute programme combining the initial Radiophonic Workshop demonstrations with the Olympic Sound session, where 'Eamonn Andrews' was recorded with the instruments processed through a VCS3.

Sep 13 — The Whole World, Roundhouse

Sep 17 — Camden Theatre, BBC Sounds of the '70's recording
broadcast Sept 25 (except E.N.J. Oct 30)
'Out-Bloody-Rageous/Slightly All The Time/Mousetrap/Esther's Nose Job' performed
Mike Ratledge, organ/electric piano; Elton Dean, alto sax/saxello; Hugh Hopper, bass; RW, drums

Sep 26 — London Sinfonietta, Queen Elizabeth Hall
broadcast Oct 20 on BBC Radio 3 'Music In Our Time'
The London Sinfonietta: Sebastian Bell, flute; Anthony Pay, clarinet; Antonia Cook, horn; Peter Reeve, trumpet; Daryl Runswick, double bass; David Atherton, conductor perform David Bedford's composition for William Blake's poem 'The Garden Of Love' augmented by David Bedford, organ/electric piano; Kevin Ayers, guitar/vocals; Lol Coxhill soprano sax/tenor sax; Mike Oldfield, bass; RW, drums/percussion

Sep — Phillipps Studios, sessions for Keith Tippett Group 'Dedicated To You But You Weren't Listening' lp released Jan/71 (Vertigo 6360 024)
Keith Tippett, piano/electric piano; Elton Dean, alto sax/saxello; Marc Charig, cornet; Nick Evans, trombone; Gary Boyle, guitar; Neville Whitehead, double bass; Roy Babbington, double bass/bass; Tony Uta, congas; Brian Spring, Phil Howard, RW, drums

Oct 4 — Neuchatel, Switzerland (venue unknown)

Oct 9 and 10 — Ronnie Scott's

Oct 13 to 16 — Olympic Sound, sessions for 'Fourth' lp

Oct 19 — BBC TV Studios, Anatomy of Pop filming broadcast Jan 10/71

Oct 23 — Eindhoven, Holland (venue unknown)

Oct 24 — Doelen, Rotterdam, Holland

Oct 25 — Concertgebouw, Holland
set consists: 'Facelift/Virtually/Out-Bloody-Rageous/Neo-Caliban Grides/Teeth/Slightly All The Time/ Eamonn Andrews/Kings And Queens/Esther's Nose Job'

Oct 27 and 28 — Olympic Sound, sessions for 'Fourth' lp

Oct 31 — University College

Nov 7 — New Union Building, Reading
High Tide supporting

Nov 8 — Roundhouse

Nov 9 — Olympic Sound, sessions for 'Fourth' lp

Nov 12 — The Whole World, Lyceum

Graham Weston (concertgoer):
"Robert Wyatt joined Ayers in what Kevin announced was an old number. As I was unfamiliar at that time with early Soft Machine I cannot tell whether they played something off the first lp or the Gomelsky demos. All I remember was that they read the lyrics from a sheet of paper and that the backing was supplied by David Bedford on piano."

For several months, Keith Tippett had been working on an extended composition for large group, resulting in the two hour suite 'Septober Energy, Music for 50 People and 100 Feet'. The realization of Centipede was an unlikely yet inspired fraternity of musicians assembled mostly by Keith. Classical musicians were brought in from the London School of Music by Sean Murphy through his friendship with violinist Wilf Gibson, who lent great enthusiasm to the project.

Keith Tippett:
"When I formed Centipede, I wanted to enfold all the friends that I knew as much as possible, from the classical world, to the jazz world, the jazz-rock world, and the rock-rock world. Robert Wyatt was an obvious choice."

FROM KEITH TIPPETT GROUP SOFT MACHINE KING CRIMSON BLOSSOM TOES NUCLEUS.....
KEITH TIPPETT · JULIE DRISCOLL · ROBERT FRIPP · PETE SINFIELD · ZOOT MONEY · MAGGIE NICHOLLS · MIKE PATTO · ROBERT WYATT · ELTON DEAN · NICK EVANS · MARK CHARIG · ROY BABBINGTON · GARY WINDO · BRIAN SPRING · BRIAN GODDING · BRIAN BELSHAW · IAN CARR · KARL JENKINS · JEFF CLYNE · THE HOORAY STRING SECTION and many others + DAVE BORTHWICK'S LIGHTS · IAN KNIGHT · COMPERE JEFF DEXTER · IS A ......
CENTIPEDE
WHICH WILL MOVE AT THE LYCEUM ON SUNDAY 15th NOVEMBER AT 7·30 pm.
A TOTAL MUSIC EXPERIENCE
+
BRIAN AUGER'S OBLIVION EXPRESS · IVOR CUTLER

Nov 16, 17, 18 — Olympic Sound, final sessions for 'Fourth' lp
released Feb 28/71 (CBS 64280)
a) 'Teeth' (M. Ratledge)
b) 'Kings And Queens' (H. Hopper)
c) 'Fletcher's Blemish' (E. Dean)
d) 'Virtually' Part 1, 2, 3, 4 (H. Hopper)
Hugh Hopper, bass; Mike Ratledge, organ/piano; Elton Dean, alto sax/saxello; RW, drums; augmented by Roy Babbington, double bass (a, c, d1, d3); Marc Charig, cornet (b, c, d1); Nick Evans, trombone (a, b, d1); Alan Skidmore, tenor sax (a, d3); Jimmy Hastings, alto flute (d3)/bass clarinet (a, d3)

Nov 20 and 21— Centipede, 'Arts Festival' Alhambra Theatre, Bordeaux, France

Roy Babbington:

"What I remember about that outing was the hotel rather than the actual gig. It was like a quadrangle and as soon as people were checked in and into their rooms their instruments were out. There were groups of people walking around this quadrangle just playing their instruments at will."

"We were going on an aeroplane to France on a tiny chartered flight with everybody clinging to their seats, except Gary Windo rushing up and down the corridor with his tenor playing like Archie Shepp. Everybody, including the air hostess, is pinned right against the wall, Gary was trying to cheer us up and make us feel alright about being in this rickety old plane! I don't think it ever occurred to us that we were all in the rickety plane until Gary started playing!"

It's the Centipede family where Robert Wyatt meets saxophonist Gary Windo, who was looking for musicians to establish a group with Steve Florence, a young guitarist he'd been rehearsing with. Robert takes the opportunity to play with trumpeter Mongezi Feza, trombonist Nick Evans, and bassist Roy Babbington to explore new musical challenges outside Soft Machine. Gary christens the sextet Symbiosis, composes a signature piece ('Standfast') and borrows television themes for what is ostensibly a free blowing ensemble. Equally free is their membership, which was dependent upon who was available to play. Keith Tippett often augmented the group with his electric piano (all 1970 gigs) and when Robert was working with the Soft Machine, drummer Louis Moholo would join, as when Symbiosis toured Holland. This socially informal milieu often produced gigs on short notice with no advance publicity for venues such as The Bull, The Greyhound, Gray's Inn, London Polytechnic, and the I.C.A. amongst others.

Gary Windo:

"That was my band, and we were fucking great!"

Nick Evans:

"The group more or less had an open door policy, and yes some musicians would jump up on stage and join us. They were free to and that seemed to happen quite a bit at a place called Bedford College where we played a lot. It was usually people we knew and had played with, people on the scene as it were. 'Cause if you were going to join in you'd better be prepared to really play. It was honesty time."

Roy Babbington:

"I don't remember ever seeing any charts, the band just went on and played. We never rehearsed. As I remember it, it was a very disorganized kind of thing, everything was chucked into the pot and Robert would chug away at the back and we would get on with having a good laugh. No post mortems after the gig. That was very much the nature of the times."

Keith Tippett:

"There was no concept, we were just playing together and making music. If I remember rightly, it was very free, spontaneous composition essentially. You must remember that the '70's was a very flourishing artistic time and Symbiosis could have been a quintet, it could have been a 12 piece. There was so much going on, there was a gig every two days. I mean London was culturally thriving, right through from theatre to contemporary visual arts. It was the extension of the swinging '60's up until the mid '70's and then the political climate changed, obviously affecting the artistic climate."

"The most interesting thing it seems to me, that has been suggested by black music, is that, as in, say, painting, the person who conceives of it and the person who plays it can be one and the same — combine both skills in one person. And this seems to me the most interesting, challenging thing that jazz music has come up with that European music doesn't really like to get to grips with. And what Symbiosis is, is a complete imbalance; in other words, we're all blowers without any of the composers — like Keith was with us the other night — he's not in a composing or controlling role at all. And so it's an incredible risk, Symbiosis every night, because we just turn up and play. The responsibility is enormous; you've got to be on form then and there because you're going to be doing all the composing and all the performing at the same time, and so is everybody else."

Dec 5 — Symbiosis, Bedford College

Dec 8 — Top Gear Choral Society, Maida Vale, BBC Top Gear recording
broadcast Dec 26
'God Rest Ye Merry Gentlemen', 'Away In A Manger', 'Good King Wenceslas', 'Silent Night', 'O Come All Ye Faithful' performed

Dec 11 — Symbiosis, Red Cow, Cambridge

Dec 15 — Maida Vale, BBC Top Gear recording
broadcast Jan 2/71
a) 'Virtually' b) 'Fletcher's Blemish' performed
Mike Ratledge, organ/electric piano (a)/piano (b); Elton Dean, alto sax; Hugh Hopper, bass; RW, drums
a) released on 'Peel Sessions' lp Oct/90 (Strange Fruit SFRLP 201)

Dec 27 — Soft Robert, Roundhouse
augmented by Pip Pyle, drums
Soft Robert is an alias for the Symbiosis septet.

Pip Pyle:

"I remember Babbington on bass, Windo on sax, Tippett on piano, but the rest is lost in the general stoned haze of the epoch. In any case I only did one gig, but it was fun enough and we played variations on the theme of 'Worker's Playtime' a terrible old radio ditty from the show popular on the air for the punters of the time. This lasted about an hour and thoroughly confused everyone there, on and off stage."

CENTIPEDE INVADE FRANCE

and NME's ROY CARR went along

OVER the week-end, the shabby little Alhambra Bar on the corner of the cobble-stoned Rue D'Alzon in the French wine capital of Bordeaux, hadn't seen so much action or served up so much local juice since the U.S. Army rumbled through in 1945.

But then, with Keith Tippett's 63-strong Centipede entourage in town for the local annual Arts Festival, the atmosphere couldn't have been anything but one of complete conviviality.

"It's just like being part of one big happy family," guitarist Bob Fripp beamed between bites of his "sandwich jambon," as a rather bewildered waiter, with County Joe's infamous Fish Cheer scribbled on the back of his white jacket, scurried back and forth between the packed tables.

A family it truly turned out to be, for singer Maggie Nicholls even brought along her beautiful 5-month daughter Aura, though she didn't make it to Alhambra theatre.

From the moment we all clambered aboard the private charter flight, Centipede became living proof that creative musicians from such diverse musical persuasions encompassing this unit can live and work together in a happy and productive enviroment.. As intended, all this energy resolved itself in the music. If the Lyceum was the dress-rehearsal, then the second of the two French concerts proved to be the euphonic climax, with the audience leaping to their feet in bursts of wild applause and the Press ecstatic in their praise.

However, the week-end wasn't without it's minor hang-ups. Julie Driscoll remains one of the biggest celebrities in France and even her withdrawal from public appearances hasn't diminished her stature. Landing at Bordeaux Airport she was hassled by some extremely un-cool representatives of Press and TV. However, they were all effectively dealt with by chaperon Richard Moody and the incident quickly forgotten.

For the next couple of days, "home" was to become the Domaine de la Salle de Villepreux, a most beautiful and expansive ranch-styled country estate, surrounded by woods.

No sooner were we settled in, then the antics of Centipede's cheerleader, silver surfed freak and tenorist Gary Windo came drifting loud and clear across the lawns. This expatriot from New York and "Soul Brother" trombonist Nick Evans were seen and heard as they both wandered casually around the grounds, blowing some fine music.

In fact, whenever the opportunity presented itself, be it dawn, in the coach or would you believe on the aircraft, they both managed to keep everyone fully entertained. During one of these impromptu sessions they composed and dedicated a number called "Bordirxs," which they were to perform constantly.

The two concerts, held in a rather ancient theatre, proved to be most rewarding and a logical improvement on their Lyceum debut. At times, during the course of "September Energy," the vocal team of Jools, Zoot Money and Mike Patto were quite uninhibited in their performance . . . dancing, gyrating and cavorting around the orchestra, who in turn roared along in a similar manner.

Solowise, everyone excelled. With Gary, Nick, Fripp, Elton Dean, Karl Jenkins, Ian Carr, Robert Wyatt and leader Keith Tippett making numerous valuable contributions. In return, they were greeted with sustained audience approval.

Both on stage and off, a most amazing and spontaneous rapport existed. For instance, in the midst of us all having dinner in the Royale Spring Restaurant someone just started tapping out a simple rhythm on a glass. Within seconds everyone joined in on anything that would make a noise and proceeded to put down layer-upon-layer of compound time signatures and cross-rhythms. As it built up to an exciting crescendo, Gary leapt to his feet and yelled: "Hey . . . we'd better watch it, otherwise Buddy Rich will be challenging the whole of Centipede." Needless to say this was greeted with much laughter and back-slapping.

As you may have already guessed, Centipede is made up of many outstanding personalities, with Patto and Money proving to be quite an unbeatable comedy duo. At a very late after-the-gig party they had just about everyone fallin' about in hysterics with their banter. A mime artist supreme, Patrick O'Patto excelled with his imaginative portrayal of "Ducks in Flight," while Zoot "I've Got Devils In Me Throat" Money acted as a fine raconteur.

All too soon, we were back on the plane and homeward bound. Tired but extremely contented, Soft Machine's ever smiling drummer admitted, "I'd be quite content to just live and work this way for the next couple of years."

A statement which more or less summed up everyone's feelings.

It's a compliment to both Keith and everybody connected with this mammoth project that it actually happened and proved to be an unqualified success.

"I remember it as a dream. You have this sort of dream where there's Sonja Kristina, Ivor Cutler, Rod Stewart, various other people all in a studio singing Christmas carols. Obviously it wouldn't actually happen in real life, but you dream things like that. And specifically in this dream Rod Stewart gets to sing 'Away in A Manger' and you think that's what happens in dreams, what a great dream, but we actually know it happened 'cause the tape's there."

■ Top Gear stars turn carol singers for a occasion at the BBC last week, recording the Boxing Day edition of John Peel's poll-winning radio show. T. Rex, the Faces and Curved Air were involved.

Left to right: (back row), Marc Bolan, John Peel, Robert Wyatt, Mike Ratledge, Rod Stewart, Kenny Jones, a "Faces roadie"; (front row) friend of Sonja Kristina, Ian McLagen, Ronnie Lane, Ronnie Wood and Ivor Cutler.

1971

"Since the summer, since I've started playing with Kevin, I've realized that in other contexts there are things in me which come out and never seem to come out, when I play with Soft Machine. It's not a question of quality at all, it's just a question of different situations demand different skills, and I hadn't realized just how much you do adapt and just play what seems necessary. I would be very loath to put a word to it and think of a concept which fits what I mean. All know is that when I get on a kit, and there's Roy Babbington on my left and, whoever it might be, Neville Whitehead or someone, and Gary and Nick, that a whole different thing happens. I just lift up my sticks and immediately something else happens and different situations arise that would never arise with Soft Machine. I just play completely different things."

Jan 5 — Symbiosis, Ronnie Scott's upstairs

Jan 7 — Liverpool (venue unknown)

Jan 11 — Symbiosis, Maida Vale, BBC Top Gear recording
broadcast Jan 30
a) 'NTU' b) 'Volume 4: Bebop' c) 'Aura' (bass variations) d) 'Standfast' performed
Gary Windo, tenor (a, b, d)/flutes (c, d); Mongezi Feza, pocket trumpet (a, d)/flutes (c, d); Nick Evans, trombone (b,d); Steve Florence, guitar (c,d) Roy Babbington, bass (c, d); RW, drums (d)/percussion (c)

Jan (mid) — Theatre 140, Brussels, Belgium
This is the only confirmed concert of the group's brief (Jan 14 to 19) tour of Belgium.

Jan 26 — Bradford (venue unknown)

Jan 29 — Darwin College, University of Kent, Canterbury

On Jan 31, the Soft Machine are to headline a concert package that includes Gong, Kevin Ayers and the Whole World, Yes, and Iron Butterfly at the Palais Des Sports, Paris. Fighting breaks out when some fans try to get in without paying and the situation quickly flares into a major riot. Most of the ground floor of the stadium is wrecked, the police use tear gas to quell the disturbance, 11 people are taken to the hospital, 18 people are arrested, and the concert is cancelled.

Sean Murphy's subsequent address of anger to the police from the stage was captured by a "bootlegger" and can be heard on the double album 'The History and Mystery of Gong' (Demi Monde DMLP 1018), erroneously identified as 'Riot 68'.

Jan — Marquee Studios, sessions for Daevid Allen 'Banana Moon' lp

Feb 5 — East Anglia University, Norwich

RELEASE BENEFIT
ROUNDHOUSE, CHALK FARM, N.W.1
SUNDAY FEB. 7   3 p.m. Admission 12/6
SOFT MACHINE * RALPH McTELL
KEVIN AYERS & THE WHOLE WORLD
IVOR CUTLER * SYMBIOIS
ELTON DEAN'S QUARTET
MARK BOYLE * DAVID ALLEN

Feb 6 — Symbiosis, University College

Feb 7 — Symbiosis, Roundhouse

Feb 7 — Daevid Allen, Roundhouse
Daevid Allen, guitar/vocals/tapes; Gilli Smyth, space whisper; Elton Dean, alto sax; Gerry Fields, violin; Archie Leggett, bass; augmented by RW, drums on 'I Am Your Animal'

Feb 7 — Roundhouse
set consists: 'Facelift/Virtually/Slightly All The Time/As If/Out-Bloody-Rageous/Kings And Queens/All White/Teeth/Esther's Nose Job' and 'Noisette' (as encore)

Feb 12 — Symbiosis, Polytechnic, Portsmouth
Quiet Sun supporting
At the end of their set Symbiosis are joined for a jam by the members of Quiet Sun: Phil Manzanera, guitar; Dave Jarrett, keyboards; Bill MacCormick, bass; Charles Hayward, drums.

"Charles Hayward was the drummer for them, right? And I thought 'what do you do with two drummers?' And I remember playing with Centipede and I thought 'three drummers fluffing about doesn't quite one Sunny Murray or Andrew Cyrille make' so what shall I do here? So what I did was to just decide to go all Solomon Burke and...(sings a hard backbeat) with my left hand on the snare drum playing the one and the three. I think everybody was comfortable with that. Being in an unknown situation, I find that having been in unknown improvising situations hundreds of times that paradoxically the least satisfactory way to enter into a total improvisation, is to enter into a total improvisation. The most satisfactory way, to really open the door to a bunch of people, is to just go into something so elementary and routine everybody just immediately bounces off it. But it's an 'it' that they can all bounce off. It just has a unity and then whatever happens...you know, you've created a one out of this disparate group and from then on whatever happens is up to everybody."

Feb 13 — Symbiosis, Bedford College

Feb 14 — Symbiosis, Country Club
For the second set, drummer Barry Altschul sits in for Robert.

SYMBIOSIS

I DON'T think it is an over-statement to say that the most exciting things happening in British music are occurring in modern jazz. Bands like Brotherhood of Breath, Spear and Tippett's walkabouts are currently injecting a much-needed spontaneity and vitality into a contemporary musical scene that seems increasingly to my ears to be jaded and too dependent upon the ethic of tastefulness.

I don't think even their greatest fan could call Symbiosis tasteful. They are loud, often raucous, and sound not infrequently quite rough around the edges. On the other hand they really have guts and play with a conviction that gets your feet stomping on its heels.

I would say their greatest quality is a certain quirky humour. Although the vast bulk of their work is improvisational, their numbers — if one can refer to such loose structures in that way — all have a basis in very corny, banal pupular tunes. The "Music While You Work" theme, for instance, is played at odd moments throughout their sets, and at London Uni-versity's University College on Saturday several bars of " My Bonnie Lies Over The Ocean " cropped up.

The ubiquitous Mr Gary Windo, on tenor sax, usually leads the way with these rendi-tions, which are pursued for short periods before the solos come in or over the top; and Nick Evans can frequently be heard aiding and abetting him on trombone.

They were joined on Saturday by Mongezi Feza on pocket trumpet, Robert Wyatt on drums, Steve Lawrence, guitar, and Roy Babbington, bass. Feza is like a little black devil on his instrument, con-tinuously stretching and push-ing out those high, banshee screams that make the blood curdle. The rhythm section of Babbington and Wyatt ad-mirably together add they sum-marised for me the spirit of the music, not only by their en-thusiasm but by the way they slipped in at times a very humorous oompah-oompah backbeat while the brass was ripping off some very anarchic lines.

Strictly blowing bands, of course, are necessarily hit and miss affairs. By and large I think I caught this one on a good night. — MICHAEL WATTS.

Feb — Marquee Studios, sessions for Daevid Allen 'Banana Moon' lp
released summer (France BYG 529 345)
Core trio: Daevid Allen, guitar/vocals; Archie Leggett, bass; RW, drums/guitar, vocals on 'Memories' augmented by guests Gilli Smyth, Gary Wright, Gerry Fields
Notes:
    1. 'Fred The Fish' is a rejuvenated Soft Machine out-take from the Kim Fowley sessions Jan 67.
    2. 'Stoned-Innocent Frankenstein' concerns Wes Brunson, 'And His Adventures In the Land Of Flip' concerns Daevid's experiences, while under LSD, at the hands of the Paris police during the student riots of May 68.

Feb 27 and 28 — Hovikodden Arts Centre, Oslo, Norway
Mark Boyle, in Oslo for his own exhibition, projected with the group on these dates.

Mar 2 — Copenhagen, Denmark (venue unknown)

Mar 5 — Arhus, Denmark (venue unknown)

Mar 11 — Paris Theatre, BBC In Concert recording broadcast Mar 26
released Mar/93 (Windsong WINCD 031)
John Peel introduces this concert as "a kind of musical chairs featuring Soft Machine and heavy friends".
a) 'Blind Badger' — Elton Dean Quintet (Dean, Ratledge, Charig, Whitehead, Howard)
b) 'Neo-Caliban Grides'
c) 'Out-Bloody-Rageous/Eamonn Andrews/All White/Kings And Queens'
d) 'Teeth/Pigling Bland'
e) 'Noisette'
Elton Dean, alto sax/saxello; Mike Ratledge, organ/electric piano; Hugh Hopper, bass; RW, drums; augmented by Phil Howard, drums (b); Ronnie Scott, tenor sax (d); Paul Nieman, trombone (d); Marc Charig, cornet (d); Roy Babbington, double bass (d)

Mar (mid) — Breda, Holland (venue unknown)

Mar 17 — Buiten Societiet, Zwolle, Holland

Mar 19 — Doelen, Rotterdam, Holland

Mar 23 — Gondel Filmkunst Theater, Bremen, Germany
Recorded by Radio Bremen (first set broadcast on June 6). Filmed by German TV and excerpt ('Out Bloody Rageous/Eamonn Andrews/All White') broadcasted on Beat Club TV.

Mar 27 — 'Arts Festival', Deutschlandhalle, Berlin, Germany
Family, Yes, Man supporting
These are the only confirmed concerts of this tour of Holland and Germany.

Mar 29 — Free Trade Hall, Manchester

Apr 3 — Royal Festival Hall
Ivor Cutler supporting

Apr 5 — The Dome, Brighton

Apr 15 — Town Hall, Watford

Apr 23 — Winter Gardens, Bournemouth

In April, Robert Wyatt makes his acting debut (typecast as a jazz-rock drummer) in an episode of BBC TV's 'Take Three Girls'. In May, Robert is voted Player Of The Month by the British magazine Beat Instrumental.

May 5 — 'Oz Benefit', Regent's St. Polytechnic

May 14 — City Hall, Newcastle-Upon-Tyne

June 1 — Maida Vale, BBC Top Gear recording
broadcast June 26
a) 'Grides' b) 'Dedicated To You But You Weren't Listening'
c) 'Eamonn Andrews/All White' performed
Elton Dean, alto sax/saxello (a, c); Mike Ratledge, organ/elec-tric piano (a, c); Hugh Hopper, bass (a, c); RW, drums (a, c)/voice and piano (b)
a, b) released 'Peel Sessions' lp Oct/90 (Strange Fruit SFRLP 201)

In June, the Centipede clan take up residence in Rotterdam, Holland and divide into a variety of musical combinations for the week prior to their Doelen concert. Venues include local youth clubs, hotels, the Arts Centre, as well as busking on the streets and shipping docks. This creative camaraderie carries on into the small cabins on the island where the musicians stayed. It is here that large quantities of alcohol and small ad hoc groupings combine to delve into what manager Sean Murphy remembers as "some of the most adventurous and exceptional music that week."

Nick Evans:
"This period around June 7-11 in 1971 at Rotterdam did allow many 'scratch' groups here and there around the city. I do remember playing with Gary Windo on the back of a low-loader lorry which drove around the streets one sunny afternoon. I remember it because a lady threw a bucket of water over the musicians on the lorry as we passed under her third storey window. A refreshing experience on a hot afternoon! You can be assured that, when Centipede was on the road, there were always odd groups of players making music all over the place. Once we were all entertained by a delightful string quartet in an airport lounge when our flight was delayed."

June 7 to 11 — Symbiosis, Rotterdam, Holland
Gary Windo, tenor sax; Mongezi Feza, pocket trumpet; Nick Evans, trombone; Brian Godding, guitar; Brian Belshaw, bass; RW, drums augmented some nights by Dudu Pukwana, alto sax

June 12 — Centipede, Doelen, Rotterdam, Holland

June 16 to 19 — Wessex Studios, sessions for Centipede 'Septober Energy' lp
released Oct 8 (RCA Neon Ne 9)
Violins — Wilf Gibson (lead), Wendy Treacher, John Trussler, Roddy Skeaping, Carol Slater, Louise Jopling, Garth Morton, Channa Salononson, Steve Rowlandson, Mica Gomberti, Colin Kitching, Philip Saudek, Esther Burgi
Cellos — Michael Hurwitz, Timothy Kramer, Suki Towb, John Rees-Jones, Katherine Thulborn, Catherine Finnis
Trumpets — Peter Parkes, Mick Collins, Ian Carr (doubling flugelhorn)
Cornet — Marc Charig
Pocket Cornet — Mongezi Feza
Alto Saxophones — Elton Dean (doubling saxello), Jan Steele (doubling flute), Ian MacDonald, Dudu Pukwana
Tenor Saxophones — Larry Stabbins, Gary Windo, Brian Smith, Alan Skidmore
Baritone Saxophones — Dave White (doubling clarinet), Karl Jenkins (doubling oboe), John Williams (doubling soprano saxophone)
Trombones — Nick Evans, Dave Amis, Dave Perrottet, Paul Rutherford
Vocals — Maggie Nicholls, Julie Tippett, Mike Patto, Zoot Money, Boz Burrell
Guitars — Brian Godding
Basses — Brain Belshaw, Roy Babbington (doubling bass guitar), Jill Lyons, Harry Miller, Jeff Clyne, Dave Markee
Drums — John Marshall (doubling percussion), Tony Fennell,

Robert Wyatt
Piano - Keith Tippett
band members not on recording session Paul Niemann, trombone; Robert Fripp, guitar (production only)

Roy Babbington:
"They had to shift people in and out of the studio as they were actually needed. There was reams of paper, they'd call your name and you'd go in and play your bit and get out. That was quite an occasion, to get that whole thing done with such an unruly bunch of musicians! I was amazed when I heard the results of that because I thought they really captured it. In fact, I think it was the first I had heard it properly, because actually being in amongst it wasn't always the best place to be, what with various acoustic problems in halls and the enormity."

Julie Tippett:
"The concerts the band gave were much better than that record. They were just wonderful experiences!"

June 27 — Coliseum

On July 5th, the Soft Machine are scheduled to open a three week tour of the United States at the prestigious Newport Jazz Festival in Rhode Island, but a riot prevents the group from playing. Except for the New York City gigs, all venues for this tour remain unknown.

July 7 to 12 — Gaslight, New York City
Loudon Wainwright III supporting
Despite problems the band was having with the hired equipment, Ornette Coleman was so impressed that he immediately organized two well attended parties for them.

July (mid) — Detroit, Michigan
supporting Yes, Savage Grace

July (mid) — Cleveland, Ohio

July (mid) — Akron, Ohio

July (mid) — Columbus, Ohio

July 20 and 21 — Beacon Theatre, New York City
supporting Richard Pryor, Miles Davis (two shows)

July (late) — Houston, Texas

July (late) — San Antonio, Texas

July 27 — somewhere in upstate New York

Elton Dean:
"I can really understand how the band fell apart then (1968). Seven weeks of playing every night is just unimaginable. It must have been hell. Our tour was fairly leisurely by comparison, although it didn't really feel that way. Musically, all the gigs were pretty good, and at times we played as well as we've ever played as individuals. Quite a lot of the time we agreed as a group, as well."

Wyatt quits Softs

ROBERT Wyatt, drummer and singer with the Soft Machine, has left the band.

The reason for his departure is believed to be a difference of musical opinion, apparent for some months, which crystalised during the band's recent and highly-successful American tour.

A member of the Softs since their very earliest days in Canterbury, Wyatt left them for a short period last year when, for the same reasons, he went to play with Kevin Ayers and The Whole World. He returned when he found that Ayers' outfit came no closer to realising his musical ambitions.

Wyatt's replacement in the Soft Machine will be Phil Howard, who has for some months been a member of the part-time quartet of Soft's altoist Elton Dean.

Melody Maker, Sep 4/71, front page

Hugh Hopper:

"It's a miracle bands ever stay together, especially creative ones - would you expect four creative painters to keep painting on the same canvas for years without arguing, losing respect for each other, hating? Robert was the opposite of Mike and me- extrovert, exhibitionist, promiscuous, given to speaking in aphorisms and saying things apparently mostly for effect. (Oscar Wilde too was probably very annoying to work with after the first ten years).

"Robert was very much my mentor in younger days, and it's not unknown for pupils to rebel against their teachers when they start to feel their own strength. He and I were close, but not that close- there was always the possibility of discord, plus I was very immature in those days. Fortunately, by the time I myself had been eased out of Soft Machine, Robert and I had become friends again, no longer forced by the pressure situation of being inside a band together."

Mike Ratledge:

"It's hard to work out exactly what the differences were, but they existed for quite a long time. For instance, Robert has always preferred playing straight 4/4 — he's never really enjoyed or accepted working in complex time signatures. But I never got a specific picture of what he does want to do."

"Everyone had very different contributions to make to the band and we couldn't really agree; it could only be paths crossing, because we started out in different places and were going in different directions — and what would be satisfactory to one person simply wouldn't be to another. It'd be baffling. Like, someone would write a composition which you'd think beautiful and then arrange it and give the solo to just the wrong person, by which time it'd be too inextricably embarrassing to rearrange it. You know, it's his tune, leave him alone. We got so we didn't really know what each other was on about.

"I think really we just grew apart from each other. We only got together in the beginning because we were the only other musicians that each of us knew. To be honest in the end I was kicked out. I could have stayed but...in political terms I'd have been better off staying — the equipment, use of the name, guaranteed full houses, road managers, etc. In a sense I've never regained the practical resources afforded by the name. Even the way I've told it is coloured by my point of view. The things they had to put up with — my vanity, my gross alcoholism, etc. Let's just call it quits."

For several months, Robert Wyatt had searched for compatible musicians as a creative outlet to work alongside the Soft Machine. In August, after being thrown in the deep end, Robert meets the Australian pianist Dave MacRae who had a wealth of session experience. The intention is to form a band, but it soon becomes clear that Dave's session schedule will conflict with the myriad demands of a working group.

Dave MacRae:

"I'd recently come from America, I'd been living there and travelling with Buddy Rich when I arrived in London. It would be during that exploratory time, looking for more interesting things to do, that I'd come across Robert. Probably at a jam session somewhere but I couldn't tell you where it was though. He was in the process of putting his band together. And having come off a fairly restrictive jazz orchestra as Buddy's was and having not really been involved in that area of jazz rock mix thing I found it very interesting. It seemed like a great opportunity and Robert was one of the more interesting intellects of the time. We played experimental type music that I'd never thought of trying before."

Ultimately, Bill MacCormick, Dave Sinclair, and Phil Miller are recruited. Bill MacCormick was an old friend who had played bass in Quiet Sun. Organist Dave Sinclair had left Caravan in August and was interested in writing new songs. A mutual friend recommended guitarist Phil Miller who along with brother and pianist Steve Miller, bassist Roy Babbington, and drummer Pip Pyle was a member of Delivery. From their concert repertoire, Phil brought along his compositions 'Part Of the Dance', 'Nan True's Hole', and a theme that joined with Robert's lyrics to become 'God Song'. The remainder of 1971 is primarily spent on developing and rehearsing songs for their upcoming CBS recording. Robert names the new quartet Matching Mole, or rather Machine Molle, French for Soft Machine.

"Phil is the only guitarist who doesn't conceptually piss me off a bit. I agree with him about how to play guitar and I really don't with anyone else. I admire lots of names — same ones everyone else does — and I don't want to start putting down other guitarists that aren't in Matching Mole, but...

"Bill's a bass guitarist, not a bass player or a guitarist turned bass guitarist. I just trust his taste and intelligence, besides which he's amazingly ambitious for his own music. He's actually an idealist and it's not just a job for him — it's important to him that what we're doing has a potential for being very good and satisfying. I knew him before I thought of him as a musician and I never thought he'd turn out to be as capable of playing like he does; I'm pre-disposed to believe that anybody who could be that clear and objective in discussion could actually turn out to have that egotistical madness, that...silliness that most good players have. Sloppy thinking on my part, really. I saw him with his group and I was surprised what a natural performer he was — in fact I think of him as quite showbizzy actually."

Personally and professionally, the autumn of 1971 is a very tumultuous period for Robert. To help relieve his depression, a mutual friend introduces him to artist Alfreda Benge. Born in Austria, Alfreda arrived in England in 1947 and went on to study painting at the Camberwell School of Art, typography at London's College of Printing, and cinematography at the Royal College of Art. Robert and Alfreda's relationship confluenced not only through their creative passions and political convictions, but also from a shared history of parallel personal experiences. Each frequented Soho's House of Sam Widge's coffee bar (with its jazz jukebox) during the early sixties, and each lived in New York City during 1968.

Sept 18 or 19 — Gong, Seloncourt, France

Daevid Allen, guitar/vocals; Gilli Smyth, space whisper; Didier Malherbe, alto sax/soprano sax/flute/percussion; Christian Tritsch, bass; Pip Pyle, drums; augmented by Pete Brown, RW, percussion

Autumn (?) — Gary Windo and Robert Wyatt, Ronnie Scott's upstairs

This duo performed on a couple of occasions for a series curated by Keith Tippett.

Autumn (?) — Amalgam (?), Towne and Country

Trevor Watts, alto sax; John Stevens, RW, drums; other musicians unknown (consider with May 31/70 entry)

Trevor Watts:
"Robert used to come down to the Little Theatre Club sometimes to see us, 'cause he was interested in improvised music. And John was always encouraging anybody who was interested to play free. So we did get to play together once."

John Stevens:
"Robert and I were in the same place at the same time. Robert and I had the same sort of consciousness. Robert and I also played the drums. Of course during that period we cross-fertilized. But now, as always, we look towards a free future."

Autumn — Abbey Road, sessions for Kevin Ayers 'Whatevershebringswesing' lp

released Jan/72 (Harvest SHLV 800)
Kevin Ayers, vocals/guitar/piano(?); Mike Oldfield, bass/guitar; David Bedford, organ/piano(?); Dave Dufort, drums; uncredited backing singers; RW, harmony vocal on 'Whatevershebringswesing'

Oct 14 — Centipede, Royal Albert Hall

Vocals — Julie Tippett, Maggie Nicols, Zoot Money, Mike Patto, Boz Burrell
Trumpets — Ian Carr, Marc Charig, Mongezi Feza
Saxophones — Alan Skidmore, Gary Windo, Ian McDonald, Brian Smith, Karl Jenkins, Dudu Pukwana
Trombones — Nick Evans, Paul Rutherford
Guitars — Ollie Halsall, Brain Godding
Piano — Keith Tippett Bass — Brian Belshaw
Double Bass — Roy Babbington, Jeff Clyne
Drums — John Marshall, RW

Nick Evans:
"The Albert Hall gig. I remember a policeman entering the band room immediately prior to Centipede going on stage. He looked rather out of place and definitely outnumbered. He asked to speak to the owner of a vehicle which was illegally parked. I believe I was the only person to hear him or see him since I was standing immediately behind the door of the band room when he entered. He made his announcement...got no response whatsoever...and quietly left us to get on with the business of preparing for the gig.
Centipede 1, Metropolitan Police 0"

Oct 17 — Robert Wyatt and Friends, 'GAP Benefit', Bumpers

Gary Windo, tenor sax; Mongezi Feza, pocket trumpet; Nick Evans, trombone; Neville Whitehead (?), bass; RW, drums

"I was playing with people like Gary Windo and Mongezi. I did some nice stuff with Gary and Mongezi, I mean it was chaotic but it was good fun. We enjoyed each others company anyway. What was nice about working with them was that socially it was a much more relaxed and friendly thing than some of the stuff I'd done before, where we hadn't got on so well. That was the nice thing about playing with Gary and Mongs and all those people, they were all drinkers like me. We were probably all bad for each other!"

In October, Robert Wyatt is invited by Joachim Brendt of MPS Records to drum in what may be described as an "international house band" backing headlining musicians for the annual Berlin Jazz Festival. To prepare the rhythm section for this event, violinist Don 'Sugar Cane' Harris, keyboardist Wolfgang Dauner, Bassist Neville Whitehead and drummer Wyatt undertake a brief tour of Germany.

Oct (late) — Don Harris, Tonhalle, Düsseldorf

Oct (late) — Don Harris, Frankfurt

'Berlin Jazz Festival' Berlin Philharmonic Hall, Berlin, Germany

Nov (early) — The Gary Burton Quartet

Gary Burton, vibraphone; Terje Rypdal, guitar; Neville Whitehead, bass; RW, drums
Recorded by German radio.
Ostensibly a solo concert by Gary with accompaniment for the opening and closing songs.

Nov 4 — Don 'Sugar Cane' Harris

Don Harris, violin; Wolfgang Dauner, keyboards/electronics; Terje Rypdal or Volker Kriegel, guitar; Neville Whitehead, bass; RW, drums

Nov 7 — Don 'Sugar Cane' Harris

Filmed by German TV. As 4th but alternate guitarist.
Recordings from these concerts comprise: Don 'Sugar Cane' Harris 'Got the Blues' lp, released 72 (Polydor 2121 283)

Nov 7 — Violin Summit

Filmed by German TV.
A two record set documents the complete concert by this international summit of violinists Jean-Luc Ponty (France), Don 'Sugar Cane' Harris (USA), Michael Urbaniak (Poland), Nipso Branter (Austria), accompanied by Dauner (Germany), Rypdal (Norway), Whitehead (New Zealand), and Wyatt (Great Britain). 'New Violin Summit' lp released 72 (German MPS 3321285-8)

"On our way to the stage we had to sign a piece of paper in the dark. On stage, drums were all in the wrong place and I couldn't hear the violins, etc. A nightmare."

Nov 13 — Symbiosis, Bedford College

Nov 20 — Paul Bley Trio, Country Club

Paul Bley, piano; Annette Peacock, synthesizer/voice; Daryl Runswick, bass; RW, drums/voice

Dec 10 — A Quartet, Country Club

Keith Tippett, piano; Elton Dean, alto sax/saxello; Neville Whitehead, double bass; RW, drums
This gig was booked and advertised for Symbiosis but since Gary Windo couldn't make it, Elton is invited to sit in. As there was never a Symbiosis performance without Gary's participation, the ensemble adopted the moniker 'A Quartet'. In the audience this evening is Lawrence Marks, a London fan who witnessed numerous concerts by Soft Machine, Symbiosis, and Centipede.

Lawrence Marks:
    "We had gone to see Frank Zappa at the Rainbow actually, but we couldn't get in, so it was off to Hampstead where I knew Robert was playing. We arrived to find a group called 'A Quartet' and their set was absolutely amazing. It was jazz, mostly improvised but with themes, from Keith and Elton I suppose. Most incredible though was Robert's playing, it was the happiest I'd ever seen him. He was having a real good night and everyone in that room on and off stage knew it. Of all the different times I'd seen him this was by far the most magical."

Dec 19 — Centipede, Rainbow Theatre

Dec 29 and 30 — CBS Studios, sessions for 'Matching Mole' lp

Nipso Brantner, Don 'Sugarcane' Harris, Jean-Luc Ponty, Michael Urbaniak

ROBERT WYATT PHIL MILLER
DAVID SINCLAIR BILL MACCORMICK

ROBERT WYATT: Born 1945, Bristol

If you ever attended one of the Soft Machine gigs during the early
part of 1971, Robert Wyatt would have been the person you'd most
likely be watching throughout the performance. During his time
with the Softs, he was the most basic, least technically minded of
the band. A bubbly, amusing, sympathetic personality with a tendency to apply his intelligence to categorise everything in his mind.
But in spite of his deep respect for Soft Machine, Robert thought
the group was too private - "too much organisation". So he depart-
ed, joined forces with three other musicians with a common
musical idea and Matching Mole was formed.

DAVID SINCLAIR: Born 1947, Herne Bay, Kent.

Educated at a Canterbury Grammar school, Dave has always enjoyed
playing piano and composing and spent most of his school breaks
playing piano in the music room. After leaving, he spent two years
labouring on motorways and saved enough money to buy himself a
bass guitar and amp, joining local soul group Wilde Flowers. After
a while Dave reverted to keyboard and when the group split six
months later, he joined the remaining members in forming Caravan.
He left Caravan, after three and a half years with the band, in
August, 1971: his place, incidentally, being taken by Phil Miller's
brother, Steve.

PHIL MILLER: Born 1949, UK

My past musical experiences include such well-worn, shabby,
degenerate notables as Roy Babbington, my brother Steve, Laurie
Allan, Pip Pryle and Lol Coxhill - all these have contributed to my
musical formation.
"Important recordings, for me, are "Emergency" by Tony Williams
and those by John Mac etc. while musical 'likes' are as wide as
B. B. King, Messiaen, Bartok, Beck and so many others. Guitar
heroes include Coryell, Mac, Beck, B. B. King and Hendrix".
Phil says he writes music at a predictable trickle of five songs
a year and became interested in music due to his parents playing
pianoforte.

BILL MACCORMICK: Born 1951, UK

After leaving Dulwich College in 1969, Bill joined a band called
Quiet Sun which broke-up when he left in September, 1971. He's
been playing in various bands since 1966 and says his major
influence was Robert with the original Soft Machine in 1966. His
favourite musicians/composers, he says, are Phil Manzanera
(ex-Quiet Sun guitarist), Randy California and John McLaughlin.
His major driving force is "an empty stomach" and Bill started
playing bass because "no one else wanted to and no-one else could
play what I wanted to hear".

1972

"Matching Mole was the next proper thing. I suppose I just hadn't got a group and felt it was time to form one. I kidnapped a few other musicians, like Bill MacCormick who was already in Quiet Sun and Dave Sinclair who was about to leave Caravan. He shared my interest in 'simple songs'. I had a few songs I wanted to do and so did everybody else, so we got into a group and played each others tunes. I was really happy with most of that first album. However, we didn't have any money or equipment, that album was made in an abandoned CBS studio that was so cold that Dave Sinclair had to play with gloves on. We'd had no money in Canterbury in the old days but what was different was that we were playing in colleges and concerts and stuff and were expected to come up with a really professional performance as musicians in amateur circumstances. Whereas as teenagers we were playing in small pubs and places as virtual unknowns. It was a very jumbled time. But that's the story of every group you've ever heard of. The name was my idea, the pun was deliberate — they got it in France straight away."

Bill MacCormick:

"Something that was as ad hoc as ever was when Robert and I went into a pub across the road from Alfie's flat. There was a rock 'n' roll band playing and we joined in and did rock 'n' roll favourites for about fifteen minutes. We cut the drummer and bass player off and did it for them."

Jan 3, 4, 5, 9, 10, 13, 14 — CBS Studios, sessions for 'Matching Mole' lp
released Apr 14 (CBS 64850)
a) 'O Caroline'
b) 'Instant Pussy'
c) 'Instant Curtain'
d) 'Part Of The Dance'
e) 'Instant Kitten'
f) 'Dedicated To Hugh, But You Weren't Listening'
g) 'Beer As In Braindeer'
h) 'Immediate Curtain'
Phil Miller, guitar (b, d, e, f, g); Dave Sinclair, piano (a)/organ (except c, h); Bill MacCormick, bass (b, d, e, f, g); RW, piano (c)/mellotron (a, e, h)/voice (a, b, c, e)/ drums (except c, h); augmented by Dave MacRae, electric piano (b, d, f, g)
All compositions by RW, except d) P. Miller and titled by Alfreda Benge

Bill MacCormick's diary documents the litany of technical breakdowns which plagued the recording and mixing of Mole's debut lp. Unless stated otherwise, CBS Studios.

Dec 29 and 30 — piano out of tune
Jan 3, 4, 5 — headphone problems
Jan 9 — mains interference, 2 til 7 pm
Jan 10 — maintenance work due to Dolby dropout, 4 — 6 pm
Jan 25 — Dolby dropout, session abandoned 4:30 pm

Jan 26 — Dolby dropout and no 30 ips on tape machine. Session moved to Command Studios
Jan 27 — Dolby dropout, noisy panpots, session abandoned 5:30 pm
Feb 15 — Nova Studios: power out 12 — 3 pm (caused by National Miners' Strike)
Feb 29 — Nova Studios: power out 1:30 — 3 pm
Mar 5 — 16 track tape machine breaks down, move to Nova

*"Making that record and forming the group were two separate things. I'd have made it whether I'd formed a group or not. It's me. I had total control over it, said I'd choose the material, do the editing, litter the whole thing with fiddling about on the mellotron — with or without anybody's approval. It seemed years since I'd done a record. At the same time, I wanted to form a group because my ideas are more intense than numerous, I'm not a great fountain of ideas and I need to be in a group. I need other people around me to use their ideas and imaginations to pull the best out of me. Besides, I had to **say** I was forming a group etcetera or they wouldn't have let me do the record. Obviously they only like to record people who are out on the road with an act or something to promote it."*

Jan 17 — Playhouse Theatre, BBC Top Gear recording
broadcast Jan 25
a) 'Part Of The Dance', b) 'Instant Kitten' performed
David Sinclair, organ; Dave MacRae, electric piano/piano (a); Phil Miller, guitar; Bill MacCormick, bass; RW, drums, voice (b)

Jan 22 — Hydraspace, Watford
Carol Grimes' Uncle Dog supporting

Jan 23 — 'UCS Benefit' Roundhouse

Feb 19 — Paradiso, Amsterdam, Holland

Feb 20 (afternoon) — Doelen, Rotterdam, Holland

Feb 20 (evening) — Globa Theatre, Eindhoven, Holland

Feb (late) or Mar (late) — Lol Coxhill, Toverbal, Maasluis, Holland

augmented by Phil Miller, guitar; RW, electric piano/drums
Saxophonist Lol Coxhill remembers that Robert arrived without his drum kit and played the room's walls and objects until a kit was found and set up.

Phil Miller:

"We were in Holland and had a day off. Lol had a gig and asked us to come along, so it was time to play with Lol, you know, make some noises."

Feb 24 — Verviers, Belgium (venue unknown)

Feb 25 and 26 — Theatre 140, Brussels, Belgium

"Dave (Sinclair) didn't stay long. It was difficult to find musicians who want to do all the different things that we were doing. We did a concert in Brussels in which the context was just to improvise — he was very imaginative but he hated it. He just wanted to do songs. You can't do eight 'O Carolines'. What do you do? O Annette? O Jaqueline? O Sue? It gets a bit unconvincing. Really he felt insecure at the very experimentalness of it. So we brought in Dave MacRae, he was happy to try anything — a really proficient musician. He really enjoyed the danger of playing in an anarchic situation."

Dave MacRae:

"It was the first time I'd ever played a concert where we'd play a complete set of music for perhaps forty minutes, as one piece of music. Even though there would be several pieces of music included we'd perform one continuous stream of music and that was an entirely new thing for me."

Mar 6 — Kensington House, BBC Sounds of the '70's recording

broadcast Mar 24
a) 'No 'alf Measures' b) 'Lithing And Gracing' performed
Dave MacRae, electric piano/piano (a); Phil Miller, guitar; Bill MacCormick, bass; RW, drums
'No 'alf Measures' is Robert's arrangement of Kevin Ayers' 1965 composition 'Vaguely'

Mar 8 — Polytechnic, Kingston

Kevin Ayers supporting. The evening concludes with an impromptu jam by Kevin, bassist Archie Leggett, and Robert.

Mar 10 — Ealing College

Mar 11 — Merton Technical College

Mar 20 — Education T.V. Studios, Music Alive filming

Kevin Ayers, guitar; David Bedford, organ; Lol Coxhill, tenor sax; RW, drums
Education TV was run by the Inner London Education Authority which produced programmes for local schools. This film features Kevin performing 'Hymn' unaccompanied, a conversation between host Brian Kenney and journalist Al Clark, and closes with a six minute collective improvisation by the quartet.

Mar 20 — Civic Hall, Chelmsford

Mar 22 — Civic Hall, Guildford

Mar 24 and 25 — Paradiso, Amsterdam, Holland

Plainsong supporting. Recorded by V.P.R.O. Dutch radio.

Mar 28 — Brussels, Belgium, TV filming

Bill MacCormick, Dave MacCrae, Robert Wyatt, Phil Miller

WHEN is Matching Mole's LP going to be released and when are they doing some more gigs? What equipment do they use, how long have they been together and where do they come from? — Nick Utteridge, Cheltenham.

■ Phil Miller: Gibson SG Special, Fender Dual Showman 100-watt amp, two Fender Dual Showman cabinets each containing two 15 inch J.B. Lansing speakers Bill MacCormick: Gibson EB3 bass, Acoustic 540 150-watt amp with one cabinet containing an 18-inch speaker. Dave McRae: Fender Rhodes electric piano specially modified to his own specifications, two H/H 100-watt slave amps, two Fender Dual Showman cabinets each containing two 15 inch speakers. Robert Wyatt: Custom-built Ludwig drum kit with 24 inch bass drum and 14, 16 and 18 inch tom-toms, plus Gretsch 14 inch snare drum. Avedis Zildjian and Super Zyn 16 and 20 inch cymbals, Avedis Zildjian 14 inch Hi-hats and Ludwig 3S sticks. PA consists of a pair of WEM Redding horns totalling 800 watts, 400 on each side of the stage. Two JB Lansing C55 bass bins with dispersal lens and super tweeters, powered by three HH 100-watt amps. Allen and Heath 12-channel stereo mixer. Monitoring on stage comprises 300 watts of WEM B columns with four AKG mikes on the drum kit and direct injection for the other three instruments, plus one AKG D1000 vocal mike. Their first LP, " Matching Mole," is now available on CBS. They formed in November 1971 and lived in the Notting Hill Gate area of London. They are present on tour with John Mayall and will be spending the whole of May in France and Germany.

Matching Mole: The beginning of another ear

Few bands have faced such a discrepancy between the enthusiasm of their welcome and the uncertainty of their economics as Matching Mole. Multiply an average musicbiz melodrama by the number of holes it'd take to fill the Wembley Empire Pool and you'll come up with some semblance of the equipment, transport and pocket-money problems that have continually confronted this merry and determined little combo of Foster's Lager addicts. This, together with a considerable affection for Robert Wyatt's drumming and voicing, Phil Miller's guitaring, Bill MacCormick's bassing and Dave McRae's keyboarding (and the now-departed David Sinclair's keyboarding on their record, the excellent CBS 64850), prompted Al Clark to wander along to a rehearsal in Dave's front room, and afterwards talk with Robert across the kitchen table . . . . .

  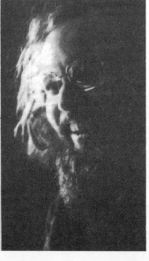

Voices and choices

It's been evident from the first Soft Machine album onwards that Robert Wyatt is the possessor of the most notched, rusty and unfailingly empathetic vocal chords in the entire area of music in which they operate. In one version of the Wild Flowers, that celebrated, ever-changing Canterbury nucleus-for-the-future, he sang for about nine months while Richard Coughlan (subsequently of Caravan) did the drumming. And it's his voice that over-shadows the early Soft Machine demos recently released by Byg. But that was an approach styled around straightforward pop singing, and evolving out of the general excitement surrounding pop music in the early and mid-sixties. Also, Kevin Ayers would occasionally write something outside his own range or might need a harmony part added, and Robert would oblige on that score.

However, by the time it came to recording the first album, his voice had extended itself into modulations, instrumentalising, harmonising, echoing, a multilaterally true voice in an arid soundscape of good voices. He even became so horrified at the original lyrics of one of his songs ('I Should've Known') that he re-wrote them the night before the recording into something so completely honest, revealing and amusing ('Why Am I So Short?') that it undoubtedly created the precedent for all his word-games to follow. In this respect the previous influence of Daevid Allen, who used to lodge with his parents and was an original member of the group, was probably quite substantial.

'Daevid, not by preaching but by example, was living out all the things he was thinking about. To me activity was reading, looking at paintings and listening to records. Meanwhile, he was writing, painting and playing guitar. What you could do consisted of what you wanted to do. He used to sing and make noises and make tapes. He made tapes with people who could play and tapes with people who couldn't play, and there was no difference in quality between them. Things like that shattered the kind of rubbish that I'd been thinking up until then . . .'

It's surprising—in view of the beauty of Robert's treatment of Hugh Hopper's 'A Certain Kind' on Soft Machine 1, his amazing vocal jigsaws on 2, the lengthy lyrical passages of 'Moon in June' on 3 and the extent to which much of the commercial success of Matching Mole's album can be attributed to the irresistibility of 'O Caroline' and 'Signed Curtain', both cracked, barely-sung diary-fragments which are indivisible from what they're about—that he isn't really all that keen on songs, or at least song situations.

'Usually they're just props for making noises. There are certain vowels and consonants that work out and have the right effect, and the people who wrote them will contrive the imitation situation whereby that's what they actually wanted to say. In my case, my pride goes if I find myself lying like that, and I think that if I'm going to use words, I should use them as carefully as possible, bearing in mind that you're talking to somebody, and that if you are trying to say something then be careful what you say. But the thing I really like about music is way outside intelligible conversation, much deeper, stronger and more moving than stringing sentences together. So I've generally played in bands which were essentially instrumental. In other words, I've never played with polite, subservient, accompanist-type musicians, and this creates a situation where if you're going to make your voice fit into the context of a set or an album, for the sake of the continuity and mood of the piece, you're just throwing your voice in to the elements, you're dealing with pure music rather than conveying some cute impression of yourself to strangers. So I've always tried to get in situations where the very fact that I also like singing songs was discouraged. Whether that means I'm totally screwed up I don't know, don't really care either'.

Moon of an ear

'Moon in June' on Soft Machine 3 is a collage of fragments assembled during the life of the group, mostly during his time in the States after the two tours they did with Jimi Hendrix. Some of it is a lament for being away from home. All of it is his own work. Mike Ratledge came in to play his organ solo and provide a drone with Hugh Hopper. Rab Spall contributed violin, but it wouldn't be unfair to call Robert Mr Moon In June, especially in the five-minute one-man aural orgy at the end. In common with most things, it came to represent something not originally intended . . . like wanting to hold on to the reins of the Soft Machine he liked while it was beginning to become one he wasn't having so much fun with. With no reflection on Elton Dean, who Robert himself after all had gone out to find, he feels it was at that stage that compromise entered the whole business.

"Moon in June' for me was the last chance I had to use all the things we'd done without being a jazz band, which was what was developing. I thought that before that we'd done something quite special that had nothing to do with being a jazz band and I wanted to get twenty minutes of it down somewhere. At the same time, I was excited about the new developments and wanted a change too. I don't know if I'll always be in this position, but I really only do those things in studios in the end, because, however much I go on about co-operativeness and that, there comes a point when I know exactly what I want something to sound like and the only way to get it is to do nearly everything yourself. I can't write complex enough scores to get other people to do it. When people ask why I don't necessarily do on stage what I do on record, the only answer is that I could not subject other musicians to the rigorous detail and discipline that I have to impose on myself to get those things right. I just don't have that kind of personality'.

How did 'End of an Ear' come about? Well, partly because CBS probably thought when they gave their okay that, as he was the singer in a primarily instrumental group, he'd come busting out all over with a long-frustrated headful of commercial pop songs. For Robert though, the motivation was slightly different . . .

'That was a direct result of wishing that I'd had more than five minutes to meander at the end of 'Moon in June'. I was just so fucking happy adding layer after layer. Mike had gone, so I made all the little noises on the Lowrey organ that I'd wanted him to make. Christ, for the first time I wasn't just planning and dreaming and hoping, I was actually doing what I wanted to do, and I suddenly thought how silly to stick it on the end of a bunch of songs. So 'End Of an Ear' came about once I'd decided to continue the ecstasy of charging about in the studio pissed out of me head for forty minutes instead of five'.

Were the title, and the 'out-of-work pop singer currently on drums with the Soft Machine' clause on the sleeve a pretty fair indication of how he felt at the time, and a nudge in the direction of his comrades?

'I seem to have inspired a certain amount of sympathy and personal enthusiasm amongst people about my own particular loneliness and battle within the Soft Machine. But the fact is that I was drunk and arrogant and didn't take them seriously enough when they didn't want to do the kind of things I wanted to. I put Mike and Hugh through ghastly emotional scenes, and the mind boggles at how they've stuck it all that long . . I've had a lot of time to think about that and—sorry, I know public confession boxes is the latest trend and all that—but it is worth saying because I'm getting vaguely sheepish and embarrassed about the sympathy for me within that context since they were simply trying to play what they wanted. If the Soft Machine was a prison, then it was a prison I built for myself out of my own indecision and lack of sense of direction. So the record isn't anti-Soft Machine, it's anti-me for not

being able to think clearly what I wanted to do. The dedications on the cover are no-pride-left, anybody-out-there-help-help type ones, claiming people by writing down their names. It was absurd. I look back on it as being a feast for some second-rate psychiatrist'.

The longest dedication of all was to Gil Evans whose Wyatt-styled 'Las Vegas Tango' came to take up about a third of the record's playing time. 'He's one of the few people who've come across an endless musical thing to do. This is what the blues is, but it's not any one particular person's invention, it's just thousands of people eventually agreeing on a format that's endlessly satisfying. And Gil Evans, almost single-handedly, got a link going in my head between Spanish cante hondo and blues singing in 'Las Vegas Tango', it's just a beautifully shifting seesaw of Spanish-influenced blues chords. That struck me as endlessly satisfying'.

The evolving mole

And then there was Matching Mole, or Machine Molle as some prophetic bilingual punsters would insist. Bill MacCormick was a civil servant at the time of joining but before that was in a group called Quiet Sun who did unusual time-signature things. Phil Miller was in Delivery but also worked with people like Roy Babbington, and spent long amounts of time learning his way around his instrument. Or as Robert put it, 'His main background is sitting around playing guitar without any money'. Robert met Dave McRae through Nucleus who were looking for a new drummer after John Marshall went to join Jack Bruce and, ultimately and ironically, the Soft Machine. Dave still plays piano for them as well as making his considerable contribution to the Mole.

'Dave McRae is an antipodean from another planet, and my life started out with them. He's such a total musician—equally happy in Australian jazz groups, knowing his Cecil Taylor, doing a Coca Cola ad or grooving behind Buddy Rich or Sarah Vaughan. The most important contribution he made to the record was being there, tuning up his piano and talking and putting on little odd plinking noises through all the instrumental things, and just creating the atmosphere of being in a room with all he can do but not doing it. It's not so much what he plays but of how different the record would've been if he hadn't been there'.

The man who did play most of the keyboard parts on the record, David Sinclair, is now late of Caravan, late of Matching Mole and currently working on some songs with a friend, and drummer Pip Pyle. Why late of Matching Mole?

'Well, although he joined to play and rave as well as do the songs, the only thing that really worked compatibly was the songplaying. He's a great freaker-outer on organ. A keyboard man with a sense of madness is very rare, keyboard people are usually very schooled and can wreck musical madness with their knowledge of what should be happening. Dave can lose himself in wonderful ways, but when you're trying to build your tune that you're going to be playing night after night, it's not enough to have a few things in common. You've really got to have so much in common. You can afford casual relationships on a record which you can't afford in a working group'.

Was there any track on the record particularly representative of the further-evolved Mole? 'Hopefully I'm now becoming a quarter of whatever gets said or played. So for me 'Part of the Dance' is the most useful pointer to the group because it was written by Phil and I'm just doing my quarter on it, like I'm doing now and like I hope to be doing on the next album'. Does that necessarily exclude any more 'O Caroline's or 'Signed Curtain's? 'Those things are like cutting off malignant parts of a diseased body. I really don't need them anymore. To be able to write and sing those, without sounding too precious I hope,

relieves some of the thing that goes into producing them. However, there's no way of making plans about that. I suppose I shall sit around pianos and sing and think up word games at certain times for the rest of my life. And if I'm in the studio, I'll do it'.

Afterpiece

A few days later, with the group having gone off to France on the Gallic Leg of their John Mayall tour, I put my brain cells in a small cardboard box and take them down to an armchair in front of a television screen in South London's ETV studios. Resting in the certain knowledge that the Mole won't be bothering with any of the right ons and rock 'n' roll medleys that might make them rich tax exiles before they get to Avignon, I settle back and watch the playback of a broadcast they taped a few days earlier.

Dave, like an electronic Gandalf with impossibly long fingers, guides the smoky, shifting rhythms over Bill's obsessive Focal Timekeeper bass line and curls elegantly up and down whatever part of the keyboard he fancies. Phil, hunched and Grecian-God-Curled, is the ideal group guitarist, waiting for the moment to contribute effectively and knowing what an effective contribution amounts to. Bill and Phil, like Bill and Ben, have a very special binding language and don't even have to say anything. Robert doing his voice bits isn't a pretty sight but makes a remarkable sound, like a man sobbing his heart out inside an echo chamber. Matching Mole seems to be the sum total of all their lives so far.

It really is a quartet now. And I only talked to Robert. Aw shucks. See them soon. Nice boys every one of them, even if they don't go for smart casuals and fast cars. They're probably the most coherent and adventurous British band that's still accessible these days, equally balancing strong themes and inspired deviations. And they're not doing much, apart from rehearsing. Music-Music never did go down all that well. Still, it's always a new pigeon-hole and there's plenty of money and support in them. In Mole-holes there's only music . . .

PS. All of which having been said, done and type-set, it turns out that Matching Mole are playing in Saturday's Midnight-to-six gig at Kings Cross Cinema with the Soft Machine (now with Karl Jenkins in place of Elton Dean) and Just Us (Elton Dean's group-on-the-side gone full-time). The wheel goes round and it should be a right old skull-fucker of a night . . .

```
******************************
Addition to Matching Mole
feature

P.P.S. Al Clark who brought
you this epic piece of
music journalism, and who
also put his balls on the
rails and turned the world
at large on to various
eccentrics of showbiz will
be leaving Time Out this
week.   Threatening letters
or tear stained signed
knickers should be sent
to the offices of Rolling
Stone where Al will shortly
resurface.
Thanks to him for the blood
sweat and beers and maybe
we can con him into a
guest review of the next
Kevin Ayers album.
******************************
```

Throughout April, Matching Mole tour Britain as support group for bluesman John Mayall. Except for a headlining gig in Canterbury, all dates this month are in support of Mayall.

Apr 3 — Royal Festival Hall (two shows)

Apr 5 — Winter Gardens, Bournemouth

Apr 6 — The Dome, Brighton

Apr 8 — St. Thomas' Hall, Canterbury

Apr 17 — Kensington House, BBC Top Gear recording
broadcast May 9
'March Ides/Instant Pussy/Smoke Signal' performed
Dave MacRae, electric piano; Phil Miller, guitar; Bill MacCormick, bass; RW, drums

Apr 26 — Free Trade Hall, Manchester

Apr 27 — City Hall, Newcastle

Apr 28 — Greens Playhouse, Glasgow, Scotland

Bill MacCormick:
"I have very fond recollections of our performance in Glasgow, mainly because it happened to be the best time I ever played with the band. The fact that I almost fell off the high stage probably helped to get the adrenalin flowing."

Apr 29 — Lancaster University, Leeds

Apr 30 — Colston Hall, Bristol

"Up until the second gig at the Festival Hall we were rehearsing in public; since then, with the exception of a disaster at Canterbury, we've to a great extent sorted ourselves out. I say this chiefly because most people would naturally think a group like this is pretty well-off, contract with CBS, album out, etc. In fact we're very poor and can't actually afford to rehearse properly even. We've had a lot of equipment nicked and the promoters in Britain aren't paying us a living wage. I'm not carping — we're paying our dues, like any other band — it's just that I want people to know that we don't use mikes that stop working every five minutes because we like them; we can't afford any better. And when the PA blows, it's not...bravura, or something. It's poverty."

May 3 — Education T.V. Studios, Music Alive filming
'Smoke Signal' performed
Dave MacRae, electric piano; Phil Miller, guitar; Bill MacCormick, bass; RW, drums, voice, toy saxophone

On May 8th Matching Mole edit 'O Caroline' at CBS Studios for release as a single. It is backed with 'Signed Curtain' and released July 8 (CBS S8101).

May 15 — L'Olympia, Paris, France
During the afternoon, the group are interviewed for French TV and the 'Pop Club' radio show.

Machine Molle, Palais de Sport, Metz

May 17 — Palais de Sport, Metz, France

May 18 — Palais de Sport, Bordeaux, France

This brief tour of France is again as opening group for John Mayall.

Bill MacCormick:
"Certainly we were not the ideal support act for them. Basically, we paid to do it, we supplied the PA system so it cost us money. It was mixed. Some of the places we played liked us better than others, particularly Paris where we were the centre of attention. I think they realized it was a slightly odd mix because we were due to go to Germany with them but we were pulled out of that."

May 27 — Essex University, Colchester
supporting Egg

June 3 — Cardiff University, Cardiff

June 4 — Flamingo, Redruth

Sorry about the last time but come to

Soft Machine Matching Mole

JUST US

FRIDAY 7th JULY. KINGS CROSS CINEMA, PENTONVILLE ROAD MIDNIGHT 6 A.M.
SUNDAY 9th JULY. NEW THEATRE. GEORGE ST. OXFORD

ELTON DEAN
64539

MATCHING MOLE
64850

SOFT MACHINE
5
64806

the mind people

June 17 — Kings Cross Cinema
also: Brotherhood Of Breath, Bond/Brown/Collins/Wallace
The first of a pair of events to showcase CBS artists Soft Machine, Matching Mole, and Elton Dean for promotion of their current records. With drummers John Marshall and Phil Howard unable to make the gig, Softs and Just Us pull out and are replaced by Chris MacGregor's Brotherhood of Breath and a last minute pickup group featuring Graham Bond, Pete Brown, Mel Collins, and Ian Wallace.

June 21 — Maida Vale, BBC Sounds of the '70's recording
broadcast July 6
'Gloria Gloom/Nan True's Hole/Brandy For Benj' performed
Dave MacRae, electric piano; Phil Miller, guitar; Bill MacCormick, bass; RW, drums/voice

June 25 — Barbarella's, Birmingham

June 29 — Mountford Hall, Liverpool
Jonesy, Roxy Music supporting

June 30 — Falcon

July 1 — Chateau Studio, Herouville, France, Rockenstock T.V. filming
'Gloria Gloom/Part Of The Dance' performed

July 7 — Kings Cross Cinema

July 9 — New Theatre, Oxford

July 13 — Weymouth Grammar School, Weymouth

July 22 — 'Europop Festival' Ostend, Belgium
also: MC5, Sweet, If, Mungo Jerry, Jericho

July 25 — The Greyhound

July 27 — Paris Theatre, BBC In Concert recording
broadcast Sept 9
'Instant Pussy/Lithing And Gracing/March Ides/Part Of The Dance/Brandy For Benj' performed. Mike Harding host.
Dave MacRae, electric piano; Phil Miller, guitar; Bill MacCormick, bass; RW, drums/voice

July 30 — Roundhouse
also: Biggles, Keith Tippett, The Flamin' Groovies

Aug 13 — 'Marquee Jazz and Blues Festival' Reading
also: Ten Years After, Quintessence, Wizard, Status Quo, Stray, Vinegar Joe, Stackridge, Sutherland Brothers and Quiver
Another high profile opportunity turns disaster. Dave MacRae's electric piano gives trouble due to several necessary gadgets being stolen, the set length is chopped from forty-five minutes to fifteen, and the microphone malfunctions when Robert attempts to sing.

Aug 14, 15, 16 — CBS Studio 2, first sessions for 'Matching Mole's Little Red Record'
Recording schedule: 14th — 'March Ides', 'Nan True's Hole', 'Lithing And Gracing', 'Brandy For Benj' 15th — 'Gloria Gloom', 'Smoke Signal' 16th — 'God Song'

Aug 18 — 'Bilzen Jazz Festival' Bilzen, Belgium
also: Curved Air, Lindisfarne, Edgar Broughton Band
Mole's performance was recorded for the King Kory Radio Show but was never broadcast.

Aug 21 and 22 — CBS Studio 1
Recording: 'Flora Fidgit', 'No 'alf Measures'
Mixing: 'Flora Fidgit', 'Smoke Signal'

Aug 25 — CBS Studio 2
Recording and mixing: 'Smoke Signal', 'Flora Fidgit', 'Starting In The Middle Of The Day'

Aug 29 — CBS Studio 2
Recording with Eno: 'Gloria Gloom', 'Flora Fidgit'

Aug 30 — CBS Studio 2
Recording and mixing vocal overdubs with The Mutter Chorus (David Gale, Julie Christie, and Alfreda Benge)

Aug 31 — CBS Studio 2, final sessions for 'Matching Mole's Little Red Record'

released Oct 27 (CBS 65260)

a) 'Starting In The Middle Of The Day We Can Drink Our Politics Away (D. MacRae)
b) 'Marchides' (D. MacRae)
c) Nan True's Hole (P. Miller)
d) Righteous Rhumba (P. Miller)
e) Brandy As In Benj (D. MacRae)
f) Gloria Gloom (B. MacCormick)
g) God Song (P. Miller)
h) Flora Fidget (B. MacCormick)
i) Smoke Signal (D. MacRae)

Dave MacRae, electric piano (except a, g)/organ (a, c, d, e)/piano (a)/ synthesizer (h); Phil Miller, guitar (except a, g, h)/acoustic guitar (g); Bill MacCormick, bass (except a, g, h); RW, drums (except a, g)/voice (except b, h, i)/lyrics (a, c, d, f, g); augmented by Brian Eno, VCS3 (f); und Der Mütter Korus , voices (b, c, d, f); Alfreda Benge, titles (f, h)

Bill MacCormick:

"Having Robert Fripp as the producer was an absolute disaster, if only for the reason that he reduced Phil Miller to a quivering wreck so that he could barely move his fingers. It was a bit difficult for Phil anyway who held Fripp in some high regard. I got along with him perfectly fine, but then again, I didn't feel particularly threatened. There was some distinct tension and the end product being certain takes of things that we would have liked to have used, which had a good feel to them, were not used because Fripp refused to allow them to be used. It got to that stage. It seemed like a good idea at the time but it turned out not to be."

"If you're going to give me credit for throwing unusual musical elements together for providing a catalyst for new things to happen, then you've got to blame me for when that creates traffic accidents."

Sep 7 — Queen Elizabeth Hall, London
Paul Wheeler supporting
set consists: 'God Song/Drinking Song/Flora Fidgit/Smoke Signal/Gloria Gloom/Nan True's Hole/Instant Pussy/Lithing And Gracing/March Ides/Brandy As In Benj'

Sep 9 — Montbeliard, France
Genesis supporting

Sep 15 — Doelen, Rotterdam, Holland

Sep 16 — Circus, The Hague, Holland

Sep 17 — Concertgebouw, Amsterdam, Holland

Sep 18 — Cine Roma, Antwerp, Belgium

Sep 19 — Salle de la Madeleine, Brussels, Belgium

Sep 20 — Conservatoire, Liege, Belgium

Sep 21 — Cine Capitol, Ghent, Belgium

Sep 22 — Stadschowbourg, Groningen, Holland

This eight day tour was in support of Soft Machine.

This postcard from the People's Republic of China served as the inspiration for the cover artwork of Matching Mole's Little Red Record

一定要解放台湾

We are determined to liberate Taiwan!
Nous libérerons Taiwan!
Wir werden Taiwan unbedingt befreien!

WYATT'S BAND SPLIT

MATCHING MOLE — the group formed by Robert Wyatt after he left Soft Machine — have broken up, according to a spokesman within the group. Although the split is not yet official, and could not be confirmed by their manager or recording company, the NME was assured that they will never play together again. The group has been idle for some time, and Phil Miller has already joined another band named Delivery in which he is featured with drummer Pip Pyle, ex-Caravan member Dave Sinclair and his cousin Richard Sinclair. Robert Wyatt is understood to be busy composing at the moment.

Bill MacCormick:

"I think it would be fair to say that when Robert decided to break it up, it came as a surprise to everyone apart from him. Certainly things had not been easy, things were sufficiently uneasy financially. I was the youngest member of the group and since I had a proper job not long before Robert asked me to join I actually had more money than they did. There was actually a two or three month period where I was paying people's wages, which is laughable...I never saw a royalty statement for Matching Mole, I never saw any publishing account let alone seen any money from them. For at least ten years, I used to be able to go into Virgin Records' shop in Oxford St. and find shrinkwrapped versions of Matching Mole albums, they were still being bloody well pressed!"

Dave MacRae:

"When you're in the business of trying to be a creative force, plumbing the insides of mental power of people involved in the band, it's understandable that many of the organizational factors would go astray. It's no reflection on management or anything like that 'cause it must have been difficult for them to place a band like this I would think. It was a relatively unusual mixture of people. If you know Robert then you know how he'd fly from one thing to the next with great speed and possibly this had something to do with the way things would work out, or not work out as the case may be. For me, not having had any great experience for the way European jazz bands and concerts organized themselves and being relatively open to anything it probably didn't seem unusual that things went wrong with regularity."

"Matching Mole finished because I don't have the qualities of leadership, I don't want to run things. The onus was on me to run it because I was better known than the others, I became the focus of attention when we played. Not because I'm a nice shy person or anything, I just wanted to be a quarter of a group. Also drink problems, equipment problems, I just couldn't handle it."

MATCHING MOLE

Dec 5— Robert Wyatt, Langham 1, BBC Top Gear recording

broadcast Dec 19
a) 'We Got An Arts Council Grant/Righteous Rhumba'
b) 'Little Child'
c) 'God Song/Hatfield'
Francis Monkman, synthesizer (a, c)/piano (b, c)/electric piano (b), backing vocal (a); RW, vocals, percussion (a, c); All compositions by RW except 'Hatfield' which is Richard Sinclair's 'Fol De Rol' and 'Little Child' which was composed by Andrei Petrov and Irwin Kostal and Tony Harrison for the 1941 Broadway play 'Bluebird Of Happiness'.

'We Got An Arts Council Grant'

Let's sow our way to the Roundhouse,
The naughty sights and sounds house,
Forget the hippies on Sundays,
'Cause culture starts on Mondays

We got to play some concerts too,
A glass of wine for the price of two,
But we don't mind if nobody comes,
'Cause friends of ours control the funds

There's Andre Previn and George Hoskin,
Making sure the loser wins,
We like our pop without the crowds,
The very best is not so loud

Dec (?) — Abbey Road, session for Kevin Ayers 'Bananamour' lp

released May 4/73 (Harvest SHVL 807)
Kevin Ayers, guitar/vocal; Archie Leggett, bass; Eddie Sparrow, woodblock; Ronnie Price, piano; RW, harmony vocal on 'Hymn'

Dec — Hatfield and the North, Red Cow, Cambridge

Phil Miller, guitar; Dave Sinclair, organ; Richard Sinclair, bass/vocals; Pip Pyle, drums; augmented by RW, vocals

Dec — Robert Wyatt, Chateau Studio, Herouville, France, Rockenstock T.V. filming

accompanied by Hatfield and the North
'God Song/Fol De Rol/Finesse Is For Fairies/untitled' performed
'untitled' is a nine minute composition by Dave Sinclair which features an extended improvisational vocal duet between Richard and Robert.

Pierre Lattes:
    "You must remember that France and England were fairly isolated because of the union system in England. So it was easier somehow for the rock bands to come to Paris and play than for the French bands to go to England. Because of this the cross-pollenization was not as much as it should have been for the times. It was only because of some guys like me around that insisted on bringing some bands over that it happened. I wasn't alone of course, there were three or four people, but I was playing all the Black music and all the weirdos."

Daevid Allen, Karl Jenkins, John Marshall, Bill MacCormick, Mike Ratledge, Robert Wyatt, Elton Dean, Francis Monkman in Paris

Hello Barry / happened to be passing this way so am able to answer a bit of your letter to John.

Dave Sinclair lives a quiet life by the sea in Whitstable where he composes sad melodies on a piano and hums into a tape recorder. However he phoned up recently to say he's written a load of new songs he wants to work on – he's been playing a little with Tim Pyle (drums) Phil Miller, and his old Caravan buddy Richard Sinclair. Best Wishes, Robert Wyatt.

O.K. ?

Anvers, Musee des Beaux Arts.

2044. James ENSOR Fleurs et Légumes (détail) (1860-1949) Bloemen en groenten (détail), Flowers and vegetables (detail), Blumen und Gemüse (Ausschnitt).

© Éditions "Viking" s.a. Bruxelles
Printed in Belgium

BARRY KING
53 AMPTHILL ROAD
SHIRLEY
SOUTHAMPTON
5013 LL 76738

Voice of the Mole

PLEASE ask Robert Wyatt, drummer-vocalist with Matching Mole, what his influences were, why he only sings for short sessions when playing live, and when will he be doing an LP? — **Ian Wome, New Addington, Croydon.**

■ Three drummers who have had an electrifying effect on my thinking about drumming are Elvin Jones, Tony Williams and Phil Howerd. I only sing for short sessions when playing live because I have responsibilities on stage which I don't have in the recording studio.

I'd like to do an album of songs because I've decided to explore the possibilities of my voice a bit more. Unlike any time before, I'm more interested in what the voice can do than what the drum kit can do. For me it's a transitional period right now and I need time to think somewhere quiet in the country. I don't want to make any decisions at the moment about what I'm going to do next. — BOB WYATT.

Alfie's flat, Notting Hill Gate, December 14

1973

NME, Mar 3 1973

Under the Influence

THIS WEEK: ROBERT WYATT

GONG: "Camembert Electrique". About the first album made by one of our "family" to have been created in sympathetic circumstances, and it shows. Appropriately enough, if our "family" has a father it's Daevyd Allen. So he deserves the opportunity.

MIROSLAV VITOUS: "Infinite Search". Vitous apparently gave up the opportunity to swim in the Olympics (for Czechoslovakia) in order to concentrate on music. What a disappointment for his school. How ungrateful to his parents. No wonder patriotis n is decaying all around us when such people are allowed to indulge their sinful practices.

BEATLES: "Magical Mystery Tour". My snobbish and elitist tendencies usually prevent me from sharing heroes with the loud majority but Lennon reached me with his two books, and some of his music is so breathtakingly imaginative that he has become a real inspiration for me.

BEE GEES: "Horizontal". About my favourite pop group.

JOHN COLTRANE: "Africa". I first heard this in Collet's record department, which was about the only place an innocent provincial lad visiting London could hear new uncommercial records without the shop staff getting hostile. Thank you, Ray Smith!

NOT A specific record, but a label: **Candid.** They made several equally amazing records, giving unprecedented freedom to the musicians on the date. Cecil Taylor's "This Nearly Was Mine" and Min-

gus's "Fables Of Faubus" are outstanding in my memory. Even Don Ellis was able to make a good record on Candid!

MINGUS PRESENTS: "Quintet of the year". My copy is on Vocalion LAE12031. Max Roach, Charles Mingus, Bud Powell, Dizzy Gillespie, Charlie Parker at the Massey Hall in Canada, in 1953. My bebop Bible.

DUKE ELLINGTON: "Such Sweet Thunder". My mid-fifties nostalgia orchestra, and about the last particular record my father and I agreed on. (When people generalise about jazz being an improviser's art, they shouldn't neglect that enormous amount of beautiful writing and arranging for which some jazz musicians have been responsible).

SONNY ROLLINS QUARTET: "Live At The Village Gate". With Billy Higgins and Don Cherry. Everybody takes ludicrous risks and they all come off a great advertisement for anarchy, and just the thing if you're in an uninhibited mood.

LARRY CORYELL: "Live At The Village Vanguard". I think someone is just as influenced by things that don't work as by those that do, and this choice falls into the category of an Awful Warning. It's a selfconscious attempt to do something that doesn't suit him, something he's been on the fringe of for several years, without really understanding what it involves. I saw him jamming with Alvin Lee in New York and it was only too clear what was going on. It's the kind of record that's so terrible it can't fail to encourage you to do someting better.

"Although drumming makes more noise, it's a pretty humbling thing for a musician to play. You're judged really as a catalyst. While you're drumming, someone else is dealing with the harmonic and melodic set-up. There's no way you could think it's all you. The communal thing is very useful — everything you do has to be met by something somebody else is doing, so that's good for the brain and keeps your ego in check. The nicest thing was that you could stop a lot and think 'I won't do all this stuff just because I'm sitting here and want to do something with my hands.' Maybe it's a reflection on my drumming, but I used to think how nice things used to sound when I stopped playing. If you stopped filling everything in, leaving enormous spaces, the stage didn't in fact blow up, disintegrate. You can listen almost as an outsider the way no one else in the group can. It's good for you NOT to make assumptions about how important you are."

The new year begins as Robert Wyatt accompanies Alfreda Benge and Julie Christie to Venice, Italy where work on Nicolas Roeg's film 'Don't Look Now' commences. While in Italy a portable Riviera keyboard bought for the equivalent of forty English pounds provides a partial catalyst for fresh musical inspiration.

Alfreda Benge:
"In the winter of 1972 I got a job in Venice for two months and I persuaded Robert to come with me. That wasn't easy then because in those days he was a workaholic. And the idea of a holiday, of him sitting somewhere...he couldn't stand because work was the only thing that mattered to him then. But I was very angry that he didn't want to come so in the end he did come, very reluctantly. He was more or less by himself every day while I was working in a house on the edge of lagoon, and we went and bought this toy organ. Just because he was a prisoner in this house for two months he had to sit there and write music. Up till then he was always so busy and nervous about the future, about getting a new band together that if he hadn't had that forced imprisonment he wouldn't have had the time to relax to do the music. Also I think Venice was a very big influence because we were just surrounded by water."

On February 14th, Robert returns home to repeated requests from Bill MacCormick to resuscitate Matching Mole. With agreement in principle reached, a premature announcement appears in the March 6 edition of the New Musical Express weekly. More concrete, however, is the parallel conception of a quartet featuring Gary Windo, tenor sax; Dave MacRae, piano/electric piano; Ron Mathewson, double bass; and Robert Wyatt, drums/voice. The ensemble play collective free improvisation and incorporate themes from Windo, MacRae, Mole, and Latin America.

Gary Windo:
"Yeah, sure I wrote some charts for WMWM. I'd draw little cartoons of Spiderman on the bar lines for a laugh! The thing is though, Robert never liked his drumming very much. He didn't think he was very good. But did you ever hear that BBC thing we did? Man, he was doing incredible things!"

Dave MacRae:

"One develops and continues to look for something else to do and Robert was like that as well, he was always looking for something else. The WMWM thing was really just another step as such. Everyone's abilities had changed, certainly mine had and I was learning about all sorts of different things so that was another aspect of playing with him. Robert was a most inventive human being so it wouldn't really matter what shape of music we'd decide to put together, he'd always be a contributor of the highest level."

"Now that was going to be something but in fact the musicians were too disparate in terms of what we were doing. You could have done the occasional gig or record but it could never have been a working group because of the terms of references. That was always the problem, I couldn't work with straight jazz musicians as it were or with straight rock musicians, only sort of strange people who fell between the cracks."

Mar (late) — WMWM, Langham 1, BBC Jazz Workshop recording
broadcast Apr 4
'Toddler', 'Caramus' performed
Gary Windo, tenor sax; Dave MacRae, piano/electric piano; Ron Mathewson, double bass; RW, drums/voice

Mar 24 — WMWM, The Tally-Ho

Mar or Apr — Nick Mason's home studio, sessions for 'Solar Flares' film soundtrack
RW, drums/Riviera keyboard/piano/voice (inc. sheep sounds)/composition
An independently produced film short about barnyard animals. Further details unknown.

Apr 13 — WMWM, Ronnie Scott's

Apr 14 — WMWM, Ronnie Scott's

Richard Sinclair:

"I was asked to sit in for the bassist who couldn't make the gig. I was behind them mostly, playing lots of bubbly notes. That Dave MacRae is such a monster musician."

"Dave MacRae is quite possibly the best musician I've ever worked with, he's such an alert, listening musician. I think I actually reached a kind of organic confidence on drums with Dave MacRae, I really started to get the hang of the drum kit there."

Apr 28 — WMWM, The Tally-Ho

May — Dave MacRae Trio, Ronnie Scott's
Dave MacRae, piano/electric piano; Ron Mathewson, double bass; RW, drums

Spring's renewal also brings the rejuvenation of Matching Mole, a new quartet consisting of Francis Monkman, Gary Windo, Bill MacCormick, and Robert Wyatt, though other considerations were explored.

Fred Frith:

"I had been approached by Francis Monkman and Bill MacCormick to be in the new Matching Mole with those two and Robert as a quartet. This would have actually led to my quitting Henry Cow. It was a rather awkward moment because Robert had been my hero for so long that this was my big chance and I really wanted to do it, and I agreed to do it basically, and Henry Cow were pretty pissed off with me."

Bill MacCormick:

"I had been trying to persuade Robert for some time to regroup. I got together with Francis Monkman who used to play with Curved Air and eventually persuaded Robert to think about it. We got together in Alfie's flat in Notting Hill Gate (Monkman, Windo, MacCormick, Wyatt, May 29) and started working around material. It wasn't a rehearsal as such, it was literally just sitting in a front room with Robert playing a little keyboard and us sort of playing around stuff."

According to Gary Windo, the new Mole's union is followed later in the day by a meeting with Richard Branson, who along with Simon Draper operated the mail order house service Virgin Records. Having just launched their new independent record label with signings from Mike Oldfield and Henry Cow they were, quite naturally, interested in the new Mole. Peripheral plans at this time also include Robert's participation in Mike Oldfield's concert debut of "Tubular Bells" at the Queen Elizabeth Hall, June 25 and in a project of Gary Windo's alongside drummers Laurie Allen and Nick Mason. Additionally, it was at this time that Gary learns from Robert of a large party at Lady June's flat in Maida Vale on June 1st.

Wyatt breaks back

ROBERT WYATT, former Soft Machine drummer and leader of Matching Mole, was rushed to hospital with a broken back and other injuries after an accident at a party last Sunday.

Robert fell out of a fourth-floor window and suffered a fractured 12th vertebra and a broken leg. He is now in Stoke Mandeville Hospital, Aylesbury, Bucks, which specialises in serious injuries.

He will definitely be in hospital for six months, bed-ridden for the first 12 weeks, and it will be some time before the possible lasting consequences of the injuries can be determined.

Robert was due to start rehearsing for the third album by Matching Mole which also includes Francis Monkman on keyboards and Gary Windo on tenor sax, as well as founder-member Bill McCormick on bass.

Rehearsals will go ahead with another drummer, as yet unchosen, and on his recovery Robert will return, probably playing keyboards and percussion.

McCormick is also in hospital — having been taken into St Thomas's, London, on Monday suffering from acute appendicitis.

"I was hanging around the studios while Hatfield were recording, hoping to be asked to rattle a tambourine or something, 'cos I'm pretty good at that, and eventually Phil getting embarrassed by my presence gave me a piece of paper and said 'Well, while you're here you might as well make yourself useful, sing this.' It was a new song that he'd just written. I thought 'Christ, I'll never be able to learn it. I'll make a fool of myself.' As it happened though, it worked out all right."

SELF-PAWTRAIT

Lady June:

"It was at a party I had organized for my and Gilli Smyth's birthdays, hers is on June 1st, mine on the 3rd. In many ways it was the end of an era."

Honor Wyatt:

"The first thing more or less he said to me in hospital when he was conscious was 'don't worry, mommy. I always was a lazy bastard.' It was so certainly the worst thing that ever happened to me apart from my husband's death. But that was in the course of nature after all."

"This was how the accident went: in order, wine, whisky, Southern Comfort, then the window. The doctor was amazed. He said 'You had to have been really drunk to fall in such a relaxed way.' If I'd been any more sober, I probably wouldn't be here today; I'd have tightened up with fear and just shattered. It's been a long time now and it's been hard, but at least the top part of me works, though I'm never quite sure about this bit here (points to his head). *I do know exactly what I can and can't do, and that makes it easier.*

"People think I must have problems talking about my accident. But I don't; what I have problems talking about is what happened **before** *the accident. 'Rock Bottom' (1974) and beyond, that I see as me. But my adolescent self, the drummer biped, I don't remember him and I don't understand him. I have a hard time dealing with the way I was before; it's almost as if the fall affected my mind. I see the accident now as being a sort of neat division line betwen my adolescesnce and the rest of my life."*

Oct — The Manor, Kidlington, session for 'Hatfield and the North' lp
released Mar/74 (Virgin 2008)
Phil Miller, guitars; Dave Stewart, electric piano; Richard Sinclair, bass/vocals; Pip Pyle, drums; RW, vocals on 'Calyx'

Greeting Robert's release from Stoke Mandeville Hospital in November is a wealth of love and support from family and friends. To alleviate a predicament compounded by poverty, actress Julie Christie purchases a wheelchair accessible home for Robert and Alfie in the Twickenham district of London. Another act of generosity arrives from old friends Pink Floyd upon announcing a pair of benefit concerts with Soft Machine at the Rainbow Theatre for November 4th.

Autumn — Kaleidophon Studios, sessions for Lady June's 'Linguistic Leprosy' lp
Kevin Ayers, acoustic guitar; Lol Coxhill, soprano sax; Archie Leggett, bass; RW, percussion /voice

Lol Coxhill:

"Everyone was trying to get Robert back to work. Kevin invited us down to do something for Lady June, he came up with the guitar chords and we just played around it. When Lady June heard what we had done she said 'I can't do anything with that!' So I said 'I can!'"

Lady June:

"I don't think I said 'I can't do anything with that.' The reality was that I loved Robert so much and the reality of what had happened to him struck me with such a force that I went shopping with Alfie and left them. So really apart from the fact that the session was created by me, I didn't have much to do with it creatively. Besides that, it was quite jazz orientated and didn't fit in with the feel of the album I felt. So when I saw it wasn't going to be used, I told Lol he could have it and use it how he wished."

The track is included on Lol's half of an album shared with pianist Stephen Miller (Lol Coxhill "...Oh, Really?" / Stephen Miller "The Story So Far" released Sep 27/74, Caroline C1507) and is credited as 'Apricot Jam' performed live at the Twist Cha-Cha Rooms Camden Over-40's Club by Sunny Sax and the Sunshine Orchestra.

1974

"I started to get to the age where instead of being a tragic youth, I started to think, well, all this is a bit of a joke. From then on it just seemed easier really. Paradoxically, I was able to take what I did more seriously. It simplified things a lot. Being in a wheelchair means you have to deliberate what you do. You can't be so impulsive. Not being a drummer anymore I then decided to concentrate on what had previously only been a sideline, which was singing. That was all I had left, so that's what I did. Instead of just being somebody's drummer banging away thinking 'How long is this solo to go on? Oh, stop this tune', when I'm my own singer I just stop when I want to stop because I'm the keyboard player as well. I just have more control. I think I became a better, more concentrated musician."

Feb/Mar — Delfina's Farm, Little Bedwyn, sessions for 'Rock Bottom' lp
released July 26 (Virgin V2017)

"The subject of 'Rock Bottom' reflects the fact that just after the accident I got married to Alfie, and Alfie is the subject underlying several of the songs, a mixture of love and curiosity, all kinds of things. The real influence of Alfie is actually on the music itself because she had been unhappy with some of the earlier music I had been doing, being so condensed, so crowded. And she said 'Why don't you have more space, just let it ride more, like Van Morrison and people like that.' And this was a very good influence on me, I learned to leave a lot of space. So the influence of Alfie on a song like 'Alifib' is actually in the music itself."

£10,000 BOOST FOR WYATT

OVER £10,000 is expected to have been raised by the Pink Floyd/Soft Machine benefit concert held for Robert Wyatt at London's Rainbow Theatre on Sunday.

The exact sum will be known next week. Both houses for the two concerts were sold out well in advance. Money raised will go towards providing home aids for Wyatt, who was injured earlier this year and who is now confined to a wheelchair. It will also help him to prepare the way for his future work in music.

Softs' manager Sean Murphy said there had been a "unique atmosphere" at the Rainbow. "The general feeling was very pleasurable," he commented.

Steve O'Rourke, manager of the Floyd, commented: "No profit was made anywhere — even trucks were loaned free."

EMI meanwhile, are re-releasing the Pink Floyd's first two albums, "Piper At The Gates Of Dawn" and "Saucerful of Secrets" as a double album package. The two record set, to be titled "A Nice Pair," will be released at the end of this month.

Wyatt benefit: where your money went

YOU may remember — and certainly I will never forget — the recent benefit concerts held by the Soft Machine and Pink Floyd on behalf of my son, Robert, who is paralysed after an accident.

This wonderful gesture brought in ten thousand pounds.

But I think you may be interested to know that Robert will receive seven thousand. Two thousand goes in tax and one thousand in VAT.

Every penny is of importance, for he must now find expensive new equipment and a new home.

Also, not having been able to earn for eight months it will probably be a year or more before he can earn again.

Yet he has been taxed on the ten thousand as though it were an annual income.

What an odd world we live in that such a manifestation of human warmth and kindness should be at the mercy of inhuman government action. — HONOR WYATT, Dalmore Road, West Dulwich, London.

A Side	B Side
Sea Song	*Alifib*
Richard Sinclair,bass guitar	Hugh Hopper,bass guitar
Robert Wyatt,voice,keyboards,James' drum	Robert Wyatt,voice,keyboards,James' drum
A Last Straw	*Alife*
Laurie Allan,drums	Alfreda Benge,voice
Hugh Hopper,bass guitar	Hugh Hopper,bass guitar
Robert Wyatt,voice,keyboards, guitar,Delfina's wineglass	Gary Windo,bass clarinet,tenor
	Robert Wyatt,voice,keyboards,James' drum
Little Red Riding Hood Hit the Road	*Little Red Robin Hood Hit the Road*
Ivor Cutler,voice	Laurie Allan,drums
Mongezi Feza,trumpet	Ivor Cutler,voice,baritone concertina
Richard Sinclair,bass guitar	Fred Frith,viola
Robert Wyatt,voice,keyboards, James' drum,Delfina's tray and a small battery	Mike Oldfield,guitar
	Richard Sinclair,bass guitar
	Robert Wyatt,voice,keyboards

Produced by Nick Mason
Drones and songs by Robert Wyatt

THE letter from a " progressive " fan in February 23 MM, telling John Peel off for playing an increasing amount of black popular music smacked of the colour prejudice few white music fans admit to, but which is more common in this post - rock generation than it ever was in my dad's day, when Kurt Weill and Duke Ellington were taken equally seriously.

I know the aspirations of some of the best popular black musicians — Las Vegas night clubs and Talk Of The Town type show-biz success — embarrass the Woodstock / Altamont generation, but this really is a sociological subject that I don't feel brave enough to go into.

My point is simply that John Peel exploring Emperor Rosko/David Simmons territory is not just being progressive — in today's atmosphere of self-righteous musical parochialism, he's being positively avant-garde! — ROBERT WYATT, Little Bedwyn, Wiltshire.

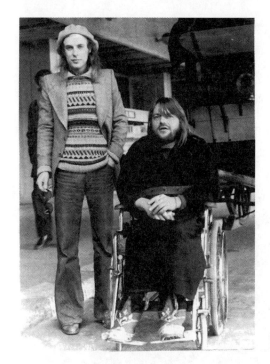

Apr 13 — Hatfield and the North, Roundhouse

Spirogyra supporting
Dave Stewart, organ; Phil Miller, guitar; Richard Sinclair, bass/vocals; Pip Pyle, drums; augmented by Alan Gowen, piano; Steve Miller, piano; Lol Coxhill, soprano sax; Geoff Leigh, tenor sax/flute; Jimmy Hastings, alto sax/flute; Jeremy Baines, flute; Amanda Parsons, Barbara Gaskin, Ann Rosenthal, vocals; RW, percussion/vocal ('Aigrette', 'Calyx')

May 10 — Hatfield and the North, Lady Mitchell Hall, Cambridge

also showing of Mike Oldfield's 'Tubular Bells' film

For the Hatfield concerts, Robert set these lyrics to Phil Miller's composition 'Calyx':

'Poetry in motion is what you've become
From the front and from behind you're a star
Sideways, underneath, and on the top
Close inspection reveals that you're in perfect nick
You'll perform like a dream'

ROBERT WYATT

WELL, it wasn't Robert's gig, exactly. He was there only to augment the Hatfield And The North Big Band, but the audience at Lady Mitchell Hall, Cambridge, had turned out in droves and continued to bawl "Robert" long after the house lights had gone up.

It wasn't that Robert upstaged the rest of the cream of English musicianship crowded on the small stage, but rather that it was just a joy to see him back in action again, playing with plenty of the old inventiveness on timbales, conga drum and other percussives and lending his unmistakeable voice to the proceedings, which consisted mostly of numbers from Hatfield And The North's debut album.

The complete line-up of this latter day Mad Dogs and Englishmen type ensemble was Wyatt (vocals, percussion), Amanda Parsons, Barbara Gaskin and Ann Rosenthal (vocals), Richard Sinclair (vocals, bass), Phil Miller (guitar), Dave Sewart, Alan Gowan and Steve Miller (keyboards), Pip Pyle (drums), Lol Coxhill, Geoff Leigh, Jimmy

Hastings and Jeremy Baines (saxophones, flutes and other blowables). Obviously, with an under-rehearsed outfit of this size, there were moments of untogetherness, but this was a warm, friendly performance.

The most amusing blunder of the night occurred when the sax section decided to deliver one part of their performance from the rear of the hall without informing the players on stage. Pip Pyle could be lip-read shouting "where's the bloody sax section?" to a nearby roadie, and believing them to have disappeared, the guys on stage kept on improvising and didn't allow any space for the unfortunate reedmen at the rear. "We thought they'd gone off for a drink," said Pip later.

Notwithstanding, the evening was a lot of fun, and hearing Richard Sinclair and Robert Wyatt harmonising together was a rare treat.

Earlier in the evening, Hatfield played a fiery quartet set, that left the crowded hall ecstatic. Dave Stewart's organ solo was genuinely amazing, and Pip Pyle's drumming a breathtaking synthesis of taste and attack. — STEVE LAKE.

June 1 — Kevin Ayers/John Cale/Eno/Nico, Rainbow Theatre

released June 28th (Island ILPS 9291)
set consists: (Eno) 'Driving Me Backwards', 'Baby's On Fire' (Cale) 'Buffalo Ballet', 'Gun', 'Heartbreak Hotel' (Nico) 'Deutschland Uber Alles', 'The End' (Ayers) 'May I?', 'Shouting In A Bucket Blues', 'Stranger In Blue Suede Shoes', 'Didn't I Feel Lonely', 'Whatevershebringswesing', 'Everybody's Sometime Some People's All The Time Blues', 'Interview', 'See You Later', 'Why Are We Sleeping?', 'Dr. Dream Theme', 'Two Goes Into Four' (all) 'I've Got A Hard On For You Baby' (Eno) 'Baby's On Fire'
Kevin Ayers, vocals/guitar; John Cale, vocals/piano; Eno, vocals/synthesizer; Nico, vocals/harmonium; augmented by Mike Oldfield, guitar; Ollie Halsall, guitar; John 'Rabbit' Bundrick, keyboards; Archie Leggett, bass; Eddie Sparrow, drums; Irene Chanter, Doreen Chanter, Liza Strike, vocals; RW, percussion

June 25 — Slapp Happy and Friends, Langham 1, BBC Top Gear recording

broadcast July 16
a) 'Europa' b) 'A Little Something' c) 'War Is Energy Enslaved' d) 'Me And Parvati' performed
Anthony Moore, piano (c)/ vocals (c)/organ (d)/harpisichord (a); Peter Blegvad, acoustic guitar (b)/guitar (a)/vocals (b, c, d); Dagmar Krause, lead vocals; and friends: Fred Frith, guitar (b, d); Lindsay Cooper, bassoon (a, b)/ oboe (c); Geoff Leigh, soprano sax (a, c, d)/flute (b)/clarinet (d); Jeff Clyne, double bass; RW, vocals (b)/percussion (a, b, c)

Dagmar Krause:
"When we came to London we had a phone call from Robert saying 'Gosh, I'd like to meet you, could you come to my house?' and Anthony and Peter couldn't believe it, and I thought 'well, he's such a star!' He was so encouraging at these early stages, so we became friends."

MAL DEAN

1941 ~ 1974

An Exhibition of Drawings, Cartoons & Paintings

at the ICA, Nash House
The Mall SW1

10 ~ 28 July

Concert 1
July 18th 8pm

National Youth Jazz Orchestra
Adrian Henri
Ken Hyder's Talisker
Frances Horowitz
George Khan's Stagecoach
Adrian Mitchell

Concert 2
July 25th 8pm

Pete Brown
Lol Coxhill
Roger McGough
Robert Wyatt
Mike Horowitz
S.M.E.

in ICA Cinema
Admission 50p
All proceeds go to Mal Dean's dependants

Arranged by G.L.A.A., Jazz Centre Society, Music Now

MAL DEAN: A PASSION FOR JAZZ

July 25 — Institute of Contemporary Arts

MAL DEAN, the illustrator, jazz critic, and trumpeter whose drawings have appeared in the MM for the past three years, died on Sunday in a London hospital after a long illness. He was 32.

Dean was best known for his bold, striking pen-and-ink work, featured in a variety of publications starting with his contributions to the early issues of International Times in the mid-60s.

Born in Widnes he studied at Liverpool College of Arts, where he was a contemporary of Paul McCartney, before moving to London. His illustrations for Michael Moorcock's Jerry Cornelius series which originally appeared in IT, were later published in book form, and he worked on volumes of poetry by his wife, Libby Houston, and Pete Brown.

A book devoted to his drawings, titled Black Dog, was published by IT in 1969.

His work appeared on the jazz records page of the MM. Using rare photographs, he would copy the likeness of a jazz musician, and then — with strokes of vivid imagination and humour — place him in a context which illuminated the player's style and personality.

He provided cover art for albums by Pete Brown's "Piblokto" and the Derek Bailey/Han Bennink duo, and last year was given an exhibition for his massive paintings of World War Two airplanes.

His trumpet-playing was perhaps the least-recognised of his many facets but for some years he had led the Amazing Band, which at various times included violinist Rab Spall, drummer Robert Wyatt, and altoist Mick Brabham. He approached his playing with a cheerful optimism which never obscured his real passion for, and knowledge of, the music.

Besides his wife, Mal leaves two children — Sam (6) and Alice (3) — and benefit concerts are being arranged for them by, among others, the Musicians' Co-operative.

It is also hoped to hold an exhibition and sale of his drawings, including some of those which appeared in the MM, with the proceeds going to his dependents.

The funeral will be at 3 pm next Monday at the Great Northern Cemetery, London — RICHARD WILLIAMS.

AFTER years of hearing Robert Wyatt's voice soaring over electronic organ and fuzz bass, or at the very least doctored with echoplex, the former Matching Mole boss seemed suddenly very naked and alone on stage at London's ICA last Thursday, making his contribution to a benefit concert for the dependents of the late Mal Dean armed with only an acoustic grand piano, and a common boom mike.

Furthermore, being confined to a wheelchair ensured no use of foot pedals, compounding the difficulties that Wyatt faced. After all, what is a drummer without a kit or a band? In Wyatt's case, the answer would seem to be an intriguing performer.

As an on-stage keyboard artist Robert has his limitations, and a few misplaced chords were gratingly conspicuous. Nonetheless this air of fragility and vulnerability proved to be an attractive and moving quality as Wyatt performed three numbers from his "Rock Bottom" album, "Sea Song," "A Last Straw" and "Alifib," Gary Windo strolling on to add a furious, convoluted tenor solo in mid-set, and the packed-to-overflowing house responded warmly.

Altogether, it was a fine evening, both atmospherically and musically. Lol Coxhill, when he wasn't playing a beautiful soprano solo, was side-splittingly funny, hidden behind huge shades and beret and lunging repeatedly into something called "Frogdance," quite the most obnoxious little tune I've heard.

Derek Bailey and Evan Parker also played exceedingly well, although it would've been nice to see the entire SME (as advertised), and between them created textures that recalled the late Music Improvisation Company.

The rest of the night was taken up by poets of varying degrees of seriousness. Pete Brown performed with Mama Flyer, a tight rock band from Scotland, while Mike Horowitz utilised a kazoo in the course of his poetry reading, and Adrian Mitchell burst into song when his verse so required.

In fact, anyway you cared to look at it, the evening was a success. Everybody played well, everybody was well received, doubtless a lot of money was grossed, and even the P.A. was OK. What more could you ask for. — STEVE LAKE.

On July 26, upon the release of the album 'Rock Bottom', Robert Wyatt Ellidge and Alfreda Benge celebrate their love through the exchanging of matrimonial vows. The euphoric reception that greets 'Rock Bottom' is indeed recognition of a genuine masterwork. A Virgin Records press bio stated the case thus: 'Figured prominently among critics favourites for year, outdistancing most of its competitors and eliciting unprecedented unanimity of enthusiasm.'

Wyatt rocks basement

REVIVE THE musical evening. As part of the celebrations for Robert Wyatt's wedding to Afreda Benge, Virgin's Richard Branson threw an elegant soiree in the basement of his house. Nick Mason, who produced Robert's "Rock Bottom" album, David Bedford, Richard Sinclair and Gary Windo were among those assembled, and Robert played the songs from the album, sitting at the piano, in an extraordinarily moving performance. Gary Windo joined in to play some beautiful bass clarinet and sax.

Alfreda Benge:
"I always feel very embarrassed that people think that some of the record is for me. When he started to do the words for 'Alifib' he was singing 'Polly, my larder', and I said 'Who's this Polly? If you're going to sing about anybody it's got to be me.' It wasn't really his idea, so I kinda forced myself onto the record."

Aug (early) — CBS Studio 2, sessions for 'I'm A Believer'/'Memories' 45
released Sep 6 (Virgin VS114)
Dave MacRae, piano (A-side); Fred Frith, guitar/violin; Richard Sinclair, bass; Nick Mason, drums; RW, vocals/piano/keyboard

Fred Frith:
"Inasmuch as it concerned me that recording took place August 5th and 6th. Since I was overdubbing (rhythm guitar/lead guitar/violin arrangements/violin solo) I assume they'd already been at it for a couple of days prior. Producer was Nick Mason."

"I think I did an interview in which they said, if you could choose your ten favourite songs — a sort of rock 'Desert Island Discs' — what would they be? So I said, oh, — 'cos I like doing that sort of thing. Simon Draper at Virgin saw the list and one of them had already been a hit for the Monkees. He said: 'Were you serious about doing that?' My bluff having been called, I said yes and went into the studio and did 'I'm A Believer'."

Sep 8 — Theatre Royal Drury Lane

Dave Stewart:

"I was a little surprised when Richard Branson phoned me suggesting I play the Drury Lane gig, because I figured Robert had quit gigging by then. Branson insisted that Robert wanted me to do it and I agreed...turned out that Branson was telling all the musicians that Robert wanted them to do it without telling him, then telling Robert that all the musicians were really keen to do it. thus, Robert was semi-coerced into doing this show, but it turned out well (despite Nick Mason's inability to play in 7/4 — whoops!)"

"I knew it was gonna be quite good, because Laurie Allen, Hugh Hopper, and Dave Stewart are basically my dream rhythm section. I felt that no matter how bad it was, those people and Fred Frith and so on would be able to pull something out of the hat. But people like me aren't basically quick thinkers and we work best without people...staring at us."

The Drury Lane programme (right) does not delineate songs in order of performance. Compere for the evening was John Peel. Julie Tippett sang 'God Song'.

Sep 10 — Langham 1, BBC Top Gear recording

broadcast Sep 26
released Nov/87 (Strange Fruit SFP 037)
a)'Alifib' b)'Soup Song' c)'Sea Song' d)'I'm A Believer' performed RW, voice/piano//marimba (b)/BBC's organ and Leslie (b, c)

On September 18th, Robert Wyatt mimes a performance of 'I'm A Believer' (charting at 35) at BBC 1 Television studios for the Top Of The Pops programme, broadcast later that evening. The stand-in backing group comprises Fred Frith, violin; Andy Summers, guitar; Dave MacRae, piano; Richard Sinclair, bass; and Nick Mason, drums.

Fred Frith:

"I remember it vividly because we had to be there in the early afternoon and our filming rehearsal wasn't until 5:55 pm. We hung around doing nothing all afternoon and then at precisely 6:00 pm all the technicians downed tools and left (union rules) even though we hadn't actually played anything. And then it was very interesting to see fat managers in suits talking to their 'boys' like it was a football team — what movements to make, how to look at the camera and so on, and the other groups were mostly kind of paunchy, middle-aged old pros dressed in ill-fitting satin suits and looking heavily made up and very uncomfortable (The Tremeloes, Slade, etc.). The audience was very small (so as not to get in the way of the technicians) but marshalled efficiently from stage to stage so as to create the illusion of a huge crowd of excited teeny-boppers. Bizarre.

"The other thing I remember was that Richard Branson had bought a beautiful antique wheelchair for Robert to sit on, but the BBC refused to allow it, and in fact wanted to cover the wheelchair completely because they thought it was in bad taste or might upset the viewers. Go figure!"

"I went on Top of the Pops and there was this geezer (producer Robin Nash) there saying 'could you sit on something else, wheelchairs don't look well on a family entertainment show'. I just exploded, the whole atmosphere frightened me, I just thought I was losing control of my life.

"Frankly, Top of the Pops appalled me, and the different things that are expected of you in situations like that...it's the singles world really, the business thing. People say this has to be changed, or that has to be changed because so and so won't play it. The rules are so strict, and I just haven't got the necessary humility or whatever to fit into that. I could see it becoming what I did — I would make singles — and I didn't want that to happen. I didn't want to get trapped in that strange, alien world. Deep down I might be competitive, I suppose, but consciously anything competitive gives me the horrors, and always has done. Suddenly, it is all a matter of comparative ratings and would this one do better than the last one or would it do better than that other one...I'd lived without charts for so long, established myself in a sort of no man's land where as long as I had enough money for cigarettes and tea I was happy."

Sep — Island Studios, sessions for Eno 'Taking Tiger Mountain (By Strategy)'

released Jan/75 (Island ILPS 9309)
core quintet: Eno, vocals/electronics/snake guitar/keyboards; Phil Manzanera, guitars; Brian Turrington, bass guitar; Freddie Smith, drums; RW, percussion/backing vocals (tracks 1, 7, 8). Augmented by various guests.

On October 2nd, Robert Wyatt mimes a performance of 'I'm A Believer' at Granada Television studios in Birmingham for the 'Forty Five' pop programme. The stand-in backing group comprised Fred Frith, violin with Hatfield and the North: Dave Stewart, piano; Phil Miller, guitar; Richard Sinclair, bass; Pip Pyle, drums

Dave Stewart:
"It was weird."

On Oct. 9th, Robert Wyatt is scheduled for a second appearance on Top of the Pops television, but the booking is cancelled when the BBC's brass learn of Robert's intention for all musicians to appear sitting in wheelchairs.

Oct — CBS Studios, sessions for 'Yesterday Man'/'Sonia' 45

unreleased until 1977 (Virgin VS 115)
Gary Windo, alto sax/tenor sax/bass clarinet; Mongezi Feza, trumpet; John Greaves, bass; RW, vocals/piano/drums
'Sonia' first recorded in 1973 by Dudu Pukwana and Spear. Composed by Mongezi Feza.
'Yesterday Man' first recorded in 1964 by Chris Andrews. Composed by Chris Andrews.
The latter is intended as a follow up single but is rejected by Virgin. Instead the song is allocated to the Virgin sampler lp 'V' released Feb 7/75 (Virgin VD 2502).

In the Melody Maker readers poll for 1974 Robert Wyatt is voted behind Leon Thomas as top International Male Singer, and behind George Melly as top British Male Singer. In Paris, critics award 'Rock Bottom' the Grand Prix Charles Cros as Rock record of the year.

WHO SAID music was dead? I witnessed on Top Of The Pops (yes, Top Of The Pops) someone who must have been music's kiss of life. I am, of course, referring to Mr Robert Wyatt and his super group. It is so ironical that Top of The Pops, a programme well known for promoting the usual humdrum of music, actually televised a group which included some of the leading musicians in British rock today: Nick Mason of the Pink Floyd on drums, Dave McRae, late of Nucleus and Robert Wyatt's Matching Mole on piano, and Fred Frith of Henry Cow on guitar and violin. The Pops for the first time in his long and superb musical career. Let's hope, indeed pray, that he will put an end to this horrible glitter music and bring those glorious days back when music was music (eg The Soft Machine's " Love Makes Sweet Music"). — CHARLES R. FRAILS, Mather Ave, Liverpool 18.

In Paris accepting
Grand Prix Charles Cros

Melody Maker letter of the week

Gong is a—gulp—psychedelic band!

A Soft Look At Gong

YOU

Gong
Virgin (V2019)

by Robert Wyatt

You Americans seem pretty strange in your choice of Europeans. I mean—Elton John? Really? But I digress already. For a start, Gong's founder member, "Dingo Virgin" Daevid Allen, is not European at all, but a native of that vast hidden continent shared by the Chinese, Japanese, Peruvians and Californians: the Pacific Rim.

Daevid left Australia in the mid-'50s (using the all-but-obsolete trains/ships traveling method) and arrived in Paris where, it seemed, the Real Action was; the Real Action being Kenny Clark and Bud Powell at the Blue-note, Bill Burroughs at the Hotel Git-le-Coeur off Place St. Michel, and Terry Riley making tape-loop cut-ups of the Chet Baker quartet on No Money At All.

But one of Daevid's most fruitful discoveries was fellow Antipodean John Esam, who, like Daevid, wrote poems that Proper Poets didn't like, drew bizarre cartoons that Proper Artists didn't like, but most unusually, danced to music that you Weren't Meant to Dance to (*i.e.* Eric Dolphy, or Johnny Griffin). Ever since then, Daevid dodged restlessly from Paris to London in search of compatible soul-mates.

Europe's not very big, and Our Hero was bound to meet Malayan-born nomad Kevin Ayers sooner or later. North Africa apart, the bottom corner of the London-Paris triangle was Mallorca, where Kevin and Daevid prepared what they fondly thought of as reasonably conventional song-tapes (the Spanish Moon makes the unlike-

Robert Wyatt, a founding member of Soft Machine, has also played with Gong.

liest fantasy seem absolutely acceptable). They were, in fact, not Proper Songs at all, of course, but with the infinite patience of the Extremely Stoned, Daevid has gradually pieced together a band consisting of a mixture of Real Musicians and Surreal Supergnomes, known to others as Gong, and to themselves as *la Compagnie d'Opera Invisible de Thibet*, whose members have in common some sort of understanding of what Daevid's actually been trying to do all this time.

So who are they, the inhabitants of Gong? Well, it's hard to tell. For a start, new members, like Muslim converts, have their names totally changed or at least mangled beyond recognition: Gilli Smyth has become Shakti Yoni. (Cynics beware: I don't mean she has just changed her name, I mean Gilli Smyth has actually become Shakti Yoni.) And since Didier Malherbe became Bloomdido Bad De Grasse (or later, Glad de Brass), all traces of half-remembered Coltrane records have disappeared, to be replaced by a slightly unearthly approach to reed playing which could not only lure a snake from the coziest basket but quite likely neutralize its venom at the same time.

Others have come and gong (forgive me) in the last few years. Drummer Pip Pyle (now of Hatfield and the North) brought his busy, urgent style to the band at the right moment, in time to record the really impressive *Camembert Electrique* record. And a little later, the great Laurie Allan's ability to do "Bat Shadow" Milford Graves-type drumming provided the basis for the most un-earthly (and least whimsical) tapes the group ever made: the live concert recording used on the Glastonbury Festival compilation.

I shan't list them all. For example I

could say "Steve Hillage is a very good guitarist" and you could answer: "Who isn't?" As in all successful rock bands, a character stronger than any individual person is projected. And when I say "successful" I don't just mean that *I* like the records, I mean they are a genuinely popular band (you know) with lots of fans and everything. They are on the road most of the year, and they still play the most un-luxurious, rain-sodden festival sites in Europe without complaining. Real rock gypsies.

But this does not mean that they play "casual" music: every piece makes original sense. They no longer risk hours of boredom in the "Let's just keep playing until someone gets a good idea" manner I associate with, say, Grateful Dead.

There are basically two things a band can do when it reaches the "long guitar solos are boring" crossroads: become a country-rock group—the usual answer—or learn how to make long guitar solos interesting. This is, of course, harder, but in Gong's case, it's paid off handsomely. More dangerously, Gong have hung onto, and developed almost beyond recognition, the Fairy Tale as a basis for the song lyrics. Of course, Daevid Allen's fairy tale is not a Tolkien-derived fantasy, but a lunar allegory of such quaintness that nearly every sober, clean "I've-been-through-all-that-shit" new-age adult squirms a little when he sees the famous little forest of pixie-hats by which members of Gong are recognized. There's no getting away from it: this is a—gulp—psychedelic band! What I'm saying is, it's also a thoroughly modern band—remember, ten years ago Rock 'n Roll was considered Old Hat.

It seems from over here as if America, always envious of our Genuine Historical Monuments, has now decided that *it's* just old enough to have Genuine Historical Monuments all it's own, and is thus gripped in a wide-ranging nostalgia fever, taking in everything from Deep South mythology (learned mainly from John Wayne movies) to surfers-with-crew-cuts culture, via Frank Sinatra and Fred Astaire. A well-deserved pause, certainly—all the real fresh ideas in music this century have come through America, it seems to me; but here in Europe, it's nostalgia itself that is old-fashioned, and bands like Gong reflect the general urgency to keep moving, to keep "experimenting" at the risk of being called "pretentious Art-rock" or even Psychedelic. And if Gong keep growing at their present rate, who knows? In ten years' time, you might be grateful that somebody, somewhere, has ignored that deathly cry, "Get back to your roots and stop trying to be clever."

originally appeared in Crawdaddy (1974)

1975

"I think it's good that people are beginning to go back and examine great songs, and not feel obliged to blunder about trying in vain to write them themselves. Sooner or later I'd certainly want to do it. I've got lists and lists of stuff in my notebooks — but right now, the selection I'd probably want to tackle would go something like this:
"Ferry's 'Do the Strand'' which is a genuinely good song; Charlie Mingus' 'Goodbye Pork Pie Hat'; Monk's 'Round About Midnight'; 'Every Little Bit Hurts'; two Beatles tunes — 'If I Fell In Love With You' and 'She's A Woman'; Caravan's 'Place Of My Own'; The Miracles 'Ooh Baby'; 'Georgia On My Mind''; Brian Wilson's 'She Knows Me Too Well'; Charlie Haden's 'Song For Che'; Duke Ellington's 'Solitude'; Randy Weston's 'Berkshire Blues'; and 'Hey, Hey, We're the Monkees' — y'know, the theme from the TV show."

Jan — Island Studios, sessions for Phil Manzanera 'Diamond Head' lp

released Apr (Island ILPS 9315)
Phil Manzanera, guitars; John Wetton, bass; Paul Thompson, drums; Eno, backing vocals; RW, lead vocals/timbales/cabasa/backing vocals/lyric on 'Frontera'

Ian McDonald:

"It was originally written in about 1970 at our house in West Norwood. Phil brought the verse chord and Bill wrote the 5th and 6th bars of the top line and the original lyric (The Day Is Coming). I wrote the rest of the top line and all of the middle section in simultaneous 4/4 and 6/8. On Phil's album it was preceded by a section from another song called 'Marcel My Dada', a paean to Marcel Duchamps by Charles Hayward."

Frontera (Border)
It's important that we make it to the border before nightfall. We must find whatever is hiding. It's doubtful that this actor is capable of such an important role. I'll end up believing that you don't want to help us. Do you think we could convince him? I will tell my employer soon to go to the aviation office. Do you deny that the accused has perjured the plaintiff in the most unforgivable way? We are sorry that it is impossible for you to assist the theatrical production. I was happy to note that the theatre was completely full of people. I'll do whatever is possible to see you again. I was amazed at what has happened. It's important that we make it to the border before nightfall. We must find whatever is hiding. It's doubtful that this actor is capable of such an important role. I'll end up believing that you don't want to help us. Do you think we could convince him? I will tell...oooh...

Mar 15 to 22 — The Manor, Kidlington, sessions for 'Ruth Is Stranger Than Richard' lp

released May 30 (Virgin V2034)
(see below for track details)

Notes:
1. 'Soup Song' is an interpretation of The Wilde Flowers 'Slow Walkin' Talk'.
2. 'Team Spirit' is an interpretation of 'Frontera'.
3. 'Sonia' was recorded October 74.
4. Fred Frith's tracks recorded at CBS Studios.

Fred Frith:

"There was a project that I instigated which never happened. It was a fairly major work involving maybe twelve or fifteen musicians that Robert was writing the words for and I was writing the music for. This was in 1975 and I chickened out at the last minute because I wasn't happy with my own work and it led to a little bit of tension between us because I think he had really worked very hard at it. But he ended up using some of it on 'Ruth'. All the stuff on 'Ruth' that I wrote, 'Muddy Mouth' and those other things, that was all written for this long piece of mine that never saw the light of day. He liked it enough that he wanted to use it anyway, so that his work wouldn't go to waste!"

"I've never really been satisfied with 'Ruth Is Stranger Than Richard'. In the beginning my idea was for a trio with Mongezi Feza and Gary Windo but I couldn't finish the record the way I wanted to. The money was a constant problem for me. You know I really envy the writer and painter who can experiment and work for hours with just a pen, a piece of paper, and a few pennies, a cup of tea, and a sandwich. It's so expensive in the studio and I'm not at ease."

SIDE RUTH

Soup Song (Hopper/Wyatt)
Laurie Allan, drums
Nisar Ahmad Khan, baritone sax
Bill MacCormick, bass guitar
Gary Windo, tenor sax
Robert Wyatt, mouth, piano

Sonia (Feza)
Mongezi Feza, trumpet
John Greaves, bass guitar
Gary Windo, bass clarinet, alto sax
Robert Wyatt, drums, piano

Team Spirit (MacCormick/Wyatt/Manzanera)
Laurie Allan, drums
Brian Eno, direct inject anti-jazz ray gun
Nisar Ahmad 'George' Khan, tenor sax
Bill MacCormick, bass guitar
Gary Windo, tenor sax
Robert Wyatt, mouth, piano

Song for Che (Haden)
Laurie Allan, drums
Nisar Ahmad Khan, tenor sax, soprano sax
Bill MacCormick, bass guitar
Gary Windo, tenor sax, alto sax
Robert Wyatt, mouth, piano

SIDE RICHARD

Muddy Mouse (a) (Frith/Wyatt)
Fred Frith, piano
Robert Wyatt, mouth

Solar Flares (Wyatt)
Bill MacCormick, bass guitar
Gary Windo, bass clarinet
Robert Wyatt, mouth, drums, keyboards

Muddy Mouse (b) (Frith/Wyatt)
Fred Frith, piano
Robert Wyatt, mouth

5 Black Notes and 1 White Note (Offenbach/Wyatt)
Laurie Allan, drums
Brian Eno, guitar, synthesizer
Nisar Ahmad Khan, tenor sax
Bill MacCormick, bass guitar
Gary Windo, tenor sax, alto sax
Robert Wyatt, imitation electric piano

Muddy Mouse (c) which in turn leads to
Muddy Mouth (Frith/Wyatt)
Fred Frith, piano
Robert Wyatt, mouth

May 8 — Henry Cow and Robert Wyatt, Theatre des Champs Elysees, Paris, France

Dagmar Krause, voice; Lindsay Cooper, bassoon/alto sax/flute; Tim Hodgkinson, keyboards/alto sax; Fred Frith, guitar/violin; John Greaves, bass/piano; Chris Cutler, drums; RW, voice/piano

For their encore, the ensemble perform an impromptu and unrehearsed version of Kevin Ayers' 'We Did It Again'.

May 21 — Henry Cow and Robert Wyatt, New London Theatre

set consists: 'Beautiful As the Moon.../Nirvana for Mice/Ottawa Song/Gloria Gloom/Ruins/...Terrible As An Army With Banners', 'Muddy Mouse(a)/Solar Flares/Muddy Mouse(b)/Muddy Mouth/(collective improvisation)', 'Bad Alchemy/Little Red Riding Hood Hits the Road'*, 'Living In the Heart Of the Beast'

* released June/76 on Henry Cow 'Concerts' lp (Caroline CAD 3002)

June 27 — Henry Cow and Robert Wyatt, Piazza Navona, Rome, Italy (photos below)

Gong supporting

Autumn — home, sessions for Michael Mantler 'The Hapless Child' lp

released Mar/76 (Virgin/Watt 4)

Carla Bley, piano/clavinet/string synthesizer; Terje Rypdal, guitar; Steve Swallow, bass; Jack DeJohnette, drums/percussion; Alfreda Benge, speaker; Albert Caulder and Nick Mason, additional speakers; RW, vocals
Compositions by Michael Mantler, words from Edward Gorey's book 'Amphigorey' (published 72).

Carla Bley:

"He has an original voice that if you took any one note you'd know it was him, and that is so rare. Just any one note, any one word, would sound like Robert. Someone like that is a rare find. And also he can sing in tune."

"It started with a panic. The first panic was when Michael brought me a cassette of him singing on his own accompaniment on keyboards. It was just a sketch, but I thought I can't do it, I can, I can't, I can, and then I finally told myself, 'well come on, you can do it'. So I couldn't reject something that was coming from Mike and Carla. They sent me tapes and the story book of Gorey which the songs are based on. I really liked them and learned them by heart. The guys in the rhythm section were some of my favourite musicians, Jack DeJohnette and Steve Swallow. Ten years ago I was following Steve Swallow just to see what kind of shoes he was wearing! They did the accompaniment and then Terje Rypdal came to play the guitar after I recorded the vocals. So the record was done a little bit everywhere but the end result really sounds like a group."

Robert Wyatt

Dagmar Krause, RW

Lindsay Cooper, RW, Dagmar

Dagmar Krause

Fred Frith

Chris Cutler

Tim Hodgkinson

John Greaves

Mongezi Feza — principal recordings
(label/year of release)

Chris McGregor — Cold Castle Jazz Festival
(Gallajazz 63)
Chris McGregor — The African Sound
(Gallajazz 63)
Chris McGregor — Very Urgent (Polydor 68)
Centipede — Septober Energy (RCA 71)
Assagai — Assagai (Philips 71)
Assagai — Zimbabwe (Vertigo 71)
Brotherhood Of Breath — Brotherhood Of
Breath (RCA 71)
Brotherhood Of Breath — Brotherhood (RCA
72)
Brotherhood Of Breath — Live At Willisau
(Ogun 74)
Dyani/Temiz/Feza — Music For Xaba (Sonet
72)
Dyani/Temiz/Feza — Music For Xaba Vol. 2
(Sonet 72)
Dyani/Temiz/Feza — Rejoice (Cadillac 88)
Dudu Pukwana and Spear — In The
Townships (Caroline 74)
Dudu Pukwana and Spear — Flute Music
(Caroline 75)
Dudu Pukwana — Diamond Express
(Freedom 77)
Robert Wyatt — Rock Bottom (Virgin 74)
Robert Wyatt — Ruth is Stranger Than
Richard (Virgin 75)

In December of 1975, Robert Wyatt is admitted to Stoke Mandeville hospital to repair a broken leg suffered from a collapsed chair. At this time also, Mongezi Feza was in Epsom hospital for treatment of a nervous condition. On the morning of Sunday, December 14th, double pneumonia took the life of this extraordinary musician, known to his friends as "Mongs". Sixteen years past, Robert Wyatt reflects:

"He was a very little person, quite small and quite shy, when he was sober. He didn't say a lot. He still seemed a bit stunned being outside South Africa. None of the people I know who came out of South Africa ever got used to it. I once asked him 'What was the most surprising thing he found coming to England?' and he said 'Seeing white women working'. He thought they were only bosses and employers. He couldn't get used to going around drinking, mixing, and all that sort of thing. Even when he was happy, I never got the impression he was relaxed. I think he had been a bit too traumatized.

"Mongezi had a bright, hard, sharp, intelligent trumpet playing which had no bullshit in it. The way he played was very non-self indulgent, although he could play very extended stuff. What he did was totally focussed. You could get people on the jazz scene who could sort of noodle about and at certain moments get it all in focus and he just seemed to play in focus all the time, he didn't warm up or go off. While he was playing, he was really playing. The point was that he was a very quick trumpet player. I'm not saying he could ever play as well as Wynton Marsalis or Clark Terry, it's just that what he could do with what he'd been given was about as good as you could expect really.

"There's a track on 'Rock Bottom' that's quite long winded harmonically. He only heard it about twice and he had the chord sequence completely in his head! — for every take. So the people who think of him as a free jazz player might think, well he didn't really know the changes, he was very good on changes, he just liked playing freer.

"I'd thought of him for future projects as the kind of soloist to bounce back, a sparring partner to make records. He would be the perfect foil for my vocals because of that hard brightness. I really thought he could do songs, he could do anything I wanted to do. I had him sketched in mind as the person to duet with as it were.

"Mongezi's death had a very dramatic effect on me. The nature of his death was really that he had come to England thinking that he had escaped the tyranny of racism, but of course in coming to England he came to the mother and father of apartheid. And although in England we don't have official racism it's very difficult for a non-white person to adjust. In his case he had to go to a mental hospital where he was considered schizophrenic, and while he was in hospital he died quite suddenly of double pneumonia. It's extraordinary, it's not necessary for a young man to die when he's already in the hospital of double pneumonia. I have a feeling that if it had been Prince Charles that he would not have died, or quite simply if he had been white he would not have died. I think that gave me a strong push towards a sense of political urgency."

1976

"From the middle of the seventies onwards I was very confused. I felt that the music I was doing was completely inadequate. And it was immensely conceited and ridiculous of a generation of people from the sixties to think that just by singing protest songs that they could make the world better. I started to become more interested in serious revolutionary activity, by which I mean revolutionary activity that changes power."

Feb — Delfina's farm, Little Bedwyn, sessions for Michael Mantler 'Silence' lp

released Mar/77 (Virgin/Watt 5)
Carla Bley, voice/piano/organ; Kevin Coyne, voice; RW, voice/percussion; Chris Spedding, guitar; Ron McClure, bass/double bass; Claire Maher, cello
Composed by Michael Mantler, 'Silence' is an adaptation of the 1969 play by Harold Pinter.

Apr — Britannia Row Studios, sessions for Gary Windo 'Steam Radio Tapes' lp

(unreleased)
Gary Windo, tenor sax; Richard Brunton, guitar; Hugh Hopper, Bill MacCormick, bass; Nick Mason, drums; Pam Windo, piano/backing vocals; RW, vocals on 'Now Is the Time'
This project also inccludes performances by Steve Hillage, Mike Hugg, Julie Tippett, and Nana Tsiboe.

Gary Windo:

"Pink Floyd had got this studio built for themselves but they weren't sure how it would sound so Nick offered to make a record with me as a guinea pig so that they could find out."

Apr — home, sessions for Jan Steele/John Cage 'Voices and Instruments' lp

released July (Obscure No. 5)
RW, voice on 'Experiences No. 2'
RW, voice; Richard Bernas, percussion on 'The Wonderful Widow of Eighteen Springs'
Composed by John Cage with text from e.e. cummings and James Joyce.

Carla Bley:

"Robert was given two songs to sing and found it too hard to learn two songs. So he said to Brian that he'd rather only do one and that I would do the other one. He kept saying he didn't read music and he can't learn things quickly so he picked the simplest song and was taught that by somebody. He still says that he can't read music and even though you tell him, well you know, if it goes up sing higher, if it goes down sing lower, he claims not to be able to do it."

May 17 — home, sessions for General Strike Project 'Will Of The People' lp

(unreleased)
Hanwell Brass Band: Laurie Scott Baker, synthesizer/percussion; Dave MacCrae, piano; Roy Babbington, bass; Tony Hicks, drums; RW, vocals on 'Nowt' Doin''
Backing tracks recorded at Maximum Sound. This project also includes performances by Cornelius Cardew, Keith Rowe, Evan Parker, and Pip Pyle amongst others.

Laurie Scott Baker:

"The song 'Nowt' Doin'' which Robert sings is a part of a longer piece, a sort of modern Folk Opera, centred on the historical struggles around the 1926 General Strike in Britain. It includes events that preceded the Strike (i.e. the 1st WW) and has references to what followed, including right up to 1976 (also relevant 1990's). The text used in the opening part is essentially made up of contemporary "Quotes" from the 1926 Strike put together in the form of a dialogue between Government ministers/Coal owners on the one hand and the Miners and their Representative on the other. This is where the song 'Nowt' Doin'' comes in and it is the opening reply which the Miners give to the Government/Owners demands for cuts.

"The project was initially financed by myself, SFA Music, Unity Records, the Arts Council of Great Britain and various Trade Unions, i.e. the musicians union paid the Professional musicians fees. This finance was aimed at getting the project to a rough mix stage — composers fees, research, musicians and arrangers fees, recording costs, etc. The bulk of the money for the final mix, mastering and the record pressing process was to have come from the Arts Council. However, on hearing the first rough mix of the tape they said that they 'didn't like it' and not only would they not fund pressing the record but also demanded the master tape be surrendered to them! Obviously we didn't comply with their censorial arrogance, and anyway their contribution was not a significant part compared to what had been put in by many other organizations and individuals. Unfortunately this activity did stop the production of the album going ahead."

STRUBBLIN' STRIFE (unreleased lyric)
Strubblin' strife, strubblin' strife, Ola Ya Ya Mama, Ola Ya Ya Mama. Me been a senstibule, considulate, fabaloofly greeny, often a parsley. Me Goota Goota, not say 'Freg' — No! No! No! Not sing him 'Freg', Oh my Goddy Goddy, Deary little God-God.
Hoooooooooooooooooooooooooo nabbin my winksey? Who heeeeeeeeeeeeeeeeee da breake ma pamerararm?
Crackle Crackle.
De Bay-con. De Sossinks.
Gone astray, gone astray. If you Goddy light I gone astray. De road turn blue, de road turn green, where my cow gone, where she been? De house turn black, de house bend and break, de house squash my Unhappamily. O no! Oh No! My Unhappamily.
Oh God, He so comprehensive, he see every sparow what fall. 'There go another sparrow', He say, 'or war it a thrush? It's hard to tell from up here'. He very well meaning, He on everyone side (but reluctantly plump for the winner-take-all approach).
'Oh Natural Selection
Oh Natural Selection
Oh Natural Selection
Evolve A While With Me'

right, RW at home, Twickenham, June 1/76

1977

"I've always had this problem right from the time I started playing music. Right back to schooldays, actually, and the Wilde Flowers. I've always worked with two kinds of musician — some that were into improvisation as a process, and some that weren't. And I've always kind of played the devil's advocate to all of them. Y'know, talking about Cecil Taylor to Dave Sinclair and taking the exact opposite stance with some jazz musician.

"All I'm saying really is that any kind of procedure can become a prison, and when that happens, watch out. It can happen just as easily in free jazz as in any other kind of music. And I think music can be more than just effective. I think there are right notes and wrong ones. I'm not into chance operations at all. In fact, I'm not interested in any kind of procedure for it's own sake."

Apr — Brian Eno 'Before and After Science' lp released (Island ILPS 9478)

recorded at Basing St. Studios

Brian Eno, voice/chorus/'jazz' piano/synthesizer; Kurt Schwitters, voice (from the 'Ur Sonata'); Percy Jones, analogue delay bass; Dave Mattacks, drums; Shirley Williams, brush timbales on 'Kurt's Rejoinder'.

Brian Eno, keyboards/bell/melody guitar/Moog; Fred Frith, cascade guitars; Bill MacCormick, bass; Shirley Williams, time on 'Through Hollow Lands'

Robert Wyatt appears incognito as Shirley Williams of Britain's Labour Party.

DISTANT VOICES
listening to short-wave radio
BY ROBERT WYATT

Perhaps the lowest-fi English language radio programme is the Voice of the Islamic Republic of Iran from Tehran, 8.30pm most evenings I think, though I haven't tried it at weekends for some reason. By low-fi I mean muffled. At best, muffled, plus the occasional fierce 'doppler effect' machine-gun rattle, and/or periodic blankets of dense grey noise. But listeners accustomed to years of free jazz, background music, and PiL aren't put off by things like that are we, in fact we wallow in it, right? So, the beauty of the medium itself (short wave radio) plus the added thrill: people out there are urgently — often desperately, trying to communicate something (I know, I know, John, aren't we all, etc. and so forth). For example, one evening whilst twiddling with the knobs, I heard a pained, mournful, rather American sounding voice saying (I paraphrase): "We're really pleased to be here on your radio programme, we're so impressed with what you've done, we're with you all the way, we've been trying to get these fuckers off our backs for 400 years..." which turned out to be a Native American Representative speaking on Iranian radio, enjoying vicarious revenge on that vast horde of European invaders and their descendants, known, quaintly enough, as the USA.

I was hooked of course, and marked the place on the dial — the busy 31m spot — to follow it up next evening.

Further listening revealed that the Voice of the Islamic republic of Iran is on the whole a very dignified, reflective station, carefully balancing rather academic little sermons based on the Q'ran with cautious but scathing commentaries on Western/Christian hypocrisy and, the sugar on the pill, lengthy chunks of earthy but elegant more or less traditional Persian chamber music. In short, real stiff-upper-lip stuff, which I found very moving, literally. That is to say, the programme helped me breakout of the Euro-centric smugness of Western radio and reach for the world outside.

The only English language radio broadcasts I've come across that have as much what did it used to be called 'class' I suppose as Iran radio are from (smirk if you like) Albania, Radio Tirana. I'm sure all that stuff James Cameron said about Albania is true — overdressed traffic cops on vast wide mountain roads, waving on about one rickety cart in an afternoon or whatever — but if you're not charmed out of your socks by Radio Tirana's unruffled routine, ending up with: "Goodnight, dear listeners..." you've a heart of ice. The folk songs sound a bit starchy — not very Ethnic, quote unquote — but with their 7/8 and 5/4 rhythms and Macedonian influenced tunes you can tell you're not far from Yugoslavia, Bulgaria, Greece.

As for the speechifying — surprisingly similar in tone to Iran, with Marx and Stalin instead of Allah and the Ayatollah Whatsisname.

Talking of Stalinists (I mean people who admit that they're Stalinists) Pekin — whoops it's Beijing now isn't it — pump out the commercials regularly, but although I've paused a short while to hear the music — which is exactly what you'd expect it to sound like, only better — they've never got me engrossed.

Even less engrossing was a monotonous catalogue of geographical features and economic targets outlined by North Korean radio about which the less said the better.

So, what a wonderful surprise to find, right near where the 25m band approaches the 31m, from 7pm to 8pm in English, then in French, as is often the way, a clear signal from the land of Hope and Glory itself, the Socialist Republic of Vietnam. I've only been on it a week or so, and time will tell whether it's just infatuation or if indeed it's the real thing, but I think I love Radio Vietnam. Lots of David and Goliath stuff about those great big bullies the Chinese of course, and quite a few sobering reminders that it ain't easy trying to grow food and nurture people in a country where the carefully developed relationship between forest and field, town and country, etc, has been totally crippled for years to come by American bombs, defoliants, and so on. Western liberals may have become bored with Vietnam, but Vietnamese mothers' children are still stepping on uncollected American mines.

And is there any sugar on this particular pill? You can bet your bottom dollar on it as they say in Japan. The news and feature items are relatively short, and they play so much Vietnamese pop music, folk music and the like, you could almost call the programme presenters disc-jockeys. Especially during the pop bits, when meandering early-English pop group type instrumental arrangements are interspersed with just-this-side-of-sentimental ballads about things like farmers who went off to be soldiers and soldiers coming back to be farmers, Spring Romances, etc. One thing I've noticed about Vietnamese pop music that makes it unique, or at least specifically 'Indo-Chinese', is the use of very wide intervals in the tunes, and lengthy, apparently irregular phrases. I'm not just referring to the pentatonic 'All the black notes, no white notes' intervals common to all Chinese influenced music, but a really elastic and eventful melodic range. None of your 'HO-HO-HO CHI MINH!' type rubbish.

Finally, I'd like to plug my old favourite, the chattiest and most breathlessly enthusiastic bunch of renegades to be found on short wave, Radio Havana, Cuba. In fact, I'll give you their address, how's that: PO BOX 6240, HAVANA, CUBA. Apart from the wonderful Yoruba/Spanish dance music, often presented in the form of a request programme (Thus the address), you get fascinating snippets of Latin-American history, as seen by the underdog, the first slave revolts, and everything. They've even just sent me some glossy little picture card calendars (with potted histories on a separate piece of paper).

Incidentally, most of these radio stations like to hear from their listeners, and they acknowledge in various ways from timetables to souvenirs, and occasionally magazines. Above all, perhaps that's why I enjoy listening to these distant voices: it's the feedback.

1978

"I got overwhelmed by other things that seemed to be more interesting, and embarked upon as process of completing the higher education that I never had, having left school early and gone straight into washing-up and working in a forest. I started to become interested in learning about things that I'd been too busy living before to get round to. Alfie and I used to really enjoy watching the Open University, with these extraordinary professors and their blackboards and charts. I'd watch them all, but particularly those ones that dealt with communication, education and politics, and the relationship between Europe and other countries. That became far more interesting to me than playing musical instruments and being with musicians.

"Alongside that, we started going to the London Film Festival, which was akin to a psychedelic experience. We'd see something like 30 films in a fortnight, including many that would never get shown again — films from places like Senegal and Java. That was an extraordinary experience, the most exciting barrage of stimuli I'd had since I discovered jazz as a teenager."

Alfreda Benge:

"Part of it was that Robert felt he just couldn't say no to any of the projects that were being offered. Once he did get his nerve to say no, and did for the first time, he then began saying no to everything."

Dec — Brian Eno 'Ambient #1 Music For Airports' lp released (Ambient AMB 001)

Brian Eno, guitar/keyboards; RW, piano on '1/1'

a cock-eyed optimist's diary

by Robert Wyatt (first published in **Licorise**, summer 1976)

1. Amnesty International, formed 15 years ago to put pressure on governments who use solitary confinement and torture as standard political tools against 'subversive' reformists etc. have obtained the release of everybody on their original lists, and continue to grow in influence, respected everywhere for their non-partisan approach; one of their most recent success stories being the release of Leonid Plyushch from Dniepropetrousk prison mental hospital.

2a. Survival International help fund the Andoke tribe in Colombia, enabling them to pay off 'debts' to the all-powerful rubber-agents, and to become independent enough to purchase their own tolls for rubber-collecting, and sell 'direct'.

2b. S.I. get some medical protection for the Yaomami tribe of Southern Venezuela and Northern Brazil, suffering from previously unknown illnesses and infections brought in by white civilization.

2c. S.I. help Murvi-Muinane Indians withstand incursions of neo-Colombian society into the native environment.

2d. S.I. help towards an integrated project for socio-economic development of the endemic people, with provisions included for animal conservation, on Siberut Island, West Sumatra, Indonesia.

2e. S.I. try to assist relations between man and wildlife living at subsistence level in Greenland, Botswana, and India, where the interests of man and wildlife sometimes seem to conflict.

2f. S.I. help establish new alternatives in food acquisition for the endemic people of Siberut, and help to reduce the impact of white commercial interests related to timber extraction.

2g. S.I. influence Paraguayan attitudes to their indigenous Indian population, away from the attitudes of social inferiority inflicted on the Indians because they are not identified as Christians, and help to create an atmosphere of concern for the future of all Amerindian groups.

3. South Africa's Progressive Reform Party demonstrated growing white disillusion with apartheid by winning an important by-election with a barrister who recently defended black students on 'terrorism' charges.

4. Meanwhile back in Britain sex discrimination is banned in employment advertising. It's only a start but it's in the right direction...

5. Baroness Wootton and Gerald Gardiner Q.C. give remarkable T.V. interviews demonstrating that maturity and responsibility don't have to make people corrupt and. or cynical.

6. Prisoners help the blind: there's a recently established Braille unit at Aylesbury prison.

7. A new government report comes out firmly in support of Free pop festivals. 'Pop festivals are reasonable and acceptable forms of recreation", says the report, "not inherently objectionable or dangerous events."

8. It looks like the fall in the pound could be just what's needed for an export boom! British steel, for example, has flourished recently with such competitive prices.

9. The housing scheme in Blackburn seems to have really worked: they have a policy of renovating the better-built old houses and small shops, keeping neighbourhoods intact wherever possible.

10. Meanwhile — outside Liverpool — Runcorn is being studied by United Nations representatives as a model of a new town building. The houses are small-scale, 'human' sized, in fact; buses have their own road; and there's plenty of grass — kids are allowed to play on it too!

11. And the new Council homes in London's dockland at St. Katherine-By-The-Tower will be traffic-free, landscaped, and will also provide areas for children to play.

12. An export boom is forecast for Britain by Sir Frederick Catherwood, chairman of the British Institute of Management. He gives five reasons: a. the undervaluation of the sterling; b. the new pay deal; c. growth of major export markets; d. secure membership of the E.E.C.; e. growing Trade Union realization of the need for export-led growth.

13. Garfield Todd, former Prime-Minister of Rhodesia, released from prison at last. Now he can campaign more actively on behalf of the others...

14. British population decreased by around 9000 last year. This should dispel any remaining fears of eventual overcrowding.

15. Get-rich quick private abortionists lost 40% business in early '76 compared with the same period last year. And the number of foreign women coming to Britain for abortions — the staple diet of the private sector — dropped by well over half, as more liberal abortion laws were introduced in France and Germany.

16. Unemployment is down throughout Europe. An indication of the more optimistic mood of West European governments came when the Italian finance minister said he hoped it would be possible to end Italy's comprehensive import controls scheme earlier than its planned duration of three months.

17. Czechoslovakia's G.N.P. increased by 38% during the last five years. They have no unemployment.

18. Recent British Government legislation stops farm labourers being thrown out of cottages when too old or too ill too work.

19. FREGG (campaign for Free Range EGGs) getting organised against the cruel (not to say tasteless) battery chicken system. Also an indication of the healthy fashion for small-scale home-grown food.

20. HABITAT studying cheap 'alternative technology' for use around the 'poor' world (most of the planet), taking easily available local resources into account. this 'self help' group, started in Stockholm, has been displaying its ideas in a special international gathering in Toronto — itself a model of trouble-free city planning for more affluent conditions. Speaking of which...

21. The Government of New South Wales is to be the next administration to legalise the private use of marijuana. Laws on soft drugs, homosexuality, prostitution, and victimless crimes like vagrancy and drunkenness are all to be liberalised.

22. The notoriously high number of heart attacks in North Karelia being checked: project financed by Finnish government and the World Health Organization has started to succeed partly by changing diet habits: more vegetables, less fatty meat.

23. A series of articles in a special report in the Grauniad on behalf of a secular, democratic Palestine. Case well and reasonably put.

24. The success of Bob Marley among others has paved the way for relatively large-scale acceptance of modern West Indian music in Britain.

25. 3rd year pupils at Stewards Comprehensive School in Harlow, Essex. learning and performing Ghanaian dances taught by director of creative studies, Felix Cobbson. they may go to the Festival of Culture and Arts in Lagos, Nigeria, next year.

26. A government white paper on the working of the Children and Young Persons Act of 1969 contains first steps towards phasing out all remands of young people to adult prisons — and will, says the white paper, come into effect as soon as possible.

27. According to 'Psychiatry in Medicine' (Vol. 7), the growing number of women doctors make better G.P.s than men: they tend to be more conscientious and thorough, as well as less irritable. And they are preferred by black and other ethnic groups.

28. Hunter Davies' book on Creighton Comprehensive School points out the unprecedented potential of the Comprehensive system.

29. George Davis released to ecstatic welcome home in Bow.

30. Workers representing the 200 people of United Biscuits plant at Isleworth took their place alongside shareholders for the first time at the company's annual meeting in Edinburgh. The firm's participation policy was based on effective, cost-conscious, profit-oriented management, who recognized that they were more likely to be successful by embracing participation which leads to greater involvement and breaks down barriers.

31. No 'War trials' bloodbath in Vietnam: old Southern soldiers going to polling booths with everyone else.

32. The film 'One Flew Over The Cuckoo's Nest' received loads of awards and has been on general release and shown in cinemas that normally only show 'uncontroversial' films.

33. Meanwhile (what a useful word that is) back in the U.S.A., Seminoles and Choctaws, remnants of a once-powerful South-Eastern group of Indians, start on the slow climb back to prosperity...

...music, curtain, lights...

— I'm glad to say this diary has no end —

1979

"I liked the music of the late Seventies. I thought the Sex Pistols were a wonderful group and I loved Poly Styrene's lyrics for X-Ray Spex. I actually became more interested because it existed side-by-side with reggae. There was a new generation of black youth that seemed to be less English than their bus-driving, nursing parents, who'd been making more of an effort to be more English, but who hadn't really been welcomed as much as they might have been. This new generation didn't bother trying and instead began recultivating rural Jamaican patois and all that. It was a grass-roots 'fuck-you-too' movement, which actually was a great inspiration for punk alongside it.

"It really climaxed in the Two-Tone era, when people began digging up the old ska records. I loved Two-Tone. That was really just about the last era of pop/rock music that I felt totally at one with. Jerry Dammers and The Beat and all those people — I thought they were lovely. That whole late Seventies environment really was like a breath of fresh air."

Oct — Grog Kill Studio, Willow, New York, sessions for Nick Mason's Fictitious Sports 'Spot the Player' lp

released Feb/81 (Harvest SHSP 4116)
Carla Bley, keyboards/compositions; Mike Mantler, trumpets; Gary Windo, tenor sax/bass clarinet/flute; Gary Valente, trombones; Howard Johnson, tuba; Chris Spedding, guitars; Steve Swallow, bass; Nick Mason, drums/percussion; Karen Kraft, RW, vocals

Carla Bley:
"Nick said he needed something and I said I had something. Then we just sat down and decided on who we would get to sing it. I think it was either Burl Ives or Yul Bryner or Robert Wyatt, so we chose Robert."

"Carla Bley made me work when I wasn't working. She said: 'Come on, who do you think you are? Some fucking pop star? You've never had a hit record, you're not good looking enough. You're just a musician like the rest of us, so get on with it.' So, she shamed me back into the studios, and I enjoyed it."

Professionally, the late Seventies becomes a hiatus from the production of music and records. Alternative satisfaction is found through time spent reading, listening to short wave radio broadcasts from second and third world nations, and an intense correspondence with prisoners of political conscience internationally. This development of political acumen and commitment leads Robert Wyatt to join the Communist Party of Great Britain in 1979.

"I was going to a lot of political gatherings. People would ask me who I thought the best vocalist I'd heard that year was, and I'd say Dennis Skinner. His gigs were a lot better than most rock gigs! Alfie (my wife) took very good care of me, was always devising things for me to do to prevent me from getting bored — like going to a festival of foreign films, that was a real eye-opener. Either because of that or in spite of it, I started to get more and more impatient with the idea that rock music is intrinsically rebellious. Compared to the marginalised lives that the people I was becoming interested in were leading, the rock thing was a very safe and easy part of the establishment. The establishment has always had a place for rebellion. Rock and Roll didn't invent that. So then I met a woman named Vivienne Goldman who was writing at the time about reggae from a political point of view. She introduced me to a friend of hers, Geoff Travis, who was head of Rough Trade Records. Geoff said, if you ever feel like recording again, let us know. I hadn't got any albums in my mind, but I thought I could at least try some of these other songs that I'd been listening to."

Alfreda Benge:
"I don't think he ever would have done anything again if they (Rough Trade) hadn't existed, because they gave him complete freedom. So Geoff and I kinda schemed to get him to carry on working, which was quite hard because he's very obstinate about when he doesn't want to do anything. But I think it's very sad when he doesn't do things because what he does is so very nice."

First of all I have to make the point that I'm 29. I think everybody's stuck in their own age group to a certain extent, where their taste is concerned. People that I know tend to believe that the music of their adolescence is the most inspiring ever, and find music from before their own generation a bit boring, and music after it a bit trivial — childish. Nearly everybody thinks that , although they rationalize it in other ways. The other point is — I'm choosing ten records I like, but actually their are fourteen records that I like, so I've had to leave out four. The third point is that I've lost most of these records so I might have details of the titles wrong.

1 'Goodbye Pork Pie Hat' by Charlie Mingus is from an album called *Mingus Ah Um* on CBS (I think). this isn't officially a song — I don't know of any words for it — but it's very singable like a lot of Mingus tunes. However complicated his tunes are, when you know them, you can sing along with them. Also I can almost play it as well as sing it because ,like many of Julie Tippetts' songs, it's nearly all on the black notes of the piano. The improvisations on this, which are by Shafi Hadi and Booker Ervin on saxophones, respect the tune — are extensions of the tune. People like Gil Evans and Mingus stand out from other jazz writers and arrangers because they integrate the improvisations of their musicians into their writing. I should think it's easier for a musician to do that playing with Mingus than with most people, simply because Mingus tunes are so beautiful anyway.

2 Next bit I've chosen is the 'Piano Quintet' by Shostakovich. The string quartet part of this quintet, as far as I can remember — as it's some years since I've heard it — play bowed, muted strings; a very haunting sound. I like the idea of a string quartet anyway; in fact I enjoy the idea of a string quartet more than I enjoy a lot of string quartet music. In this case, perhaps, I liked it because the cello is often used rather in the way the double bass is used in jazz — i.e. not bowed but plucked; relatively simple rhythmically, as far as I remember. it's an incredibly melodic piece, which you must admit is a great achievement for someone who is, after all, only a brainwashed communist.

3 'Friday The Thirteenth' by Thelonious Monk. The particular version I have in mind is from the Town Hall Concert he did — the first main Town Hall Concert — where the arrangements were done by someone called Hal Overton. I think when Monk dies there'll be a rash of colour supplement potted biographies, little television programmes — arts programmes and so on, about him. 'The zany loony of the bebop world' is what they'll call him no doubt. they won't do it till he's dead of course, in case he makes a lot of money, which they probably think would be bad for him. In my opinion he's one of the greatest writers of tunes that I've ever heard, within my range of appreciation. The thing about this particular concert is that Hal Overton's arrangements are really imaginative. he's taken old recordings of Monk playing these tunes and written them out, including the solos Monk played, and orchestrated them for a large band. So you have the spontaneity of the improvised ideas strengthened by Hal Overton's inspired orchestration. 'Friday The Thirteenth' I particularly like because its got a secondary bass line which is sort of out of synch with the tune itself, and it sort of tilts the whole tune at a strange angle (If that sounds like Pseuds' Corner, I'm sorry, but that 's what happens when you try and explain what you like about music).

4 'Epilogue' by Miroslav Vitous, from the album *Infinite Search*. Miroslav Vitous is technically in a class with Barre Phillips, Stanley Clarke, and Barry Guy. But as composer of music for the bass he is my favourite since Charlie Haden. Maybe his Slavic origins have something to do with his particular melodic inclinations. On *Infinite Search*, the double bass — an instrument usually in a subservient role — is the group's 'lead' instrument. The group — Herbie Hancock, John McLaughlin, Jack DeJohnette, and Joe Henderson — support Miroslav' s lines with the accuracy, speed, and imagination you associate with a first-class tennis match. Although the individual musicians are accustomed to working together in a live context, they are also accustomed to drowning out double-bassists, on the expedient premise that the loud instruments lead, the quiet follow. The recording studio can liberate musicians from this 'hierarchy of volume'. In this case, the effect of such energetic players pulling their punches to leave space for Miroslav to set the direction in each piece creates a fine, translucent texture, like a spider's web. Tennis matches, spider's webs — the whole world in a song, what more can you ask?

5 'Blues For Pablo' by Gil Evans and Miles Davis. This is from an LP originally called *Miles Davis Plus Nineteen*, which was Evans' first attempt to arrange a complete series of inter-related mini-concertos for Miles, who plays mainly flugelhorn in a big-band context.It's harder to play the flugelhorn than the trumpet, which tends to make even flugelhorn virtuosi like Clark Terry, Art Farmer and the great Johnny Coles play more carefully, thoughtfully than many trumpeters. As the title suggests, there is a certain similarity between the music of southern Spain and early blues of the southern States, which Gil Evans exploits beautifully without using the obvious link instrument, the guitar. In fact Gil Evans was, as far as I know, the first 'jazz' arranger to supplement the traditional 'ethnic' dance band instruments with French horns, flutes and other instruments usually associated with the European orchestral tradition. Incidentally 'Blues For Pablo', like the other tracks on this record, is only a couple of minutes long, which demonstrates Gil Evans' roots as an arranger for 'pop' dance bands, and makes each individual piece nice and tight (if I'd been a radio DJ at the time I'd have pushed them as worthy competition to Sandy Nelson and Duane Eddy on the instrumental singles market).

6 'Sex Machine' by Sly and the Family Stone. Sometimes, when I've got nothing else to do, I sit and speculate about Sly Stone's innovations in the recording studio. He used to be a disc jockey and as anyone who admires the work of Kenny Everett knows, DJs have a unique opportunity to muck around with tape recorders and create a sort of surreal continuity with their between-record link pieces-to make a musical entity out of an otherwise more-or-less random series of records. Also a successful American DJ has to be fast, slick, tasteless and dramatic-a great education for a musician. One major difference between Sly Stone's courageous production stunts and, say Frank Zappa's, was that the basic band recording always had the immediacy and excitement of a good live gig. Larry Graham in particular, is a spectacularly useful bass-player and singer.

7 'Flying' by the Beatles. A lot of people didn't like the *Magical Mystery Tour* film because it was amateurish (the cameras didn't dart in and out of the lead singer's nostril's like they do in professionally made music films) or pretentious (they were actually trying to do something interesting); or something. Belonging as I do to the gullible hippy generation whose critical faculties are irredeemably blunted by drugs and sex, and bad PA systems, I thought it was great. The LP of the same name was even better, because they filled it out with their recent amazing singles. The most magical and mysterious piece on the record though, for me, was 'Flying', which essentially seems to consist of a twelve-bar blues, except that all the chords are major, and the singing 'white'. So white actually, that it sounds like the 'Volga Boat Song', part two. The effect is um what can I say oh you know the usual string of misleading, inadequate adjectives, um, how about 'this record is very nice so I like it'. P.S. I thought the Beatles much more daring and inventive than most of us 'progressive' groups of the late sixties (apart form the Pink Floyd). Something to do with endless studio time replacing endless live gigs, I should think.

8 'Leaning On A Lamppost' by George Formby. Yet another Daring, Wacky Northerner. Apart form being Daring, Wacky, and Northern, George Formby was a shit-hot ukulele player, not half so stodgy as his many imitators — he'd have made a good rhythm guitarist. Apart form which this is a useful record to play to anybody who still thinks that Bob Dylan invented good lyrics. while I'm at it I'd like to mention Frank Crummit. Ahem, "Frank Crummit". Thank you.

9 'Hold On I'm Coming' by Sam and Dave. I vividly remember as if 'twere yesterday the day I saw the amazing Stax circus come to town. And best of all I remember Sam and Dave striding on stage form either side and meeting in front of Booker T's gang all hammering away like it was the encore already-very exciting. Once again how can mere words convey etc. etc.

Goldie does a version of this song which apparently accentuates the title's erotic possibilities — more power to her, er, elbow and everything, I say; but nevertheless I doubt if her version matches the original in terms of pure musical excitement. On the other hand, there's probably no such thing as pure musical excitement — apart from *The Old Grey Whistle Test* of course.

The way Stax records were recorded made them perfect for discotheques rather than posh stereo systems etc, on which, like many good dance records e.g. West-Indian dance records, they sound comparatively stark and dry. Conversely, many so-called "well-produced" records, when pumped out over a busy dance floor, are about as helpful to dancers as a carpet of wet cement. I mention this because it's puzzling trying to work out why things are or have been popular, if you don't take into account the original context. I'd like to continue in this vein and discuss the amphibious life of the sea lion but I know that you're supposed to stick to the point. So here's my last record.

10 'Get Out of My Life Woman' by Lee Dorsey/Allen Toussaint. These two made a series of great singles, and if anybody's got a spare copy of the LP of this title they made together, I'll give anything except perhaps my right arm for it. I gather Lee Dorsey's not working as a singer any more, runs a garage of something. Never mind we've still got John Mayall. Toussaint belongs to the great tradition of musicians form New Orleans with the names include Bechet, 'Slow-drag' Pavageau, Alphonse Picou, Barney Bigard, Joseph 'Zigaboo' on drums on this particular record but whoever it is ought to be famous. He saved my bacon, anyway, by showing me a way to combine the triplet feel of the earlier wing bands with the more violent military-band-derived eighth note feel favoured in modern rock circles. Now I hastily leave you to ponder the exact meaning, if any, of the phrase 'modern rock circles'.

First published in UK magazine Let It Rock, 1974

1980

"Good tunes don't pour out of my fingertips like the morning dew. I only ever wrote about three or four songs a year anyway. Not very prolific. I don't write enough songs to sustain a recording career. I mean it used not to matter when I could drum as well and was part of an arranged group, but when I'm left stranded, a bit high and dry now in the chair, loads of the things I could do before I can't do and I'm left with the things I can do. But there isn't enough of my output to sustain a career and that sort of stumped me for a couple of years until I realized the obvious thing. I thought 'Fuck me, Elvis and Frank Sinatra never wrote a song in their fuckin' lives. What's the point of knocking yourself out for it.'"

Jan 26 — Matrix Studios, sessions for 'Arauco'/'Caimenera' 45

released Mar (Rough Trade RT037)
A side — Bill MacCormick, bass; RW, keyboards/piano/guitar/vocal

"'Arauco' is by Chilean folk-singer Violetta Parra. It's a despairing exhortation to all the great Indian chiefs and the cultures and communities they represent to rise up and throw off the Christian colonialists. It's despairing because the exploitation's been going on for 400 years and there aren't that many Indians left."

B side — Bill MacCormick, bass; Harry Beckett, flugelhorn; RW, keyboards/piano/percussion/vocal
For Maurice Bishop

"'Caimenera' is a version of 'Guantanamero' which is virtually the Cuban national anthem. I sing it since there's been so much press for the thousands of Cubans who left Cuba I thought I'd sing a song for the millions who stayed."

Jan 30 — Matrix Studios, sessions for 'Stalin Wasn't Stallin''/'Stalingrad' 45

released Feb/81 (Rough Trade RT046)
A side — RW, vocals
First recorded in 1943 by acapella gospel group the Golden Gate Jubilee Quartet. Composed by Bill Johnson.

"I just thought it was amusing to realize that the song had been done and how impossible it was going to be to find a composer, because he wouldn't dare say he'd written it anyway, when it comes to royalties."

B side — written and performed by Peter Blackman whom Robert saw read at an Art Against Racism and Fascism event.

"As that song on the other side points out, England and America were for five extraordinary and unlikely years anti-fascist countries, because they weren't being the fascists. I didn't know anything about Peter Blackman, and when he read this poem I was very moved. He's not young, he belongs to quite another generation, the Thirties Left movement, and he's stuck to it where others haven't. He hasn't made a career out of being Left wing or a poet."

Feb — Matrix Studios, sessions for 'At Last I Am Free'/'Strange Fruit' 45

released Nov (Rough Trade RT 052)
A side — Frank Roberts, piano; Mogotsi Mothle, double bass; RW, keyboards/percussion/vocals
For Angela Davis
First recorded in 1978 by Chic.

"In this case, I listened to it and thought, what on earth is this? The chorus goes 'Now at last I am free' — yes, well, that's a great feeling, that's good — but the verse is a bitter and miserable let-down. The gist of it is a betrayal, and the chorus is 'Hooray, made it!' I thought, COR! — that's right up my street! My voice always comes out disappointed to say the least. I've got that sort of sound. It's too lugubrious to be a hit. Nothing I could do would ever cheer anybody up, and I don't even sound fashionably down. So, if I sing 'At Last I Am Free' it wouldn't sound as if I meant it anyway, and that would suit the sense. I got Frank Roberts to do the piano, and I just did what I liked about it, and left the rest out."

B side — Frank Roberts, piano; Mogotsi Mothle, double bass; RW, keyboards/vocals
For Winnie Mandela
First recorded in 1939 by Billie Holliday.

"'Strange Fruit' was interesting for me because it was an American protest song. But when they talk about the American protest song tradition they don't really mean songs like that, which is a song of the thirties against the lynchings. I thought it had a very modern meaning. It's not just a historical song because although the song is about the racism in the deep south of America, I feel that the whole attitude of the northern hemisphere to the southern hemisphere in the world echoes the racism of the north and south of old America."

Feb — Matrix Studios, sessions for 'Grass'/'Trade Union' 45

released Aug/81 (Rough Trade RT 081)
A side — Kadir Durvesh, shehnai; Esmael Shek, tabla; RW, vocals
First recorded in 1975 by Ivor Cutler.

"Cutler says I sing it alright except that I sing it as though it has meaning."

B side — written and performed by Dishari whom Robert also saw perform at the Art Against Racism and Fascism event.

Abdul Salique:
"When I came to this country, I was aware that there were lots of Indian and Pakistani groups but none from Bangladesh, which was now independent. I thought I should do something about it especially when there was a lot of trouble in 1978 in Brick Lane (National Front racist attacks). I don't play enough music to do something very creative but when I spoke with people they all asked me to do something. So I made this group, Dishari Shilpee Gosthi, which is a cultural organisation, with Esmael Shek the tabla player and Kadir Durvesh the shehnai player and other musicians. A lot of people asked us to play and represent our country; we performed at many multi-cultural events, at a benefit at the Royal Albert Hall, on the TV programmes *Skin* and *Nationwide*, and at the Blair Peach memorial concert. Dan Jones, the secretary of the Trades Council, has been very helpful and I began to develop interest in Trade Union activities. Out of that I wrote the song to encourage my people to join the unions."

'Trade Union'

We came from a distant land
Counting the waves
of thirteen rivers and seven seas
With hopes of a better life.
We are the workers!
We labour in the factories and the workshops.
If we unite
We can grasp our rights in our hands.
Of course we must unite
If we want to defeat the racists
If we want to draw the teeth
Of those who suck our blood and exploit us.
We must stand together
Under the trade union banner.

Mar — Alvic Sound, sessions for Kevin Coyne 'Sanity Stomp' lp

released Nov (Virgin VGD 3504)
On the second disc of this double album: Kevin Coyne, guitar/keyboards/vocals; Brian Godding, guitar/keyboards; Bob Ward, guitar; RW, drums/keyboards

June — Berry Street, sessions for The Raincoats 'Odyshape' lp

released June/81 (Rough Trade Rough 13)
Gina Birch, bass/balaphone; Vicky Aspinall, guitar/vocal; Ana da Silva, guitar; Ingrid Weiss, finger cymbal; RW, drums on 'And Then It's O.K.'

June — Berry Street, sessions for Vivien Goldman 'Launderette'/'Private Armies' 45

released Aug/81 (Window Wind 1)
Vivien Goldman, vocals; Keith Levene, guitar; Vicky Aspinall, violin; George (Oban) Levi, RW, percussion on 'Launderette'.

Summer — home, sessions for 'Rangers In The Nights'

released Nov on compilation lp 'Miniatures' subtitled 'a sequence of fifty-one tiny masterpieces' (Pipe 2)
Morgan Fisher, tape manipulation; RW, vocals

Morgan Fisher:
"Invitations were sent out to a highly personal selection of creative artistes, asking them to contribute pieces of not more than one minute's duration, to what has turned out to be this extraordinarily eclectic album. The response was excellent; only a handful of artistes declined. Many of them visited Pipe Studios to record their pieces; others were recorded in their homes on the pipe Mobile (i.e., a Revox)."

1981

"Going back to work is in some ways a defeat. Because I've now come to the conclusion that I can only do what I used to do in the first place. I'd like to think that after the last four or five years I could now see further, do more, and so on. But this isn't the case — I find I'm reduced to this built-in introspection and narcissism of being A Creative Person, and it's very hard to harness the amazing things I've seen or heard. Suddenly all the windows disappear and are replaced by mirrors. I can't graft all the experiences and thoughts that I've had since I dropped the craft on to what I remember of the craft. I know lots of things I didn't used to know, but they're not specifically about how to make better records. If anyone told me they'd been doing something for five years and felt really disillusioned and wanted to give it a break and go off and do something else, I'd say something like DON'T. Stick to whatever it is you can do, because you have to grow through whatever it is that you do."

Feb 16 to 20 — RAI Studios, Rome, Italy, RAI Un Certo Discorso recording

a) 'Opium Wars' b) 'L'albero Degli Zoceoli' c) Heathen Have No Soul' d) 'Holy War' e) 'Billie's Bounce' f) 'Revolution Without Tears' g) 'Born Again Cretin' performed
RW, vocals/percussion/piano (except e, f)/keyboards (except c, f)/jews harp (c)
'Billie's Bounce' first recorded in 1945 by Charlie Parker.

Pasquale Santoli (series producer):
"We wanted to use the specific role of the radio to give listeners a different point of view on music and culture. Normally radio is an amplifier of the point of view and the products of the culture and record industry. We're used to listening to music as a finished product, signed, sealed, and delivered. If you write a letter and scrap the first attempt, that's just as interesting as what you finally write, so we wanted to look at the different drafts, to show the work in progress. Then we can use the drafts in different ways, maybe just play one of Robert's tracks, or mix them differently."

"I was invited to go for a week just to record the actual process of my working. Of things like that which I've seen, for example on painters, with the honorable exception of Picasso who worked on a piece of glass, people tend to cheat a bit and do an actual finished performance in front of the cameras. But I thought 'If they really want to see how I work before I know what I'm doing, then that's what they're going to get and if during that week something comes out of it, then it will do, but if it doesn't then that will be more honest.' I deliberately went in there and improvised what I was doing as well as how I did it. The point wasn't to have a finished result that could be listened to, the point was to see a process. It's only in retrospect that I can see that bits of some of them have some kind of coherence."

Apr — 'Born Again Cretin' released

NME/Rough Trade compilation cassette (Copy 001 C81)
recorded at Wave Studios
RW, keyboards/piano/percussion/vocals
Note: The opening scat vocal is based on Ornette Coleman's composition 'Peace'.

Apr — Scritti Politti 'The Sweetest Girl' released

NME/Rough Trade compilation cassette (Copy 001 C81)
recorded at Berry Street
Musicians uncredited except Green, vocal; RW, keyboards

On May 17, the BBC Radio 4 programme 'Woman's Hour' broadcasts an interview with Robert Wyatt and his mother Honor, who had been a producer for 'Woman's Hour' years earlier. Together they candidly discuss their relationship and the challenges they've faced since the accident of '73.

May — Alvic Sound, sessions for Epic Soundtracks 'Popular Classical' 45

released Aug (Rough Trade RT 084)
Epic Soundtracks, piano/bass/drums/harmony vocal; Vicky Aspinall, violin; Georgie Born, cello; Flossie (Robert and Alfie's dog), barks; Robert Ellidge, (muddy) mouth on 'Jelly, Babies'

Aug 7 — Wave Studio, sessions for 'The Animals Film' (other session dates unknown)

released May/82 (Rough Trade Rough 40)
RW, keyboards/piano/percussion/vocals
Written and produced by Victor Schonfeld, narrated by Julie Christie. Premiered at London Film Festival Nov 8.

Julie Christie:
"When Victor Schonfeld contacted me about his film I was interested, but have to admit I suspected it would be a kind of Disney 'Let's be kind to the fluffy bunnies' type of thing. However, I went and saw it, and gruelling experience though it was, I saw a film that reached to the roots of all our confusions about our treatment of animals. Because it's not about animals — it's about us. It's about human nature and the atrocities some factions of it can quite blandly commit. It's about the deadness of the mind that can commit these atrocities without blinking, every day, exactly in the same way they're being committed, for example, in El Salvador today. And it's about our participation in these atrocities even when we're not the perpetrators. People who 'love' animals wear furs, wear make-up, use products, eat food, that is the direct result of the extremest forms of cruelty to animals."

Victor Schonfeld:
"When I started working on the film I perceived it was trying to show a form of exploitation that most people weren't even aware of or didn't recognize. But as we worked on it and actually visited places and found footage, I realized that was describing it in very mild terms. What that film is really about is torture."

Aug 28 and 29 — Wave Studio, sessions for 'The Internationale'
released May 1/82 on 'The Recommended Records Sampler' lp (RR 8/9)
RW, keyboards/percussion/vocal

Summer — Wave Studio, sessions for 'Red Flag'
released Mar/82 on 'Nothing Can Stop Us' lp (Rough 35)
RW, keyboards/percussion/vocal
'Nothing Can Stop Us' collects the four 45 rpm singles with 'Born Again Cretin' and 'Red Flag'.

Summer (?) — Wave Studio, sessions for 'So That You Can Live' film soundtrack
RW, piano/keyboards
Produced by a Socialist film making co-operative concerning the decline of a Welsh working class community, and including a slow tempo performance of 'Born Again Cretin'.

Summer (?) — Wave Studio, sessions for City Limits radio advertisement
Bill Patterson, speaker; RW, keyboards/percussion
Commissioned by Duncan Campbell for the weekly London based magazine City Limits and broadcast on Capitol Radio.

Summer (?) — Wave Studio, sessions for Shiny Men 'Again' lp
released Oct (Experimental EX 002)
Group members credited under pseudonym; RW, singing/scat gurgling on 'Dream Pussy'

Dec 19 — The Raincoats, Albany Theatre
Vicky Aspinall, violin; Ana da Silva, guitar; Gina Birch, bass; Charles Hayward, drums; RW, vocal on 'Born Again Cretin'
As of 1993, this is Robert's only stage appearance since the Henry Cow concerts of 1975.

Dec — Alvic Sound, sessions for Ben Watt 'Summer Into Winter' ep
released Apr/82 (Cherry Red Cherry 12)
Ben Watt, voice/guitar; RW, voice/piano on 'Walter and John', piano on 'A Girl In Winter'.

At some point during this busy year Robert is roped into a recording project by the rock group Mex at Paul Mex's home studio in the town of Watford. Robert contributes piano, percussion, and vocals during the rehearsal recordings, but Mex soon disbands and the record is never realized.

Selling the Morning Star in Twickenham with CP delegate Digby Jacks

1982

"Jazz was my education, but the only thing that sounded convincing to me was what I do. I'm not a black American in Harlem, I'm an English bloke born in 1945, so if that's what I am and what I sound like, then that's what I should be doing. It's been a long process, finding my own voice."

---

portrait of the artist as a CONSUMER
ROBERT WYATT

SONGS
Hopelessly Without You.........................Carroll Thompson
You Bring The Sun Out..............................Janet Kay
Love Don't Live Here Any More ....Rose Royce
Every Little Bit Hurts.............................Brenda Holloway
I Put A Spell On You................................Nina Simone
Love Me Tonight ....Trevor Walters

TUNE
Peace .... Ornette Coleman
(from 'The Shape Of Jazz To Come' LP)

RECENT LP
Wynton Marsalis

DRUMMERS
"Max Roach to Connie Kay to Brian Abrahams — a quick rush through 30 years of jazz."

ARRANGERS
Melba Liston ("A trombonist who's worked with Dizzy Gillespie, Charles Mingus, Quincy Jones and — a particular favourite — on Randy Weston's 'Tanjah' LP.")
Fela Kuti ("I know he's only got one arrangement, but it's so good it doesn't matter.")
Philip Koutev ("A Bulgarian choir arranger, kind of a Bulgarian folk version of what Gil Evans did for Miles Davis.")

SOVIET MUSICIANS
Alexei Koslov — jazz reeds player and arranger
Igor Brill — jazz keyboards
Folk & jazz from the Southern USSR
("I like Soviet jazz very much. It's unusual in that the musicians are often highly trained formally, but they also play very fiercly, deliberately avoiding formal straitjackets.")

FILMS
Ceddo........................ Sembene Ousmane (Senegal, 1976)
Death Of A Cameraman............ Faliero Rosati (Italy, 1978)
The Outsiders................................Mrinal Sen (India, 1977)
India Song .... Marguerite Duras (France, 1976)

SOME AUTHORS I LIKE
Jean Rhys
Franz Fanon
Jack Santa Maria

RADIO PROGRAMMER
Alex Pascall — BBC Radio London
("He does the *Black London* programme, which is a community programme that actually responds to what people want to talk about — a breakthrough in radio. He also plays records nobody else plays: Soca, Calypso and music for older black people in England — Nat King Cole and suchlike — which I like because I'm old too, I remember Nat King Cole.")

POLITICAL COMMENTATORS
Noam Chomsky
John Pilger
Jonathan (as opposed to David) Dimbleby

NEWSPAPER
Morning Star

Winter — Redan Recorder, sessions for Marsha Hunt 'Man To Women' 45

released and withdrawn Apr 15(Virgin VS499)
Musicans uncredited except vocalists Jeanette Landrey, Eddie Kemp, Christine Ellerbeck, and RW, vocal on 'All She Wanted Was Marlon Brando'.
'Man To Women' was a stage play Marsha Hunt wrote based on four women and their relationship to men. When uncontrollable circumstances at the April 15th Zig Zag Club press reception proved disastrous, Virgin Records immediately withdrew financial support for both play and prospective album. All programmes and three thousand copies of this four track single were destroyed. See Marsha Hunt's biography, "Real Life", published in 1986.

Spring (?) — Berry Street, sessions for Scritti Politti 'Asylums In Jerusalem'/'Jacques Derrida' 45

released July (Rough Trade RT111)
Green, vocals/guitar; Joe Gang, Nial Jinks, bass; Lorenza, Mae, Jackie, chorus; Tom Morley, Linn drums; Mike McEvoy, RW, keyboards

Spring — home, sessions for 'Round Midnight'

released Oct on NME compilation cassette 'Mighty Reel'
Dave MacRae, piano/synthesizer; RW, vocal
First recorded in 1947 by Thelonious Monk.

Spring — home, sessions for 'Memories Of You'

released Aug as B-side of 'Shipbuilding'
Dave MacRae, piano/synthesizer; RW, vocal
First recorded in 1930 by Eubie Blake.

July 23 — Eden Studios, sessions for 'Shipbuilding' 45

released Aug (Rough Trade RT 115)
Clive Langer, organ; Steve Nieve, piano; Mark Bedford, double bass; Martin Hughes, drums; Elvis Costello, backing vocals; RW, percussion/vocals

Elvis Costello:
"It's been the happiest experience I've had as a producer/songwriter. The song has been realised perfectly. It sounds completely like the intent of the lyric and melody, Wyatt has an amazing voice. I'd always wanted to hear Dusty Springfield record one of my songs and when she did 'Just A Memory' it was a great bland disappointment. I think that people have been so overwhelmed by the melancholy of Robert's singing that the political comment in 'Shipbuilding' hasn't been immediately spotted. The lyric seems to filter through afterwards; the BBC probably wouldn't like it otherwise."

"They sent me a cassette through the post beccause they thought I'd like a go, which I did. It was brilliant of them to think it sounded like a Robert Wyatt song, and not to have met me and got it so right. I was very moved."

In December, the London based pop group Gambit of Shame issue the single 'Gambit of Shame'/'No Bounds' (Gambit of Shame DHE 7009) with a credit for Robert Wyatt as producer.

1983

"Most composers get their ideas, I've read the interviews, they get their ideas in the shower or in the bath or in the traffic. I'm very eccentric, I get my ideas when I'm sitting down at the piano trying to compose!"

With Rough Trade's spring reissue of the 'Shipbuilding'/'Memories Of You' single quickly climbing the British pop charts, Robert and Alfie's off season stay in the Spanish seaside resort town of Casteldefells is cut short to oblige a series of promotional media appearances. These include the customary interviews with various pop music papers, a one hour profile programme by Mark Allen for BBC Radio One, and a taping of BBC television's 'Loose Talk' programme alongside Elvis Costello.

On May 29th, Robert, Elvis, Clive Langer, and Mark Bedford are filmed for the promotional video of 'Shipbuilding'.

"It seemed a bit aloof not to. They said 'Come on, give a hand, everyone else is doing a bit of work on this record, it's all for you, havin' a good time in Spain are you? Nice is it sittin' about there while we're workin' for your record?' So here I am."

June 3 — BBC Studios, 'The Old Grey Whistle Test' T.V. filming

broadcast June 3
'Born Again Cretin', 'Shipbuilding' performed
Clive Langer, organ; Mark Bedford, double bass; Kiernan O'Connor, drums; Niccck Clyfus, piano; RW, vocals

---

Don't Quote Me, Comrade

Quiz set by an old Softie

Who said:

a) "I know that many of you under-rate the women and even laugh at them. This is a mistake, comrades, a serious mistake."

b) "Materialism in general recognises objectively real being as independent of consciousness, sensation, experience... Consciousness is only the reflection of being, at best an approximately true reflection of it."

c) "It is impossible to separate thought from matter that thinks."

d) "The question of the relation of thinking to being, the relation of spirit to nature, is the paramount question of the whole of philosophy..."

e) "Fuck this for a game of soldiers."

f) "There are two types of survival and two types of peace: survival for the rich and survival for the poor, peace for the rich and peace for the poor."

The Final Solutions:

a) J.Stalin, 1936 b) V.I.Lenin, Selected Works, Vol.11 c) K.Marx, Selected Works, Vol.1 d) F.Engels, Selected Works, Vol.1 e) S.Tracey, Westminster Abbey, 1970s f) F.Castro, December 5th 1988

Autumn — Power Plant, sessions for Working Week 'Venceremos—We Will Win'/'Bottom End' ep

released Feb/84 (Paladin/Virgin VS 684-12)
Simon Booth, guitars; Larry Stabbins, soprano sax/tenor sax/flute; Harry Beckett, trumpet/flugelhorn; Annie Whitehead, trombone; Stuart Matthewman, tenor sax; Dave Bitelli, clarinet/baritone sax; Chuchow Mercham, double bass; Kim Burton, piano; Mark Taylor, drums; Dawson, Bosco D'Oliveira, percussion; Tracey Thorn, Claudia Figueroa, RW, vocals on 'Venceremos—We Will Win'
Dedicated to the people of Chile and the memory of Victor Jara.

Dec 19 — Blackwing Studios, sessions for 'Amber And The Amberines'

released 84 on NME cassette compilation 'Dept. Of Enjoyment' (NME 011)
Hugh Hopper, Casio keyboard; RW, Wasp keyboard/vocal

Alfreda Benge:

"We were at home in Twickenham when we heard on the mid-day news that the U.S. had invaded Grenada. We were so angry, we had to do something. I quickly made a placard with a strip of wood and a piece of hard-board I'd just primed to do a painting on and asked Robert what to write on it. He decided on 'U.S. SCUM OUT OF GRENADA' or something along these lines. We all got in the car (Robert, my mother, me and the pregnant dog) and drove straight to the U.S. Embassy in Grosvenor Square.

"There was no-one outside except a couple of policemen and a policewoman. They had already put up a barrier outside the Embassy and were obviously expecting protesters. For about an hour and a half we were the only people there. It occurred to me that no doubt someone inside the Embassy would be taking photos for 'the files', and it still makes me laugh to imagine what an odd group of subversives we would seem to the people responsible for checking these photographs. A man in a wheelchair, an old lady, a pregnant dog, me, and a very rude placard. The policewoman asked my mother who she 'represented'. 'Old Age Pensioners' she replied.

"More police arrived, and eventually the 'real' protesters turned up organised by the N.J.M. Among them was Chris Searle, who had recently returned from working in Grenada and was devastated by the whole business. He was near to tears and said to Robert that he should do a song for Grenada. That's how 'Amber and the Amberines' came about."

"'Amber And The Amberines' is actually the name of a military rehearsal conducted by the US military covertly; 'Amber And The Amberines' being a euphemism for Grenada and the Grenadines. It was a rehearsal in case they ever had to invade a Caribbean island. I think they used some small islands in and around Puerto Rico to practice beachhead landings and so on."

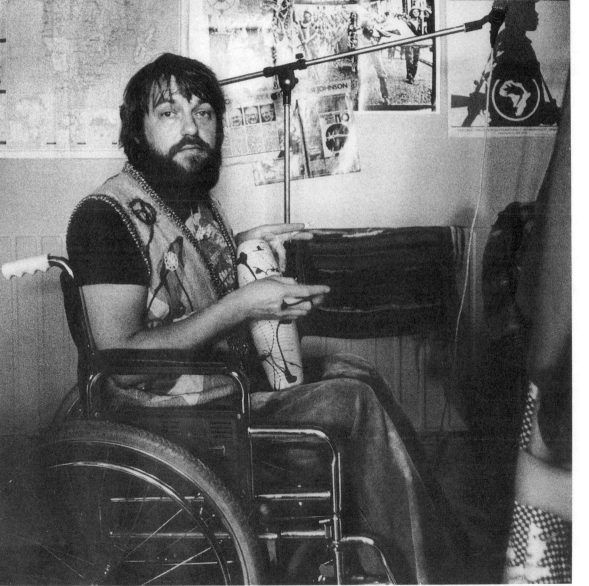

1984

"I have a very traditional attitude to music. With songs, I think, what are the chords, the harmonies, what's the rhythm, what's the tune, how are the words? Then I try to sing them right, and all the emotional energy goes into that. I just try to get it right. I don't consciously address myself to style. I think my voice is just a blank, but it comes out sad. What I do is more or less predictable. I'm not in the novelty industry. I just plough my furrow. Here's another Robert Wyatt protest song."

Spring — Blackwing Studios, sessions for 'Work In Progress' ep

released Aug (Rough Trade RT 149)
a) 'Biko' (P. Gabriel)
b) 'Yolanda' (P. Milanes)
c) 'Te Recuerdo Amanda' (V. Jara)
d) 'War Without Blood' (unknown)
RW, keyboards/percussion/vocals
This twelve inch extended play release consists of tracks a, b, c with 'Amber And The Amberines'. Track d is Robert's lyric set to a song regularly heard on Radio Moscow in 'the bad old days' and was never released.

"Why Biko? I have to defuse any big claims about this, you know. I have to restate that I'm just earning a living making records. It's what I do, and I think I may as well sing songs about what interests me. I don't really claim much more than that for them. I think the relationship between music and politics is that the kind of music you get is the result of the political situation, the result rather than the cause. Biko wouldn't have placed any hope in me singing about him, or Peter Gabriel writing about him. As a member of the Black Consciousness Movement, Biko was almost a Malcolm X to Mandela's Luther King — except Biko was religious and a pacifist and never tried and convicted for any criminal offence before they beat him to death. They had to reinterpret the laws of South Africa, posthumously, to justify his death on grounds of incitement to terrorism."

June 19 — Blackwing Studios, sessions for 'This Is The End'

released on first thousand copies of 'Work In Progress' ep though uncredited on record sleeve and label
Alfreda Benge, voice; RW, percussion/vocals

"It may not seem like much, but that little song means a lot to me. That's me and Alfie on that, and we used to sing it together in the car whenever we did any long distance driving. She's the one thing in my life that's made the most sense since...well, since I was Robert Wyatt."

Oct 31 — Cold Storage, sessions for various 'The Last Nightingale' ep

released mid-Nov (Re 1984)
Lindsay Cooper, piano/electric piano/bassoon/sopranino sax; Chris Cutler, drums/etc.; Bill Gilonis, guitar/bass; Tim Hodgkinson, piano/Moog/baritone sax/alto sax; RW, vocals on 'Moments Of Delight', 'In The Dark Year'

Chris Cutler:

"For nine months now, miners and their families have had roofs, food, clothes, and utilities to pay for — and no strike pay. Families living on £12 a week. How can anyone believe that they'd put up with that kind of hardship if they weren't fully behind the strike? A political strike, not a strike to be settled by pay negotiations. A strike to do no more than to uphold a signed agreement which the government want unilaterally to tear up. The miners are suffering their hardships to save not only their jobs but also the mining industry itself — a nationalised industry and therefore a national asset — for us, for the country as a whole. Not only are the miners and their families suffering to protect our national assets, but also, on 'our' behalf, the present government is busy trying to grab all the union assets (freezing millions against a £200,000 fine), offering Xmas bribes, importing expensive coal, paying for well over the odds oil and nuclear powered electricity, stunning policing bills, court costs, etc. to the tune of more than £3 a week per head of us. This is an involuntary contribution we are all forced to make so that our leaders can renege on a signed agreement and waste our national assets. I took no part in any ballot to break the coal strike. This money is financing hardship. It seems clear that the least we can do is to give money voluntarily to the miners and their families. It is them we want to support; their part is our part, unequivocally. Hence this record. Our work and all earned from it (from the record company and the distribution company too) are a concrete contribution to the miners' struggle. To this end, the entire income from the full pressing has been given, in advance, to the strike fund. So long as the strike continues, all monies from any future pressing will go the same way — and in an unsiezable form. I hope this proves to be the first of many."

Nov 14 — West 3 Studios, sessions for 'Old Rottenhat' lp

a) 'Castles Built On Sand' b) 'Old School Ties' c) 'East Timor' d) 'PLA' e) 'Chairman Mao'
These working titles are the first for several recording sessions towards a new album of original music.
'Chairman Mao' released Sep/86 on 'Re Records Quarterly Vol. 2 No.2' (Re 0202)
RW, keyboards/drums/vocal/lyric
First recorded in 1979 by Old and New Dreams. Composed by Charlie Haden.
'Castles Built On Sand' is retitled 'The Age Of Self' backed with 'Raise Your Banners High' by Grimethorpe Colliery Brass Band and G.C.H.Q. Trade Unions with 7:84 Theatre Co. England. Released Sep/85 (TUC/7.84). All proceeds to the TUC Miners Hardship Fund.

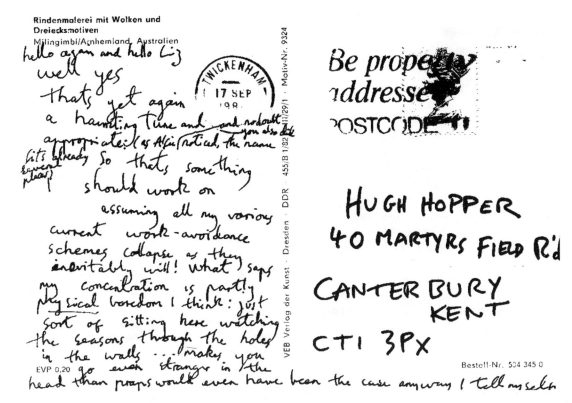

East Berlin in winter is no tropical island. Neither the beautiful broad boulevards running from the Brandenburger Gate through the historical part of town nor its vast modern squares such as Alexanderplatz were built to shelter Berliners from the bitter winds blowing across Central European plains.

But as I was in the German Democratic Republik for its third Rock For Peace Festival I spent most of the weekends indoors, inside the gigantic Palast der Republik. The walls of the palast's four floors were lined with stalls and exhibition stands, selling everything from metal jewelry and rock memorabilia, pottery, painting and wooden doves.

An enormous card addressed to the Pentagon and bearing a "Hands Off Nicaragua" message drew large crowds to sign it. There was no doubting as to who was the villain of the piece!

A very state of the art singer who was hot on the connection between capitalism and fascism flashed up big back projections to illustrate his songs. His images would edit together old and new — Guernica and Nicaragua — intercut with images of Hiroshima and so on. And each time shots of old Nazi leaders or new NATO leaders appeared they would be greeted with loud hooting from the terraces.

The disconcertingly named group Silly were anything but — sharp vocals, good subtle undertow in the drummer's loping wallops. A gent called Diestelmann, apparently the G.D.R.'s very own Taj Mahal, did a nice tribute to the late Alexis Korner. And Puhdys, whose brainchild these festivals were, proved to be immensely popular, drawing hundreds of only just teenagers to their feet. Sparklers were whisked out for the moodily lit numbers, that kind of thing.

Paradoxically Puhdys might attract the youngest fans but they are the oldest band. A very untrendy looking quartet of rock survivors, their all embracing show comes on like Pink Floyd doing an Xmas panto: giant inflatables, searchlights, chunks of heavy metal interspersed with programmatic synthesized minidramas, a John Lennon tribute featuring a pause for an appropriate slice of the original 'Imagine' — *"...nothing to kill or die for...and no religion too..."*

With so many groups all alien to me, coming in a very efficiently run relay marathon over the three days and all singing in a language I didn't think I would understand, I unsurprisingly got too wrapped up in the event itself to fix exactly who did what at a given moment. But I can't remember a better organized event or one whose message was conveyed with such impact.

NOTHING TO KILL OR DIE FOR

by Robert Wyatt

(first published in NME, March 10, 1984)

That said, one song in particular stands out. called 'No Bomb' it was performed by Berluc, who have obviously been Pistols fans in their time. Despite this unlikely route into the G.D.R. charts they were rewarded with the biggest hit of '83 — this blistering little ditty sung half in English for the benefit of a "Mr. President of America".

All the groups, mostly German, but also Italian, polish, and Russian, incidentally, agreed to do at least one song each to justify the Peace Festival's name. Any worthy-but-dull clouds you might expect to hover over the event didn't materialize however. For all the performances.

The last night's show, when just about every group encored with its "peace song" was particularly impressive. Such a totally focussed sequence of rock theatrics, normally an organizer's nightmare, went without a hitch, drawing steaming performances and a highly charged audience reaction.

Such cooperation was indicative of the event and illustrative of its central theme. None of the dirty tricks marring Western rock festivals was evident. No long drawn out soundchecks or tuning sessions. Groups didn't need to get louder the more famous they got.

The peace theme, too, suffused the city for the weekend. I am told there's a permanent exhibition of anti-warmongering graphics on the walls of Alexanderplatz Underground station.

After hours, in the university students club where upturned plastic buckets served as seats to a tiny stage, you could hear Ian Dury and The Blockheads records filling the intervals between the live acts. Recalling Berlin cabaret the club's acts this weekend were mainly satirical punk artists with assorted puppets who, to drum machine accompaniment, robot danced and jive talked through tight routines.

Ironically, though, the audience here assumed they were bang up to date London style, not realizing the fashion time warp dated them in comparison to some of the button smart, short back and sides establishment types hanging around the fringes of the Palast.

Personally, I refuse to apologize for saying I had a great weekend in East Berlin. The concentrated atmosphere of careful people trying that bit harder was paradoxically a welcome contrast to the lordly self assurance projected across the Atlantic from the vaticans of our mighty pop industry.

In addition I'm certain all those Lennon tribute peace anthems of the weekend indicate a kid of immortality that would have made the great man himself feel good. "...but I'm not the only one..."

No, John, I don't think you are.

1985

"I want to show you something which is my finger pointing. That's my finger pointing. Now there are two interesting things about a pointing finger. First of all you can look at the finger and secondly you can look where the finger is pointing. The problem I have as a musician is that I'm a pointing finger but it's not enough for me if people only look at my pointing finger. I would only be happy if people looked at what I was pointing at, because otherwise it's just a totally subjective game we're playing with the artist and the person looking at the artist."

Aug 30 — Powerplant, sessions for Robert Wyatt with The Swapo Sisters, 'The Wind Of Change'/'Namibia' 45

released Oct (Rough Trade RT168)

Jerry Dammers, piano/synths/guitar; Ben Mendelsohn, guitar; Lynval Golding, rhythm guitar; Mark Lockheart, soprano sax; Claire Hurst, saxophone; Dick Cuthell, cornet; Annie Whitehead, trombone; Ernest Mogotsi Mothle, double bass; Roy Dodds, drums; Bience Gawanas, Vaino Shivute, Lohmeier Angula, Theo Angula, Clarina Simbwayi, Richard Muzira, RW, vocals on 'The Wind Of Change'

'The Wind Of Change'/'Namibia' release is a joint effort by SWAPO (South-West Africa People's Organisation), the SWAPO singers, and the Repression and Political Prisoners Campaign, who elected Jerry to produce the music and Robert to be the lead singer. Both men undertake a series of media interviews, including an appearance on BBC TV's 'The Old Grey Whistle Test' program, to raise public awareness for the national liberation movement of Namibia. Rough Trade defers their standard percentage with all proceeds going to SWAPO. The promotional video for 'Wind Of Change' includes footage of the group performing the song on the steps of the South African embassy in London.

"There was a euphoria in the '60's when Dylan picked up on Woody Guthrie and it was felt that you could protest\your way out of Vietnam. However, the result of that movement is Ronald Reagan so the power of song to move continents was, er, overstated. That said, my friends in the anti-apartheid movement said that Jerry's record was a great boost and helped enormously in getting up interest when they were organising the protest's against Botha's visit here. So that had a real and tangible effect and the South Africans do seem afraid of pop. They've even banned Stevie Wonder. Maybe to find out how effective political pop is, we should ask our enemies!"

Summer — Acre Lane Studios, sessions for 'Old Rottenhat' lp

released Nov (Rough Trade, Rough 69)
a) 'Alliance'
b) 'The United States Of Amnesia'

c) 'East Timor'
d) 'Speechless'
e) 'The Age Of Self'
f) 'Vandalusia'
g) 'The British Road'
h) 'Mass Medium'
i) 'Gharbzadegi'
j) 'P.L.A'

Alfreda Benge, voice (i); RW, keyboards (except i)/piano (i)/percussion (except a, f, h)/vocals (except d)/compositions

For Michael Bettany

"Michael was an English lad from working class origins who was a conservative and worked his way up through the ranks of the British civil service to the top. And it was only when he got there that he found he had been misled. It wasn't a benevolent organisation he was working with, but a very snottish one, involved in manufacturing a cold war when there was no need to. And it was run by people with a hatred for the working classes whether they had made it or not. So for personal and moral reasons he decided to take sides with their enemies and was eventually imprisoned for trying to hand over secrets to the Russians — to warn them about what was being worked up. He's now in prison for a very, very long time — as a traitor always is. The funny thing is that the reason he didn't get anywhere was because the people he thought were Russians turned out to be double agents working for the British! The way he was treated by the press was either as a ridiculous naive person or a filthy traitor. But for a lot of reasons there's something very touching about his story for me, trying to realign your allegiances in the light of choice. We're always told we're fighting for freedom of choice, yet if you choose a different set of allegiances you get imprisoned for it.

*"Each song was chosen on quite a consistent basis, all part of a conscious attempt to make **un-misusable** music: music that couldn't be appropriated by the Right. This is also why the new stuff is much more straightforward. I was pushed into this by an alarming occurrence: I was fiddling around on the short wave radio when I heard one of my old songs being played on one of those Western propaganda programmes — The Voice Of America or Radio Free Europe. Blow me, I thought, I don't want my music used in this way. So I consciously set out to make records where the ambiguity was removed, records that would have to be rejected by anyone promoting Western culture. Now I make sure I always put a spanner in the works. A desperate move, but..."*

Sep — Akimbo 'So Long Trouble' ep released

(Forward Sounds International Forward 003)
(musicians, studio, and location unknown)
RW, vocal on 'The Machine', human woodblock on 'The Criminal'

Nov 26 — Cold Storage, sessions for News From Babel 'Letters Home' lp

released July/86 (Re Records, Re 1..14)

Lindsay Cooper, piano/keyboards/bassoon/sopranino sax/alto sax; Chris Cutler, drums/percussion; Zeena Parkins, harp/accordion; with Bill Gilonis, bass/guitar; Dagmar Krause, Sally Potter, Phil Minton, RW, vocals

2 Maurward
Close Stinsford
Dorchester
Dorset

DT2 8PY

Robert
Wyatt
c/o Rough
Trade
Records

Dear Mr. Wyatt,

I like your record 'old Rotten hat'.

I like the song 'poor little Alfie'.

who is Alfie?
How old is he?
why can't he sleep?
Why can't he draw?

love PLease write
to me
love Beatrice Dyer
age 5

1986

"It's so bloody difficult to do my own stuff: that's why I'd much rather do covers or quite happily get roped into other people's projects. I go into this state of trance when I'm working on my own and really I have very little control of what I'm going to come up with. The songs tend to suggest themselves so the word 'creative' is a misleading one. For me it's more like fishing, dangling a line over the keyboards and hoping something will jump out at you."

Spring (?) — Blackwing Studios, sessions for 'Pigs...(In There)'
released Sep on 'Artists For Animals' compilation (Slip SD 003)
RW, keyboards/percussion/vocal

Aug — sessions for Paul Haines 'Darn It!' CD
(studio unknown)
To be released late 93 by American Clave
Evan Parker, soprano sax; RW, piano/keyboards/drums/vocals on 'Curtzy'
'Darn It!' is a double CD project setting Paul Haines' poetry and lyrics to music by various friends and players, including Derek Bailey, Carla Bley, Paul Bley, Jack Bruce, George Cartwright, Milton Cardona, Alex Chilton, Tom Cora, Andrew Cyrille, Melvin Gibbs, Wayne Horvitz, Mary Margaret O'Hara, Gary Peacock, Don Pullen, Steve Swallow, John Oswald, John Tchicai, Carlos Ward, and Robert Wyatt among others.

Paul Haines:
"I met him through Evan Parker, well really through Carla I suppose, but mostly through Evan. We just walked over because Evan lived in Twickenham too. The curious thing is, when we walked in Alfie was painting something to 'Song Of The Jungle Stream', you know, that song from 'Tropic Appetites' (Bley/Haines lp). She didn't know I was coming over and I didn't know she'd be having that on! Since then he's become a very dear friend. We are in constant letter and tape exchange."

Sep or Oct — West 3 Studio, sessions for Michael Mantler 'Many Have No Speech' lp
released May/88 (German Watt 19)
The Danish Radio Concert Orchestra; Michael Mantler, trumpet; Rick Fenn, guitar; Marianne Faithfull, Jack Bruce, RW singing poems by Samuel Beckett, Ernst Meister, and Philippe Soupault.

In the autumn of 1986, Robert and Alfie receive an invitation from TV3 in the Catalan region of Spain to film an interview for the television series 'Arsenal'. The offer is accepted upon condition that the air-fare tickets are open-ended thus enabling a second six month stay in Casteldefells.

Nov 12 — TV3 Studios, Barcelona, Spain, Arsenal T.V. filming
broadcast Feb 4/87
RW, vocal/piano on 'Born Again Cretin'
A forty minute film entitled 'The Voyage Of Robert Wyatt', produced and directed by Juan Bufill. This career profile juxtaposes interview segments from Robert and Alfie with thoughtful video images set to a cross-section of songs.

Anti - Apartheid conference, Reggio Emilia, Italy, September 6/86

1987

"I've really thought alot about singing. I think it's an interesting instrument, the voice. For obvious reasons it's the only instrument everybody can use anyway. Any noise the voice makes is liable to have connotations spinning off it of the meaning of the words. So in that sense it's a very rich instrument to use. On the other hand it's a very difficult instrument to play, if you've only got my technique anyway, you can't really leap about. There was a time when I used to try and do scat influenced singing and try to be more like an instrument. And I thought that was the way out, just really develop speed and a wide range of octaves. But I can't listen to singers the way I listen to other musicians — I get really embarrassed when singers start doing funny things with their voice that clearly they wouldn't do in the normal course of your average telephone conversation. In a way I find it a limitation, I'm only comfortable singing fairly close to speech patterns. It's all down to confidence."

Jan 31 — TV3 Studios, Barcelona, Spain, sessions for Atlas TV
RW, keyboard/percussion/scissors
This episode of the Atlas series examines the frenetic conditions of urban Hong Kong. From the five minutes of music Robert recorded for the soundtrack, two minutes of a trombone sounding keyboard piece was used.

Feb 19 — Aprila Studios, Barcelona, Spain, sessions for Claustrofobia 'Repulsion' lp
released summer (Justine C-102)
Pedro Burruezo, guitars/vocal; Maria Jose Pena, piano; Antoni Baltar, drum programming/bass synth; RW, vocal on 'Tu Traicion'

In or around 1987, Robert and Alfreda make the decision to relocate their residence from Twickenham, London to the rural town of Louth in Lincolnshire county.

"There were just too many flashy cars, and we suddenly started to feel like aliens — like American Indians or something! Alfie, my wife, said 'I don't want to die in Twickenham', so basically we've come to die in Lincolnshire."

Thoughts of Wheelchairman
Robert Wyatt

They add dirt to the potatoes you see in shops, to make it look like they just came out of the ground.

The thing is, agriculture isn't what it was. There doesn't seem to be an economic farm in England! Farmers get 3 billion quid a year from the government. That's at least 16,000 quid per farm. Public grants to drain land. Guaranteed sale above world price. That's the Free Play Of Market Forces for you. The monetarists' Hidden Hand. No wonder they want to keep it hidden! I mean, imagine if the Workers found out and demanded the equivalent State subsidies to keep *working in guaranteed security*: bleedin' Communism that'd be wouldn't it...God forbid, eh?

Yes, and of *course the farmers are* all in the hock to the chemical industry. You needn't take my word for it! Have a look at *'Food for Thought'* (yours for the asking from PO Box 418, London SE99 6YE).

Whenever I think of refined sugar and flour, my quaquaversal thoughts turn to refined culture and Radio 3. I'm an atheist, you see; *I don't believe* in High Art. I'm not talking about aesthetics (which are pretty subjective: *if you doubt it consider your average* dog's favourite sniffing posts), I'm talking about Morals. It's just that I haven't noticed vast doses of Shakespeare, Beethoven, and Leonardo Da Vinci improving anyone's behaviour, or increasing anyone's capacity for compassion or generosity. In short, I see no really substantial evidence that <u>Great Art Is Morally Elevating</u>.

Mind you, I like a bit of Art (the deliberate evocation of magic? daydreaming?). A little framed something on the wall brightens up the shop no end, don't you find?

No, I'm only joking. I think aesthetics are rooted in function, and nurture my own aesthetic inclinations with the grim determination of a - well of a - *conscientious potato salesman delicately* powdering his freshly laundered, moontinted wares with Real Countrified Earth, just so as to - er - *Brighten Up the Shop,* I suppose...

It should be extraordinary the way people take people at their word:
"We call you, the Pope."
"I accept. I am the Pope."
"Look everybody! There's the Pope."
"We call you, intelligent."

"I accept. I am intelligent."
"I call myself, Avant-Garde."
"Well then, you must be more Avant-Garde then the people who don't call themselves Avant-Garde."
"I am an Art Expert."
"Then, tell us about Art, since you must know more about Art than those of us who don't get called Art Experts."
"I accept. I accept the name I have given myself. And, you must accept it too, otherwise This Show Can't Go On..."

ESMERELDA

Picasso did a sculpture of Esmerelda, his goat. In some kind of metal, I think. He had Esmerelda's tether attached to it. The sculpture, having never lived, is, of course, 'immortal'. Meanwhile, living goats come and go, die and metamorphose, and so on.

I saw an Art Expert on the telly who said: "This sculpture is the Essence of Goat. It is more real than the goat itself. It is eternal Goatness!" (I paraphrase.)

Now, this seems to me to be a typical Art Expert's remark. An artist wouldn't say that. Not what I call an *artist. Art Experts who are not themselves 'artists' often get their priorities upside down horse and cart wise.

Picasso shows us the beauty of life, and then is punished by being praised for 'transcending' it. Now that, to me, is blasphemy.

The Art Expert sees only A Picasso. Picasso sees the goat.

1988

1989

"There's been talk recently, in the last few years, of world music, people listening to music from outside the North Atlantic countries and so on. But to me the music that first inspired me, I suppose jazz and related musics, was a world music in a sense that I know of that Western, Northern European music has actually had as one of its basic ingredients an African element. Just as sculpture was totally transformed in the twentieth century — people like Picasso discovering African sculptures — so music, or popular music in the twentieth century, is totally transformed by Black Americans which is to say African Americans contribution. And while I was not particularly interested in politics originally, I couldn't reconcile the difference between the immense inspiration I got from this wonderful culture of Black America with the status of non-white people in the world around me. I couldn't make sense of it and I started to get very defensive. And when you start defending the music you start in the end defending the people who make it. So when you hear people who have given you more pleasure in your life than anybody else you can think of constantly being described as a problem, whose numbers must be limited, you think...you get angry. Not because you're nice or kind, you're defending what you love."

Sep — C.T.I. 'Core — A Conspiracy International Project' lp released

(Belgian Play It Again Sam BIAS 095)
Chris Carter, Cosey Fanni Tutti, keyboards/perussion/vocals; RW, vocal on 'Unmasked'; allartists, RW, voice on 'Core'. Each track is a joint project between Chris and Cosey and various artists/groups (Monte Cazazza, Boyd Rice, John Dunccan, Joe Potts, Lustmord, Coil). Sounds were mailed or brought to Studio 47 in Norfolk where they were manipulated, processed, composed, and mixed with the full collaboration of those involved.

"Chris Carter and Cosey Fanni Tutti, who used to be in Throbbing Gristle, now live in Norfolk and were putting together some tapes and asked me to collaborate. It was the first time I heard my own voice being used with a sampler. I actually had a tape of me singing 'Autumn Leaves' and some other words, and Cosey shuffled them about into little fragments. Though it's basically her singing and their music, it comes out feeling like me. They've got their own studio, are self-sufficient and do stuff. It was a true collaboration in that they did the work. I did the 'co', they did the 'laboration'."

"I left the CP a couple of years ago. It just seemed to be a launching pad for media pundits. I can see no difference between the stance of 'Marxism Today' and the David Owen/SDP viewpoint. When I joined the party in the late Seventies, the people I actually liked and got on with were very often the aging battle-scarred anti-Fascists who'd been in it since the Thirties and had been through a thing or two. There was a plumber who, despite the opportunity to get promoted, chose to stay at the hard end, and really lived the meaning of what he was doing. We used to go to 'Morning Star' bazaars and I completely fell in love with the people there.

"But then I felt disappointed when a much trendier bunch of post-Beatle people picked up on it, and sat around making sarcastic jokes about these old people because they listened to Paul Robeson and didn't know about what was going on today. I didn't like those people at all! I felt I was being patronised — 'Oh, we've got a musician, a real useful badge for our new image.' I wasn't interested in helping the right wing do what they do so well anyway, which is laugh at old lefties. Nearly every other Radio 4 play was doing something like that. It's too easy, and it's ageist as well."

Autumn — home, Louth, sessions for Ryuichi Sakamoto 'Beauty' lp

released Mar/90 (Virgin America VUSLP 14)
The Neo Geo Ensemble — Dali Kimoko-N'Dala, guitar; Paco Ye, percussion/vocal; Sibiri Outtara, percussion/vocal; Seidou 'Baba' Outtara, percussion/vocal; Pino Palladino, bass; Milton Cordona, shekere; Yoriko Ganeko, vocal; Misako Koja, vocal; Kazumi Tamaki, vocal; Ryuichi Sakamoto, keyboards/vocal; Brian Wilson, vocals; RW, lead vocal on 'We Love You'

Ryuichi Sakamoto:
   "I knew him from the Soft Machine, but the main thing was the single 'At Last I Am Free', which was a very big thing for me. I'll just never forget that voice. So I wrote a letter to him and said: 'The reason I need you Robert is to cover 'We Love You', a song about people's love you know, and I want the saddest voice in the world to sing it, and that's your voice.' So he agreed."

Dec 12 — Axis Studio, Sheffield, sessions for The Happy End 'Turn Things Upside Down' lp

released Apr/90 (Cooking Vinyl Cook 033)
Twenty-two piece big band; RW, vocals on 'Turn Things Upside Down'

The late eighties also saw the publication of Gigi Morinoni's book 'Robert Wyatt' by Stampa Alternativa in Rome. This ninety-six page book presents several interviews in Italian, reprints all post-Soft Machine lyrics, and comes with a one sided pink vinyl single of 'Chairman Mao'.

1990

"First of all, I am a real Minimalist, because I don't do very much. I know some minimalists who call themselves minimalist but they do loads of minimalism. That is cheating. I really don't do very much."

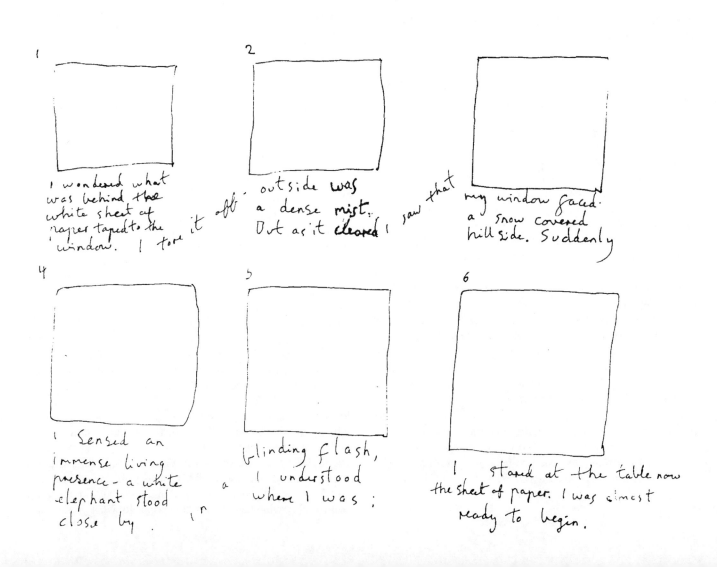

1

I wondered what was behind the white sheet of paper taped to the window. I tore it off,

2

outside was a dense mist. But as it cleared I saw that

my window faced a snow covered hillside. Suddenly

4

I sensed an immense living presence — a white elephant stood close by. In a

5

blinding flash, I understood where I was;

6

I stared at the table now the sheet of paper. I was almost ready to begin.

1991

"In a way I've got more technical confidence in doing my own things, for example not getting in another drummer or even another bass player but trying to do those parts myself. Not because I can play these instruments as well as other people but because when I do them it keeps the music more exactly in character and particular. If you're the pianist and the drummer and the bass player and the singer you really line those four up and make each one do exactly what he wants the other one to do. I've got more confidence about that now."

Feb 18 to Mar 4 — Chapel Studios, South Thoresby, sessions for 'Dondestan' lp

released Aug 27 (Rough Trade R2741)
a) 'Costa'
b) 'The Sight Of The Wind'
c) 'Catholic Architecture'
d) 'Worship'
e) 'Shrinkrap'
f) 'CP Jeebies'
g) 'Left On Man'
h) 'Lisp Service'
i) 'N.I.O. (New Information Order)'
j) 'Dondestan'
RW, vocals/keyboards (except c, e)/piano (except a, f, g)/acoustic guitar (e)/melodica (h)/percussion (except b, g)/compositions, except h) Hugh Hopper; Alfreda Benge, poems (a, b, c, d, e)
Note: 'Shrinkrap' is based on Charles Mingus' composition 'Boogie Stop Shuffle'.

"The fresh element for me here was — I found some poems that my wife wrote in the mid-eighties while we were in Spain and I thought I could put music to words, I always thought the other way round rather. And I found, maybe because I'd known these poems for five years they were, they started to sing themselves in my head, they started to turn into tunes. So I simply got out there with my fishing net, which is to say my piano, and caught them as they fell really, and put them onto tape. So that was a new thing for me and it was very exciting doing that. Also I like her poems because they just seem to be a list of observations but there is a kind of lot being said but isn't said.

"I call the record 'Dondestan' as a double meaning. 'Dondestan' is Spanish for 'where are they?' but it also sounds like some Eurasian republic you can't quite recall, or is about to declare itself independent of somebody else or something. I do feel at the moment like an exile from some country that I don't even know what the name of it was in the first place, and more, so many people I know seem to be nomadic exiles from something they were not quite sure where it was they came from. The songs have a kind of uprooted characteristic I think, that threads both my wife Alfie's lyrics and my own songs. It came out in different ways. It's kind of a record about uprootedness, floatingness."

In June, Alfreda Benge, Brian Conlan, Gina Kalla, and Vojislav Nesic begin work on a twenty minute promotional film for Rough Trade's release of 'Dondestan'. The video features Robert's reflections on, and splendid visuals for a selection of titles, and is broadcast on several television programs across Europe.

The media focus welcoming 'Dondestan' is an intensive summer long affair. Robert and Alfie find the guest room in their 19th century Lincolnshire home put to much use as accommodation for journalists from across Europe. Upon the release of 'Dondestan', a week at Chelsea Bridge House in London is arranged to receive the British press. The words and accolades are plentiful as evidenced by Alfie's collection of magazines and papers dubbed 'the Dondestan suitcase'.

Nov — home, Louth, sessions for France - Culture The Rhythm And The Reason radio series

broadcast Mar/92
RW, piano/vocal
A brief impromptu song with the introductory lyric 'The Rhythm and the Reason on France - Culture with Robert Wyatt, good evening' is used to begin this seven part career profile program.

Nov — home, Louth, Robert Wyatt - Part One video filming

broadcast Apr/93 on ARTE TV (France)
This twenty-four minute film consists of interview segments with two brief excerpts of Soft Machine filmed in Paris Mar 2/70 and performances of 'Catholic Architecture', melodica to lp recording of 'Lisp Service' on home stereo, drums to lp recording by Cuba's Orchestra Reve.

Nicholas Klotz (director):
"Robert's work has always been very important to me, today I have the feeling that his route embodies my generation's route. Musically, his inventions were so free and different from any other kind of music we were listening to at the time. But in those days being, thinking, and singing differently wasn't a handicap as it is today. The great thing about Robert is that he never tried to be different, he just was, and still is.

"As a film director one of my dreams was to film Robert singing. When I asked him to play the piano and sing something from 'Dondestan', he chose to perform 'Catholic Architecture.' I asked him not to make it too short, just for my pleasure. He laughed and said that it would last exactly two minutes and forty seconds. In order not to interfere with his singing I decided to shoot the song in one single shot. We made three prints, each exactly four minutes and fifty seconds long. During the shots I felt Robert was very tense, that's why he slowed down. The cameraman was moving all around the piano, closing up on his hands, his mouth, his eyes, then sliding across the score. When it was over, Robert told me he was very happy to have done it because it was the first time in a very long time since he had sung in front of people.'

"I don't think that anyone who hasn't been to the Wyatt's house in Louth can imagine the gentleness, the explosive humor, and the friendship you can feel flowing all around the house. In a few hours you will do and undo the world, speak about astrophysics, drink some white and red wine, listen to music from all over the world, visit the GB communist party on top of a pataphysical camel and talk about just anything you feel like, knowing that Robert knows exactly what you mean."

at home with Alfie and piano

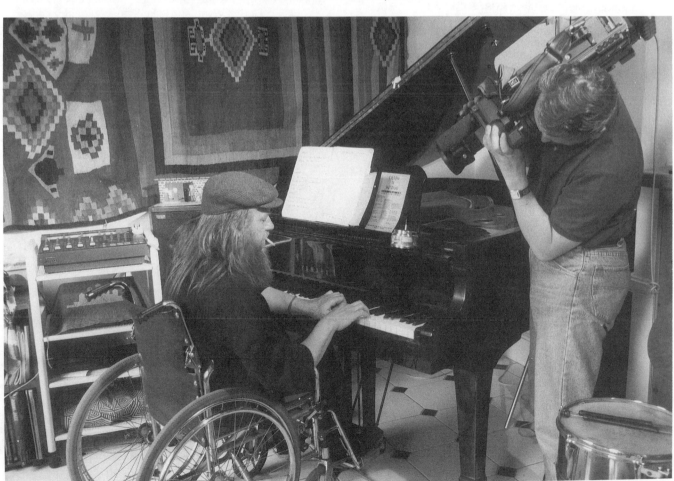

1992

"In Paris, Burroughs did this strange thing. Sitting with lights projected on him, sitting there not moving his mouth while a tape recorder read out his poems, which I thought was pretty cool! I've thought since, if it comes down to it, maybe that's the kind of performance I could do. Somebody who sits me there like Ironside in my chair and just plays tapes of my records! You want an appearance? Here I am! But don't expect me to sing at the same time — I'm not multi-talented!"

June — home, Louth, sessions for 'A Short Break' mini CD

released Sep 19 (Voiceprint VP108)
a) 'A Short Break'
b) 'Tubab'
c) 'Kutcha'
d) 'Venti Latir'
e) 'Unmasked'
RW, voice/piano/percussion/keyboards (except a)

Could you track down any information on a film made about ROBERT WYATT? It was being made around the time that 'Shipbuilding' was released, but that's all I know.
Bob Pearce, Warminster, Wilts

I read somewhere that a ROBERT WYATT biography is being pieced together. Any details? Also, I wouldn't mind reading a list of his favourite albums.
B Stacy, Chiswick, London W4

■ *First, the list of favourite albums. Robert says: "I love doing this desert island stuff – much easier than writing tunes. Mind you, favourites aren't necessarily the ones I listen to most, funnily enough. I mean, some favourites are special occasion ones, an atheist's version of carols.*
"What I play every day are hundreds of interchangeable flamenco, soul, and be-bop-hip-hop tapes. Anyway, I hope this list makes sense! (1) 'Three Windows' – MJQ & The New York Chamber Symphony; (2) 'The Jazz Giants '56' – Lester Young, Roy Eldridge, Jo Jones; (3) 'Blue Trane' – John Coltrane (with Kenny Drew etc); (4) 'Contemplation' – Yusef Lateef (with Nat Adderley etc); (5) 'Casta' – Lole y Manuel (Andalusian singer/arranger); (6) 'The Legendary Grupo Irakere In London – Vol 2'; (7) 'Kwela' – Gwigwi's Band ('67 LP with Dudu Pukwana); (8) 'Do It Yourself' – Ian Dury & The Blockheads) (9) 'Confessions Of A Pop Group' – The Style Council; (10) 'Metal Box' – PiL."
Regarding the film, Wyatt says that he and his wife, Alfie, were filmed for a Catalan TV programme called Arsenal around the time of 'Shipbuilding', but adds that Rough Trade put together a 20-minute video (presumably a promo for Wyatt's 'Dondestan' album) during the summer. Finally, that biography. Says Robert: "A Mike King of Ontario, Canada, is conscientiously putting a kind of disco-gigography together but I think he's beginning to wonder why he decided to do it! We haven't yet met he's visiting in the spring to check through the final draft."

On July 25, 1992 , the life of Gary Windo was taken by a heart attack at age 52. For fifteen years Gary had been living in New York City where he gave private saxophone lessons, worked in saxophone shops, and played with a variety of jazz, rock, and rhythm 'n' blues groups (including his own). The body of work he created and contributed to since the late '60's is a legacy boundless in volume and borderless in breadth; imbued throughout with an unmistakable original tone and artistry, by turns explosive and tender. It was Gary Windo's lust for life, exuberance, and wild humour which left an indelible impact on his music and unforgettable memories for old and new friends alike.

above: Frank Lowe and Gary Windo, Knitting Factory, NYC91
below: Robert Wyatt and Mike King, Louth, Feb 28/92

extraordinary - people never seem so
ALIVE as the moment they're at rest at last:
my ears have been tingling just right
now, the last few days, to the tape you
sent us of Gary, Ron Mathewson, Richard Sinclair etc
which I was re-assessing for possible
budget CD on some little friendly label -
extraordinary, I sort of shrugged them off
on first re-hearing, then came back to
them struck by the sense of adventure
into the unknown of them, frustrated though
by relatively poor quality of posterity
technically speaking, but thinking, really these
uncelebrated moments, like the things with
Laurie Baker, and in Spain, are the most
resonant of my musical memories.

§ Terribly enough, I must
admit to another sensation: anger,
that my old comrades are escaping one
by one to 'the bush of ghosts' and leaving
the dwindling rest of us stranded to
fumble on ... definitely, yes, especially since
so many friends recently died -- the woman
who got my records in the local shop, another
who worked in another nearby shop, the nice butcher
who got me scraps for flossie, and Lulu, and a dear
old commie friend of my mothers. Suddenly, all gone..

1993

"You take things in and you make them your own, and then it's hard to know what is an influence and what is now you. I think my biggest influence in a way is constantly thinking that I still haven't got it right, and listening to what I've done that I didn't like and trying to get it right next time. In practical terms that is the thing that influences what I do, trying not to make the mistakes I made last time."

Mar 2 and 3 — Chapel Studios, South Thoresby, sessions for Ultramarine 'United Kingdoms' CD
released Aug 23 (Blanco Y Negro TBD)
Ian Cooper, acoustic guitar/keyboards/programming; Paul Hammond, bass/keyboards/programming; augmented by various guests including RW, vocals

Notes:
 1 — a) The lyrics of 'Kingdom' are adapted from 'The Song Of the Lower Classes' by Ernest Jones (c. 1848) b) The lyrics of 'Happy Land' are adapted from a parody of the popular Victorian song of same name c) The co-writing credit to Wyatt acknowledges the melody he composed for these lyrics.
 2 — a) 'Kingdom' was first released in June as a CD single (Blanco Y Negro TBD) along with an extended mix and 'Goldcrest', which includes samples of Robert's vocals b) The promotional video for 'Kingdom' features Robert in their garde dressed as King Arthur.

"P. S. — My very last word — It's an eye opener to see what others see. My subjective experience is probably as unreliable as anyone else's, so I wouldn't quite know what I'd change if I were writing my own story, especially since I've tried to bulk-erase the more debilitating experiences from my memory bank, to regain my confidence at the expense of the objective truth."

ADDITIONS & CORRECTIONS

1963

June 3 - Daevid Allen Trio, Marquee. Victor Schoenfield's tape is labelled June 3, but Melody Maker's gig advert for Live new departures is Tuesday June 4th. (By the way, Victor Schoenfield declined Soft Machine's invitation to manage the group's affairs in 1967. He thought they were too pop).

1966

April 1 - Wilde Flowers at Toft's in Folkestone. In fact this gig flyer was published in 1967. Robert Wyatt had left Wilde Flowers by this time.

Jun 24 - Wilde Flowers, Margate. (This was Pye Hastings first gig with the Wilde Flowers).

Autumn - Soft Machine demo recordings. Robert remembers a session that included Ron Rubin on double bass that "must have been very early on because I didn't know what musicians had to be paid for their sessions."

1967

That's Mark Ellidge holding the camera in the mirror in the Speakeasy photo.

March - unnamed collective, ICA, is March 19 (Sunday), March 24 - London School of Economics

Spring - For Greenwich Theatre, Deptford (augmented by Gilli Smyth, poems/vocals)

April 8 - The Electric Poets, Roundhouse (supporting Pink Floyd)

The St Tropez Town Square gig credited as August, in fact took place on July 4th.

Autumn - Cambridge (venue unknown), French radio sessions, Amsterdam (venue unknown)

December 5 - BBC Top Gear recording. A recently excavated recording confirms that Strangest Scene was the original title of Lullabye Letter. Robert doesn't play piano on this session.

1968

January 12 - Drury Lane Arts Lab included dancer Graiella Martinez's last appearance with the group.

1969

Before autumn the trio were recorded individually by soundman Bob Woolford in his sitting room; Hugh and Mike with bass and keyboard loops, Robert with echoplex. These tracks were mixed together with a gig tape by Bob and played at a multi media event at the Roundhouse called Spaced.

December 27 - Superstar Jam Session, Roundhouse. Noel Redding: "My diary re: 27 December 1969 - Went to the Roundhouse had a blow with Mitch, Jack Bruce, Capaldi, Dave Mason and Neil Landon. I also recall Robert being involved. There were many occasions I played with Robert, The Scene Club - probably more stuff in the studio (Eddie Kramer may even have these tapes?) My memories of Robert as a drummer were very good. We even talked about getting a band together."

1970

June 12 - Hull (venue unknown)

September - sessions for Tippett's Dedicated to You... LP. Robert Wyatt, voice on Five After Dawn.

October 19 - Anatomy of Pop filming includes interviews with all group members, and a performance of As If.

1971

March (late)- Radio Bremen recording session includes a remarkable bass/drum duet and an unaccompanied scat vocal minus the usual echoplex treatment.

Oct 15 - Kevin Ayers, Daevid Allen and Gong, City University.

Oct 24 - Kevin Ayers, Daevid Allen and Gong, Roundhouse (augmented by RW)

November 11 - Kevin Ayers and Gong, Hammersmith Town Hall.

November 13 entry was in fact Louis Moholo drumming.

Centipede - RCA produced a promotional film with footage of the group on and off stage, and various interviews.

1972

The February to March entry for Lol Coxhill, Toverbal, Maashuis is in fact September 14 at Paradiso, Amsterdam. The March 20 entry is for Kevin Ayers. March 21 - Kevin Ayers, Kensington House, BBC Top Gear recording.

December - Matching Mole on Rockenstock (French TV), Pierre Lattes was the producer.

1975

January 8 - Pacific Eardrum, The Phoenix. Bob Bertles, Brian Smith (saxes), Big Jim Sullivan (guitar), Dave MaCrae (kybds), Bruce Lynch (bass), Tony Hicks (drums), augmented by RW (percussion) second set only.

1976

April - Gary Windo's Steam Radio Tapes sessions. In fact Robert's vocal was recorded at his home as Britannia Row wasn't wheelchair accessible.

1981

(circa) - Robert also recorded with the punk group Oxy and the Morons, playing piano and singing on a track entitled War. Further details unknown.

 ROBERT WYATT & THE SWAPO SINGERS

INTERNATIONAL DISCOGRAPHY

Compiled by Manfred Bress, editor of Germany's Canterbury Nachrichten.

The following notation has been used in this discography:
FOC - Fold out cover
NFC - No fold out cover
GC - Gimmick cover
NGC - No gimmick cover
DC - Different cover
LC - Lyrics on cover
FOS - Fold out sleeve (7" only)
DPS - Different picture sleeve
LIS - Lyrics on inner sleeve
OST - Original soundtrack

ROBERT WYATT

LP:

01) The End Of An Ear
 (70) UK CBS 64 189
 (80) UK CBS 31 846
     F Barclay 920 308

02) Rock Bottom
 (74) UK Virgin V 2017
     US Virgin VR 13-112
     I Virgin Orlando ORL 8307

03) Ruth Is Stranger Than Richard
 (75) UK Virgin V 2034
     D Ariola 89 061 XOT
 (81) J Victor VIP 4100

02/03) Rock Bottom / Ruth Is Stranger Than Richard [2LP, FOC]
 (80) UK Virgin VGD 3505

04a) Nothing Can Stop Us [sampler of 7"s & "Born Again Cretin" & "Red Flag", BKL]
 (82) UK Rough Trade ROUGH 35
     NL Roadrunner RR 9983

04b) [RI, w extra track "Shipbuilding"]
 (83) UK Rough Trade ROUGH 35
 (86) US Gramavision 18-8614-1

05) The Animals Film [OST]
 (82) UK Rough Trade ROUGH 40

06) 1982 - 1984 [Sampler, LC in English/Spanish, cont 12" No: 02 & 03, & "You're Wondering Now" by Clement Seymour, non-LP]
 (84) US Rough Trade RTSP 25
     J Tokuma 25 RTL-20

07a) Old Rotten Hat [FOC, LC]
 (85) UK Rough Trade ROUGH 69

07b) [NFC, LIS]
     NL Megadisc MD 7981

08a) Dondestan [w LS]
 (91) UK Rough Trade R 2741

08b) [LIS]
     D Rough Trade RTD 101-1234-1

CD:

02) Rock Bottom
 (89) UK Virgin CDV 2017

 (89) J Virgin VJD 5022

03) Ruth Is Stranger Than Richard
 (89) UK Virgin CDV 2034
 (89) J Virgin VJD 5023

04) Nothing Can Stop Us [w extra track "Shipbuilding", w BKL]
 (86) F Rough Trade ROUGH CD 35

07a) Old Rotten Hat [w BKL & lyrics]
 (86) F Rough Trade ROUGH CD 69

07b) Late 70's - Early 80's / Old Rotten Hat [2CD-Box]
 (87) J Tokuma 27 JC-195

08) Dondestan [w BKL & lyrics]
 (91) UK Rough Trade R 2741 CD
     D Rough Trade RTD 101-1234-2

09) A Short Break [Mini-CD, w BKL]
 (92) A Voiceprint VP 108CD

10) The End Of An Ear
     F Col 473005-2

11) Mid Eighties
     UK Rough Trade R2952

CD Sampler:

01) Robert Wyatt [Sampler cont 7" No: 05, 06, 07 & 08]
 (81) I Rough Trade/Base RT 0007

02) Late 70's - Early 80's [Sampler cont 12" No: 02 & 03 + 7" No: 05, 06, 07, 08 - except "Trade Union" & "Stalingrad", w BKL & lyrics]
 (85) J Tokuma 32 JC-109

03) Robert Wyatt Compilation [parts of LP No: 06 & 09 & 12" No: 02, w BKL]
 (90) US Gramavision R2 79459

12"

01) Arauco, Caimanera / At Last I Am Free, Strange Fruit [PS]
 (81) D Phonogram 6005 139

02) Shipbuilding / Memories Of You, Round Midnight [PS]
 (82) UK Rough Trade RT 115T
     D Rough Trade RTD 03T

03) Work In Progress: [Biko, Amber and the Amberines / Yolanda, Te Recuerdo Amanda TLC, PS]
 (84) UK Rough Trade RTT 149

04) I'm A Believer, Yesterday Man / Team Spirit, Memories [A1+2, B2: non-LP, PS, rec 1974 - 1977]
 (84) UK Virgin Wyatt 1

05) The Wind Of Change / Namibia [LC, all non-LP, w SWAPO Singers, ext vers, Wyatt only A-side]
 (85) UK Rough Trade/SWAPO RTT 168
     NL Megadisc MD 125 292

06) Shipbuilding / At Last I Am Free [DJ]
 (86) US Gramavision 18-1212-1

07) The Peel Sessions: Soup Song, Alifib / I'm A Believer, Sea Song [all different versions, B1: non-LP, rec solo 10.09.1974, PS]
 (87) UK Strange Fruit SFPS 037

CD - Single:

01a) The Peel Sessions: Soup Song, Alifib / I'm A Believer, Sea Song [same as 12" No. 07, lim edition]
(89)   UK Strange Fruit SFPSCD 37

01b) [dif cover]
US Dutch East India DEI 8336-2

01c) [dif cover]
F Strange Fruit 672 005

7":

01a) I'm A Believer / Memories [all non-LP]
(74)   UK Virgin VS 114

01b) [PS]
D Ariola 13 617 AT

01c) [DPS]
SP Ariola 13 617 AT

01d) [DPS]
NL Virgin 13 591 AT

01e) [DPS]
F Virgin 640 040

01f) [DPS]
YU TRB S 53 881

01g) I'm A Believer [mono / stereo]
US Virgin VR 56 000

02) Yesterday Man / Sonia [A: non-LP]
(74)   UK Virgin VS 115

03) Yesterday Man / I'm A Believer [all non-LP, PS]
(74)   F Virgin 640 059

04) Arauco / Caimanera [PS]
(80)   UK Rough Trade RT 037

05a) At Last I Am Free / Strange Fruit [PS]
(80)   UK Rough Trade RT 052

05b) [FOS]
(81)   J Rough Trade RT-6

06) Stalin Wasn't Stalling / Stalingrad [B-side: Peter Blackman, PS]
(81)   UK Rough Trade RT 046

07) Grass / Trade Union [B-side: Disharhi, INS]
(81)   UK Rough Trade RT 081

08) Man To Woman [OST of musical by Marsha Hunt, 4-track-EP, 1 track of Robert Wyatt: "All she wanted was Marlon Brando", non-LP, PS]
(82)   UK Virgin VS 499

09a) Shipbuilding / Memories of you [PS]
(82)   UK Rough Trade RT 115

09b) [RI in 4 different foldoutsleeves]
(83)   UK Rough Trade RT 115

10) Amber and the Amberines / ? [DJ, white label]
(84)   UK Rough Trade RTT

11) Biko / Yolanda [DJ, white label]
(84)   UK Rough Trade RTT 149

12) Age of Self / Raise Your Banners High [A: Robert Wyatt, B: by John Tams & Grimetorpe Grass Band, PS]
(85)   UK 7.84

TUC 784

13) The Wind Of Change / Namibia [Robert Wyatt only A-side, w SWAPO Singers, all non-LP, PS, LC]
(85)   UK Rough Trade/SWAPO RT 168

14) Chairman Mao [one-sided, red or pink vinyl, non-LP, PS]
(87)   ISCONC 002

Tape:

01) Robert Wyatt / Meccano [C 40, w BKL, illustrations & interview w R. Wyatt, music only by Meccano]
(81)   F Tago Mago 4751

ROBERT WYATT with SOFT MACHINE

LP:

01) Rock Generation Volume 7 [one side: The T-Bones, rel 1971]
(67)   F Byg 529 707

02) Rock Generation Volume 8 [one side: Mark Leeman Five, rel 1971]
(67)   F Byg 529 708

03a) Faces and Places Volume 7 [cont Soft Machine sides of LP: 01 & 02]
(72)   F Byg 529 907
J Byg YX 6027

03b) Soft Machine [DC]
(73)   D Metronome 2001.137

03c) At the Beginning [DC]
(77)   UK Charly CR 30 014
(80)   I Oxford OX 3157

03d) At the Beginning [DC]
D Bellaphon CR 3058

03e) At the Beginning [DC]
(77)   F Charly 2933 212

03f) Soft Machine [DC]
(80)   US Piccadilly PIC 3331

03g) At the Beginning [DC]
(82)   UK Charly CR 30 196

03h) Memories [DC]
(82)   US Accord SN 7178

03i) Jet Propelled Photographs
(88)   PO Decal LIK 36

04a) The Soft Machine - Volume One [FOC, GC = wheelcover]
(68)   US ABC Probe CPLP 4500

04b) [FOC, NGC]
US ABC Probe CPLP 4500 X
J Probe SR-303
(86)   UK Big Beat WIKA 57

04c) [DC, NFC]
F Barclay 0 920 082

04d) We Did It Again [DC]
(76)   NL Ariola 27 135 ET

04e) Soft Machine Vol 1 [DC] (RI)
I Record Bazaar RB 73

(73)   J Toshiba IPP 80899

05a) The Soft Machine Volume Two [FOC]
(69)   US ABC Probe CPLP 4505 S
        J Probe SR-348
(86)   UK Big Beat WIKA 58

05b) [NFC, DC]
        UK ABC Probe SPB 1002
        US ABC Probe 4505

05c) [DC]
(78)   I Record Bazaar RB 159

05d) [DC]
(83)   I Orizone ORL 8663

05 e) [DC] (RI)
        F Barclay 0 921 019

04/05a) The Soft Machine Volume 1 & Volume 2 [2LP, FOC]
(69)   UK Probe GTSP 204 (GTT 2041/2)
        I Probe 3C 154-50185/6

04/05b) The Soft Machine Collection [2LP, FOC, DC] (RI)
        UK ABC ABCD 602

04/05c) The Soft Machine Milestones [2LP, FOC, DC] (RI)
        UK Probe 5C 184-50185/6

04/05d) The Soft Machine [2LP-Box, DC]
(73)   US Command RSSD 964-2

04/05e) Soft Machine 1 & 2 (Architects of Space Time) [2LP, FOC, DC]
(75)   F WEA Atlantic 60 113

06) Third [2LP, FOC, w "Facelift" rec live at Fairfield hall, Croydon 04.01.1970 & Mothers club, Birmingham 11.01.1970]
(70)   UK CBS 66 246
        US Columbia G 30 339
        J CBS Sony 50336-37

07a) Fourth [GC]
(71)   UK CBS 64 280

07b) [NGC]
        US Columbia C 30 754
        J CBS ERIA 53003
LPs No 08 to No 13 (Fifth, Pop Spectacular 23, Six, Seven, Bundles, Softs are without Robert Wyatt)

14) Triple echo [3LP-Box, BKL, Sampler cont 7" No: 1, parts of LPs: 03, 04, 05, 07, 08, 09, 10, 11, 12 & unreleased material & different versions recorded 1967 - 1976]
(77)   UK Harvest SHTW 800
LPs No 15 & 16 (Alive and Well In Paris, The Land of Cockayne are without Robert Wyatt)

17) Live at the Proms 1970 [rec live at Royal Albert Hall, 13.08.1970]
(88)   UK Reckless RECK 5

18) The Peel sessions [2LP, FOC, LC, BBC sessions rec 1969 - 1971]
(90)   UK Strange Fruit SFRLP 201

CD:

03a) Jet Propelled Photographs [w BKL]
(89)   F Charly CD 197

03b) Soft Machine (& Graham Bond Organisation - Live 1964)
(89)   J Century 29ED 6026

04/05) The Soft Machine Volumes One & Two
(89)   D Big Beat CDWIKD 920

06) Third
(88)   EEC Charly LIKD 35
        US Columbia CGK 30339

07) Fourth [w BKL]
(91)   J Epic/Sony ESCA 5417

17) Live at the Proms 1970
(88)   UK Reckless CD RECK 5

18a) The Peel Sessions [2CDs, w lyrics]
(90)   UK Strange Fruit SFRCD 201

18b) [dif cover]
        F Strange Fruit 672 009

Live In Concert
(93)   UK Windsong WINCD 031

Sampler:

01a) The Soft Machine [edited from "Volume 1" and "Volume 2"]
(69)   DEMI Hrzu SHZE 908 BL

01b) [DC]
        NL EMI / Stateside 5C 054.91600

01c) [DC, side 2 of LPs: No 04 & 05]
        NL S. R. International 201 657

01d) [DC, side 1 of LP: No 04 & 05]
        NL EMI / Stateside D 109/5
Sampler - CD:- Sampler No 02:"The Untouchables" (without Robert Wyatt)

03) As If ... [compiled of LPs No: 06, 07, 08 & 10]
(91)   UK Elite 006CDP

7":

01a) Love Makes Sweet Music / Feelin' Reelin' Squeelin'
(67)   UK Polydor 56 151

01b) [PS]
        NL Polydor 65 151

02) Joy Of A Toy / Why Are We Sleeping
(69)   US ABC Probe 45-452

ROBERT WYATT with MATCHING MOLE

LP:

01) Matching Mole
(72)   UK CBS 64 850
(82)   UK CBS 32 105

02) Matching Mole's Little Red Record [IS]
(72)   UK CBS 65 260
        US Columbia KC 32 148

CD:

01) Matching Mole [w BKL & lyrics]
(91)   J Epic/Sony ES CA 5425
(92)   A Columbia COL 471 489-2

F Columbia COL 471 489-2

02) Matching Mole's Little Red Record
    (92)   A Columbia COL 471 488-2
            F Columbia COL 471 488-2

7":

01) O Caroline / Signed Curtain
    (72)   UK CBS S 8101

Related records with Robert Wyatt:

AKIMBO
12":
01) So long trouble, The machine / C & C Blues, The criminal, Kalimbo 2 [PS]
    (85)   UK Forward 003

DAEVID ALLEN
LP:
01a)Bananamoon [FOC]
    (71)   FByg 529 345
    (78)   UK Charly CR 30 165
01b) [NFC]
    (78)   D Bellaphon CR 3050
01c) [DC]
    (75)   UK Caroline C 1512
CD:
01) Bananamoon [w BKL]
    (90)   F Charly CD LIK 63

DAEVID ALLEN TRIO
CD:
01) "Live 1963" [rec 03.June 1963 & Mr Head & one Soft Machine track]
    (93) UK Voiceprint VP122CD

KEVIN AYERS
LP:
01) The Joy Of A Toy [FOC,LC]
    (69)   UK Harvest SHVL 763
            US Capitol SKAO 421
02) Shooting At The Moon [& The Whole World]
    (70)   UK Harvest SHSP 4005 DEMI IC 062 04556
    (90)   UK Beat Goes On BGOLP 13
01/02a) The Joy Of A Toy / Shooting At The Moon [2LP, FOC]
    (75)   UK Harvest SHDW 407
            F Pathe 2C 1845 2277/8
01/02b) [2LP-Box, INS]
    (85)   SP EMI Harvest 156 260 362/3
03) Whatevershebringswesing [FOC]
    (72)   UK Harvest SHVL 800
    (88)   UK Beat Goes On BGOLP 11
04a) Bananamour [FOC, BKL, LC]
    (73)   UK Harvest SHVL 807
            F Pathe SHVL 807
04b) [DC]
    (86)   UK EMI EMS 1124
04c) [DC, w extra song: "Carribean Moon"]
            US Sire SAS 7406
03/04) Whatevershebringswesing/Bananamour [2LP, FOC, LC]
            F Pathe 2C 1505 2507/8
06) June 1, 1974 [live w John Cale, Nico, Eno]
    (74)   UK Island ILPS 9291
            D Ariola 802 150
            AUS Island L 35 241

CD:
01) The Joy Of A Toy
    (90)   UK Beat Goes On BGOCD 78
02) Shooting At The Moon
    (90)   UK Beat Goes On BGOCD 13
03) Whatevershebringswesing
    (89)   UK Beat Goes On BGOCD 11
04) Bananamour
    (92)   UK Beat Goes On BGOCD 142
06) June 1, 1974
    (90)   UK Island IMCD 92
Sampler:
02) Banana Productions - The Best Of Kevin Ayers [2LP, FOC, Sampler, cont songs of LPs No: 01, 02, 03, 05, 07, 08 & 10]
    (89)   UK Harvest EM 2032
Sampler-CD:
02) Banana Productions - The Best Of Kevin Ayers [4 songs less, w BKL]
    (89)   UK Harvest CZ 176

CENTIPEDE
LP:
01a)Septober Energy [2LP, FOC, LC]
    (71)   UK RCA Neon NE 9/1-2
01b)[DC, LC]
    (74)   UK RCA DPS 2054
            US RCA CLP2-5042
CD:
01) Septober Energy
    (92)   D Dandisc CENT 1

CORE
LP:
01) CORE - A Conspiracy International Project [INS, w Robert Wyatt, Coil, a.o.]
    (88)   B Play It Again Sam BIAS 095
CD:
01) CORE - A Conspiracy International Project
    (91)   B Play It Again Sam BIAS 095 CD

LOL COXHILL
LP:
01) Ear Of the Beholder [2LP, FOC]
    (71)   UK Dandelion DSD 8008 (K 69001)
            US Ampex C 10 132
04) The Story So Far ... / Oh ... Really? [one side Steve Miller]
    (74)   UK Caroline C 1507

KEVIN COYNE
LP:
13) Sanity Stomp [2LP-Box, one LP w Ruts, one LP w Robert Wyatt]
    (80)   UK Virgin VGD 3504
            D Ariola 301 427-406
CD:
13) Sanity Stomp [w BKL]
    (91)   UK Virgin CDVM 3504

EIRE APPARENT
LP:
01) Sunrise [with help of Robert Wyatt, produced by Jimi Hendrix]
    (69)   US Buddha BDS 5031
CD:
01) Sunrise [w one extra track]
    (91)   D Repertoire REP 4174-WZ

BRIAN ENO
LP:
02) Taking Tiger Mountain (By Strategy) [FOC]
    (74)   UK Island ILPS 9309
               D Ariola 88 443
               F Island 9299 328
    (77)   UK Polydor 2302 068 (EGLP 17)
               US Polydor EG ENO 2
               D Polydor 2344 080 (RI)
               J Polydor 23 MM-0123
03) Another Green World
    (75)   UK Island ILPS 9351
06) Before And After Science [w 4 different prints]
    (77)   UK Polydor 2302 071 (EGLP 32)
               D Polydor 2304 087
               US Polydor EG ENO 4
08) Music For Airports [IS]
    (78)   UK Ambient AMB 001 EGED 17
               D Polydor 2344 132
               US Polydor EG EGS 201 (RI)
               J Polydor/EG MPF 1229
CD:
02) Taking Tiger Mountain (By Strategy)
    (87)   UK Virgin EGCD 17
06) Before And After Science
    (87)   UK Virgin EGCD 32
08) Music For Airports
    (87)   UK Virgin EEGCD 17
Sampler:
01) More Blank Than Frank [compiled of LPs No: 01, 02, 03 & 06, IS]
    (86)   UK Polydor EG EGLP 65
               D Polydor 829 036-1
Sampler-CD:
01) Desert Island Selection [cont some different songs as LP]
    (86)   UK Virgin EGCD 65
               D Polydor 829 036-2

EPIC SOUNDTRACKS
7":
01) POPULAR CLASSICAL: Jelly, babies / A 3-acre floor, Pop in packets
    (81)   UK Rough Trade RT 084

VIVIEN GOLDMAN
12":
01) Launderette / Private armies, P.A. dub [PS]
    (81)   US Window 99-05 EP
7":
01) Launderette / Private armies [FOS]
    (81)   US Window WIN 1

PAUL HAINES
CD:
01) Darn It
               D Clave AMCL 1014 2

HAPPY END
LP:
01) Turn things upside down [FOC, LC]
    (90) UK Cooking Vinyl COOK 033
CD:
01) Turn things upside down [w BKL & lyrics, w 2 extra tracks]
    (90) UK Cooking Vinyl COOK CD 033

DON "SUGARCANE" HARRIS
LP:
01) Got the blues (recorded live at Berlin Jazz Festival, 04. & 07.11.1971)
    (72)   DMPS 68.029

HATFIELD AND THE NORTH
LP:
01a) Hatfield and the North [FOC]
    (73)   UK Virgin V 2008
               US Virgin VR 13-110
               D Ariola 87 803 IT
    (82)   J Victor VIP 4154 (VIP 6910)
    (84)   UK Virgin OVED 131
01b)[NFC](RI)
               I Virgin ORL 8306
03) Afters [Sampler cont 5 livesongs rec 1973 - 1975 & 7" No: 01, LS]
    (80)   UK Virgin VR 5
CD:
01) Hatfield and the North [w 2 extra songs of 7" No: 01]
    (87)   UK Virgin CDV 2008
    (89)   J Virgin VDJ 5020

JIMI HENDRIX
CD:
01) Jimi Hendrix 50th birthday-CD - Long Distance Calling...
    (92)   UK Univibes 001

HENRY COW
LP:
04a) Concerts [2LP, FOC, rec live at London, 08.05. & 21.05.1975, Udine, Italy,13.10.1975, Oslo, Norway, 25.07.1975 & Groningen, Holland, 26.09.1974]
    (75)   UK Caroline CAD 3002
               D Ariola 800 345-406
    (78)   UK Compendium FIDARDO 1
    (82)   UK Broadcast BC 2
04b) [DC]
               FLTM 1011/2
04c) [DC, LIS in english and italian]
    (77)   I L'Orchestra OLD 01/02

LAST NIGHTINGALE
12":
01) THE LAST NIGHTINGALE: Moments of delight, In the dark year / Back in the playground blues, Bittern storm revisited, On the beach of Cambridge [B1&3: by Adrian MITCHELL, B2: remixed version, LS, INS, PS]
    (84)   UK Re 1984

MICHAEL MANTLER
LP:
04) The Hapless Child and Other Inscrutable Stories [FOC, LC]
    (76)   DWatt /4
05) Silence [FOC, LC]
    (77)   DWatt /5
19) Many have no speech [LIS]
    (88)   DWatt /19
CD:
04) The Hapless Child and Other Inscrutable Stories [w BKL & lyrics]
    (88)   DWatt /4 (831 828-2)
19) Many Have No Speech [w BKL & lyrics]
    (88)   DWatt /19 (835 580-2)

PHIL MANZANERA
LP:
01) Diamond Head [LIS]
    (75)   UK Island ILPS 9315
               D Ariola 88 750 XOT
    (77)   UK Polydor Deluxe 2302 062
               D Polydor 2459 352
               US Atco SD 36-113 (RI)
               J Polydor MPF 1101
CD:
01) Diamond Head [w BKL & lyrics]
    (88)   J Virgin VDJ 28 055
Sampler:
01) Guitarrissimo [IS, compiled of LPs No: 01, 02, 03, 04 & 801 - "Live"]
    (86)   UK Virgin EGED 69
Sampler-CD:
01) Guitarrissimo [w 4 extra songs]
    (86)   UK Virgin EGCD 69

NICK MASON
LP:
01) Nick Mason's Fictitious Sports [LIS]
    (80)   NL Harvest 1A 062-64216
12":
01) Hot River / ? [white vinyl, DJ]
    (80)   US EMI

NEW VIOLIN SUMMIT
LP:
01a) New Violin Summit - Live at Berlin Jazz Festival, 07.11.1971 [2LP, FOC]
    (72)   DMPS 33 21285-8
01b) [RI with DC]
    (76)   DMPS 22 22720-0

NEWS FROM BABEL
LP:
02) Letters Home [BKL w lyrics]
    (86) UK Re 1..14
CD:
01/02)Work Resumed On The Tower / Letters Home [w BKL & lyrics]
    (89)   UK ReR nfbcd

RAINCOATS
LP:
01) Odyshape
    (81)   D Rough Trade ROUGH 13

RYUICHI SAKAMOTO
LP:
01) Beauty [LIS]
    (89)   US Virgin VUS 14
CD:
01)Beauty [w BKL& lyrics]
    (89)   US Virgin CDVUS 14

SCRITTI POLITTI
LP:
01) Songs to remember [GC]
    (82)   UK Rough Trade ROUGH 20
CD:
01) Songs to remember
    (86)   UK Rough Trade ROUGH CD 20
12":
02a) The Sweetest Girl / Lions After Slumber [PS]
    (81)   UK Rough Trade RT 091
02b)[DC]
               US Rough Trade TRADE TWO/TWELVE

04) Asylums In Jerusalem, A Slow Soul / Jacques Derrida (ext vers) [PS]
    (82)   UK Rough Trade RT 111 T
7":
03) The Sweetest Girl / Lions After Slumber [PS]
    (81)   UK Rough Trade RT 091
05) Asylums In Jerusalem / Jacques Derrida [PS]
    (82)   UK Rough Trade RT 111

SHINY MEN
LP:
01) Again ! [LS]
    (81)   UK Experimental EX 002

SOFT MACHINE-GONG
Daevid Allen, Gong, Robert Wyatt, Gary Wright, Kevin Ayers - The Complete Family
LP:
01) Soft Machine & Gong - Complete Family [2LP, FOC, contains one side of Soft Machine "Volume 7", one side of Gong "Camembert Electrique", one side of Gong "Magick Brother, Mystic Sister" & one side of Daevid Allen "Bananamoon"] (RI)
    F Byg Double Actuel 529.201

JAN STEELE / JOHN CAGE
LP:
01) Voices and Instruments
    (76)   UK Obscure OBS 06

KEITH TIPPETT GROUP
LP:
02) Dedicated to you, but you weren't listening [FOC]
    (71)   UK Vertigo 6360 024

ULTRAMARINE
LP:
01) Every man and woman is a star [2LP]
    (92)   UKRough Trade R 2892
CD:
01) Every man and woman is a star [2CD]
    (92)   UKRough Trade R 2892 CD
02) United Kingdoms
    (93)   Blanco Y Negro 4509-93425-2
CD Single:
01) Kingdom/Goldcrest
    (93)   Blanco Y Negro 4509-93074-2

BEN WATT
CD:
01) North marine drive [includes 12": Summer into winter]
    (87)   UK Cherry Red CD BRED 40
12":
01) Summer into winter: Walter and John, Aquamarine / Slipping slowly, Another conversation with myself, A girl in winter [PS]
    (82)   F Cherry Red 12 Cherry 36

WILDE FLOWERS
CD:
01) The Wilde Flowers [rec at Wout Steehuis Studios, Spring 65]
    (93) UK Voiceprint VP123CD

WORKING WEEK
LP:
04) Payday [2LP, FOC, compilation w 12" & 7" songs]
    (87)   UK Venture VE 19
CD:
04) Payday [w BKL]
    (87)   UK Venture CDVE 19

12":
01) Venceremos - We will win (jazz dance 12" vers) / Bottom end, Venceremos, We will win (7" Bossa vers) [PS, LC]
    (84)   UK Virgin VS 684-12
7":
01) Venceremos - We will win / Bottom end [PS]
    (84)   UK Virgin VS 684

Samplers:
LP/CD:

Robert Wyatt
1. "Age of self" on A Rough Trade
    (85)   NL Megadisc MD 7982

Wyatt, Robert
1. "Pigs ... (in there)" on Artists for Animals
    (86)   UK Slip SD 003
    D Abuse / Artists for Animals Rough Trade L10-2545

Soft Machine
1. "Out-Bloody Rageous" (extract) on Different Strokes
    (71)   US Columbia AS 12

Soft Machine
1. "Teeth" on Epic Sampler Album
    (71)   J Epic SONF 01116

Matching Mole
1. "Marchides" (edited) on Progressives [2LP, FOC]
    (73)   NL CBS 68 210

Wyatt, Robert
1. "Rangers in the Nightst" on Miniatures [w poster]
    (82)   UK Pipe 2

Wyatt, Robert
1. "Grass" on Raindrops Plattering on Bananaleaves and other tunes
    (85)   UK Womad 001

Soft Machine
1. Love Makes Sweet Music
2. Feelin' Reelin' Squeelin' (first 7") on Rare Tracks 7
    (7?)   UK Polydor 2482 274

Robert Wyatt
1. "The Internationale" on Recommended Records Sampler [2LP,LS,clearbag]
    (82)   UK Recommended RR 9

Wyatt, Robert
1. Red Flag
2. Biko on Requiem [CD only]
    (84)   J Rough Trade Japan 35 JC-104
Wyatt, Robert
1. "Pigs" on Re Records Quaterly Vol. 1 No. 3 (LP + Book)
    (86)   UK Re 0103
Wyatt, Robert
1. "Chairman Mao" on Re Records Quaterly Vol. 2 No. 2 [LP + Book]
    (87)   UK Re 0202
Wyatt, Robert
1. "Chairman Mao" on ReR Quaterly Selections from Vol. 2 [CD w BKL]
    (91)   US ReR QCD2
Wyatt, Robert
1. To Mark Everywhere

Soft Machine
1. "Out-Bloody-Rageous" (excerpt) on Rock Buster

    (73)   D CBS SPR 48/49

Wyatt, Robert
1. "Stalin wasn't stalling" on Rough Trade Compilation
    (81)   D Phonogram 6435 086

Wyatt, Robert
1. "Shipbuilding" on Rough Trade Compilation Deutschland
    (83)   D Rough Trade RTD 5

Mantler, Michael
1. A l'abattoir (& Robert Wyatt)
2. The doubtful guest (& Robert Wyatt) on Together The WATT works family album [CD only]
    (90)   D ECM WATT/22

Soft Machine
1. "Teeth" on Together
    (74) UK CBS SP R 52

Wyatt, Robert
1. "Yesterday Man" on Virgin sound "V" [2LP, FOC]
    (74)   UK Virgin VGD 2505

Wyatt, Robert
1. "At Last I Am Free" on Wanna buy a bridge? [IS]
    (80)   US Rough Trade ROUGH US 3

Matching Mole
1. O Caroline
2. Signed curtain on 7":Playback [PS, BKL]
    (72)   US Playback AS 39

Wyatt, Robert
1. Little red Robin Hood hit the road
2. Sea song on 3 Virgins [PS]
    (74)   US Virgin PR 225

Wyatt, Robert & Bley, Carla
Diverse extracts from Obscure - session for Jan Steele / John Cage "Voices and Instruments" - The Tectonic Ptolsecope EP [supplement to magazine]
    (92)   UK Ptolemaic Terrascope POT 9
Tape:

Wyatt, Robert
1. Strange fruit

Scritti Politti
1. The sweetest girl on Best / Rough Trade - le quartier reservede la musique
    (81)   F Rough Trade HS 88

Wyatt, Robert
1. Grass
Epic Soundtracks
1. Extract from "Popular classical" on Morocci Klung!
    (81)   UK Morocci Klung

Wyatt, Robert
1. Amber and the Amberines on N.M.E. - Departure of Enjoyment
    (84)   UK N.M.E.

Wyatt, Robert
1. Round midnight on N.M.E. - Mighty Reel
    (83)   UK N.M.E.

Scritti Politti
1. The sweetest girl
Wyatt, Robert
1. Born Again Cretin on N.M.E / Rough Trade
    (81)   UK Rough Tapes COPY 001

Wyatt, Robert
1. Interview on Touch [w BKL]
   (82)   UK Touch Magazine

Video:

Soft Machine
1. We know what you mean (aka Soon, soon, soon)
2. It wouldn't last (aka I should have known) (recorded 1967)
on Psychomania! 20 Golden Greats [82 min]
   (92)   AUS GEMV 474

Paul Haines
1. Third World Two
50 poems (French and English) read by an all-star cast, with original music by Carla Bley, Derek Bailey, Steve

Swallow and Sheila Jordan.
   (81)
2. Jubilee
features a visual chorus to the Carol Taylor narrative and spoken or played contributions of Robert Wyatt, Evan Parker, and Derek Bailey.
   (92)

Viva Mandela!
Spanning the years from 1918 to 1990 and narrated by Kenneth David Kaunda, President of Zambia. Throughout this two hour film, documentary and newsreel footage is augmented by background music (including Born Again Cretin) and live performances from over thirty artists.
   (90)

GOING BACK A BIT: A LITTLE HISTORY OF ROBERT WYATT

Released 5th April 1994. Virgin CDVM 9031

'Going Back A Bit: A little History of Robert Wyatt' is a neat retrospective of his musical ventures following his departure from The Soft Machine in 1970. It plots his musical history from his first solo album 'End Of An Ear', through his Matching Mole days, his Virgin years, and subsequent musical collaborations. Compiled with Robert's blessing it features a host of rare or previously unreleased tracks.

ROBERT WYATT
FLOTSAM AND JETSAM
A Special CD Of Rare Recordings Featuring Robert Wyatt.

"Slow Walkin' Talk" - Robert Wyatt And Jimi Hendrix
Recorded in Hollywood, October 1968
"Moon In June" - Robert Wyatt
Recorded In Hollywood / NYC, October 1968
"Standfast" - Symbiosis (featuring Gary Windo)
Recorded At Maida Vale, January 1971
"No 'Alf Measures" - Dave MacCrae Quartet
Recorded At Kensington House, March 1972
"God Song / Fol De Rol" - Robert Wyatt
Recorded At Maida Vale, December 1975
"Apricot Jam" - Lol Coxhill
Recorded At Kaleidophon, Autumn 1973
"A Little Something" - Slapp Happy And Friends
Recorded At Maida Vale, June 1974
"We Did It Again" - Henry Cow And Robert Wyatt
Recorded At L'Olympia, Paris, May 1975

"Now Is The Time" - Gary Windo
Recorded At Brittania Row, April 1976
"N' out Doin'" - General Strike
Recorded At Home, May 1976
"Speechless / Billie's Bounce" - Robert Wyatt
Recorded At RAI Studios, Rome, February 1981
"Jelly Babies" - Epic Soundtracks
Recorded At Alvic Sound, May 1981
"Oban Tancat" - Robert Wyatt
Recorded At Catalan TV3 Studios, January 1987
"Tu Traicon" - Claustrophobia
Recorded Aprila Studios, Barcelona 1986
"Turn Things Upside Down" - The Happy End
Originally Released April 1990

FLOTSAM AND JETSAM WILL BE AVAILABLE ON ROUGH TRADE IN MAY 1994

Other music titles available from SAF Publishing.

Kraftwerk: Man, Machine and Music

by Pascal Bussy

200 pages – paperback – 8 page section – ISBN 0946719 098
Price: £11.95
Rock writer Pascal Bussy has written a uniquely definitive account of Kraftwerk's history, delving beyond their publicity shunning exterior. Ralf Hütter, Florian Schneider, former group members and collaborators have broken their usual silence, providing an in-depth examination into their working methods and complex technological imagery.

"Bussy engagingly explains why they're one of the few groups who've actually changed how music sounds." **** Q Magazine
"I doubt this book will ever be bettered." Vox
"Bussy's crisp business-like biography purrs along like one of the top-of-the-range Mercs Ralf Hütter and Florian Schneider used to collect." NME

Meet The Residents: America's Most Eccentric Band!

by Ian Shirley

200 pages – paperback – 8 page section – ISBN 0946719 128
Price £11.95
Ian Shirley takes an outsider's view of The Residents' operations, exposing a world where nothing is quite as it seems. *Meet The Residents* is a fascinating tale of the musical anarchy and cartoon wackiness that has driven this unique bunch of artistic mavericks forward.

"This is the nearest to an official history you're ever likely to get, slyly abetted by the bug-eyed beans from Venus themselves." Vox
"The Residents have been on the rubber-walled edge of of popular culture for 21 years and this exposé follows their complex marketing strategy." *** Q
"Few enthusiasts will want to put this book down once they start reading." Record Collector
"It's a highly informative, immensely readable account of one of the most self-consciously elusive groups." Top

Cabaret Voltaire - The Art of the Sixth Sense

by Mick Fish & Dave Hallbery

224 pages – paperback - Over 50 photographs - ISBN 0946719 039
Price: £6.95
Now into its second and updated edition, this definitive book is a critical appraisal of the career of an innovative and influential group.

"The book covers everything from video and voodoo to Dada and Doublevision .... an essential and lively read." Sounds
"A fabulous book which really lifts itself above the mire that is the tacky pop music book world. Essential reading." Zipcode Magazine

Wire... Everybody Loves A History

by Kevin Eden

192 pages – paperback – Over 70 photographs - ISBN 0946719 071
Price: £9.95.
Including interviews and commentary about Wire's complete history and solo projects, this book successfully unravels the complexities of this multi-faceted group.

"Eden delivers a sharp portrayal of the punk industry's behaviour, influence and morality." **** Q Magazine
"Any band or their fans could feel well served by a book like Eden's." Vox Magazine
"Everybody Loves A History is a fine complement to the band's music, from its self-effacing title to sheer wealth of interview and photographic material." Record Collector

Tape Delay

by Charles Neal

256 pages - paperback - Over 60 photographs - ISBN 0946719 020
Price £11.95
A unique collection of interviews and exclusive writing featuring: Marc Almond, Cabaret Voltaire, Nick Cave, Chris & Cosey, Coil, Einstürzende Neubauten, The Fall, Foetus, Diamanda Galas, The Hafler Trio, Matt Johnson, Laibach, Lydia Lunch, New Order, Psychic TV, Boyd Rice, Henry Rollins, Sonic Youth, Swans and Test Dept .

"A virtual Who's Who of people who've done the most in the past decade to drag music out of commercial confinement." NME
By far the most ambitious attempt so far to link together the large number of noise-orientated bands to have emerged from the indie ghetto." Sounds
Arguably the best genre book of all time." Music From the Empty Quarter
"Useful and timely" iD Magazine   *"Intriguing and interesting"* Q

The Can Book

by Pascal Bussy & Andy Hall

192 pages - paperback - Over 80 photographs - ISBN 0946719 055
Price: £8.95
A complete history of this 'cult' band. Includes biographies of all the group members, a chronology and discography, as well as up-to-date commentary from the group.
"If Can's music is a mystery, this book will make you want to investigate." Q Magazine
"A book trying to make sense of their myths and weird psyches has never been more welcome." Sounds
"Bussy's account of the characters and chronology of Can is helpfully musicalogical for the fan and iced generously enough with information and anecdotes to attract the as-yet unaligned." Melody Maker

Dark Entries: Bauhaus and Beyond.

by Ian Shirley

200 pages – paperback – 8 page section – ISBN 0946719 136
Price £11.95
Aided by interviews with group members, Ian Shirley recounts the full story from the dramatic early successes with Bauhaus, through various solo projects, to the huge Stateside popularity of Love And Rockets.

Plunderphonics, 'Pataphysics & Pop Mechanics

by Andrew Jones

256 pages - paperback - illustrated - ISBN 0946719 152
Price £12.95
Features: Chris Cutler, Fred Frith, Ferdinand Richard, Heiner Goebbels, Willem Breuker, Henry Threadgill, Sergei Kuryokhin, Rova Saxophone Quartet, Amy Denio, Lindsay Cooper, Zeena Parkins, Tenko, John Oswald, John Zorn, Charles Hayward, Roberto Musci & Giovanni Venosta, Les Granules, Fat, Bruire, Justine, The Residents, Kalahari Surfers, After Dinner, Tom Zé.

"The talent assembled between Jones's covers would be interesting under any rubric..... Thought provoking and stimulating." Mojo

Forthcoming title:

The One And Only: Peter Perrett - Homme Fatale

by Nina Antonia

A fully authorised yet no-holds barred investigation into the life and often dangerous times of The Only Ones mentor and songwriter Peter Perrett. Features interviews with Peter Perrett and all the ex-members of the group.

Ordering/ Mail Order

All titles are available from most good bookshops, or order from your local bookshop quoting the ISBN number, author, title and publisher.

To order direct by mail order contact SAF Publishing, 12 Conway Gardens, Wembley, Middx. HA9 8TR UK.
Telephone/Fax: 0181 904 6263
Payment can be made by cheque or Mastercard/Visa/cheques (All foreign cheques must be in pounds sterling and drawn on a British bank.) Postage: UK Free - Europe £2 - Rest of the World £4

Distribution:

UK & Europe: Airlift Book Company, 8 The Arena, Mollison Ave, Enfield, Middx. UK.
Tel: 0181-804 0400 Fax: 0181-804 0044
USA: Last Gasp, 777 Florida Street, San Francisco, CA 94110. Tel: 415 824 6636 Fax: 415 824 1836
Canada: Marginal Distribution, Unit 103, 277 George Street North, Peterborough, Ontario, Canada K9J 3G9.
Tel/Fax: 705 745 2326
Titles also available through Virgin Records, See Hear (USA), Wayside Music (USA), Tower Records (UK & USA), Rough Trade Shops (UK), Compendium Bookshop (UK), Sordide Sentimental (France), These Records (UK), Touch (UK).